Solving the Literacy Puzzle

Practical Strategies for Integrating the **Science of Reading** Into Classroom Instruction

D1608325

Norene A. Bunt

Solution Tree | Press
a division of
Solution Tree

555 North Morton Street
Bloomington, IN 47404
800.733.6786 (toll free) / 812.336.7700
FAX: 812.336.7790

email: info@SolutionTree.com
SolutionTree.com

Visit **go.SolutionTree.com/literacy** to download the free reproducibles in this book.

Printed in the United States of America

Library of Congress Cataloging-in-Publication Data

Names: Bunt, Norene A., author.
Title: Solving the literacy puzzle : practical strategies for integrating
   the science of reading into classroom instruction / Norene A. Bunt.
Description: Bloomington, IN : Solution Tree Press, 2024. | Includes
   bibliographical references and index.
Identifiers: LCCN 2024003813 (print) | LCCN 2024003814 (ebook) | ISBN
   9781958590874 (paperback) | ISBN 9781958590881 (ebook)
Subjects: LCSH: Reading (Elementary) | Reading (Secondary) |
   Literacy--United States.
Classification: LCC LB1573 .B836 2024 (print) | LCC LB1573 (ebook) | DDC
   372.4--dc23/eng/20240222
LC record available at https://lccn.loc.gov/2024003813
LC ebook record available at https://lccn.loc.gov/2024003814

Solution Tree
Jeffrey C. Jones, CEO
Edmund M. Ackerman, President

Solution Tree Press
President and Publisher: Douglas M. Rife
Associate Publishers: Todd Brakke and Kendra Slayton
Editorial Director: Laurel Hecker
Art Director: Rian Anderson
Copy Chief: Jessi Finn
Production Editor: Gabriella Jones-Monserrate
Proofreader: Elijah Oates
Text and Cover Designer: Rian Anderson
Acquisitions Editors: Carol Collins and Hilary Goff
Content Development Specialist: Amy Rubenstein
Associate Editors: Sarah Ludwig and Elijah Oates
Editorial Assistant: Anne Marie Watkins

To my husband, Pat, who supports all of my
endeavors, and to all literacy teachers who are
passionate about teaching children to become
proficient, lifelong readers.

Acknowledgments

Solution Tree Press would like to thank the following reviewers:

Lindsey Bingley
   Literacy and Numeracy Lead
   Foothills Academy Society
   Calgary, Alberta, Canada

John D. Ewald
   Education Consultant
   Frederick, Maryland

Colleen Fleming
   Literacy Specialist
   Calgary, Alberta, Canada

Jennifer Renegar
   Data and Assessment Specialist
   Republic School District
   Republic, Missouri

Robert B. Taylor
   English Language Arts Instructor
   Solon Community School District
   Solon, Iowa

Visit **go.SolutionTree.com/literacy** to download
the free reproducibles in this book.

Table of Contents

Reproducibles are in italics.

Chapter 3

Vocabulary Instruction and Word Retention 43

Chapter 4

Phonemic Awareness and Language Arts
Within Vocabulary Instruction. 65

Chapter 5

Comprehension as the Heart and Goal of Reading . . 83

Chapter 6
Text Discussion and Questioning

Chapter 7
Fluency and Reading Proficiency

Chapter 8
The Role and Impact of Independent Reading 143

Chapter 9
Literacy Development Through Writing 157

Chapter 10
Whole-Group, Small-Group, and Independent Work 167

About the Author

Norene A. Bunt, EdD, is an author and former teacher, principal, curriculum coordinator, school improvement strategist, and superintendent. She is an expert on best practices in literacy instruction and integrating the science of reading effectively and efficiently to support high levels of learning for all students. Dr. Bunt has more than fifteen years of teaching experience and seventeen years serving in leadership roles in schools with widely diverse populations of students.

Her expertise has been developed through these professional experiences, as well as through action research, classroom observations, and extensive reviews of current research. She continues to serve as an adjunct professor, student teaching supervisor, Solution Tree associate, and author.

Dr. Bunt earned a master's degree in elementary education from Northwestern College and a doctorate in educational administration, with an emphasis in curriculum and instruction, from the University of South Dakota.

Introduction

Since 1978, I have had the opportunity to serve in various capacities within the field of education. My experiences include classroom teacher, Title I teacher, principal, curriculum coordinator, and school superintendent. In addition, since 2012, I have served as an adjunct university instructor, student teaching supervisor, researcher, and author.

Through my experiences as a school administrator and my doctoral research, I spent literally hundreds of hours observing in K–12 reading and English language arts (ELA) classrooms. During these classroom observations, it became evident that ELA and reading teachers cared deeply about helping their students become proficient readers, who are skilled in reading fluently, comprehend what they read, and find enjoyment in reading. It was also clear that literacy teachers worked diligently to implement programs and strategies that promoted high levels of reading proficiency. Unfortunately, the programs and strategies that schools select to use, and often require teachers to implement, change frequently, leaving teachers to question what the best practices for teaching reading truly are.

Based on these many observations of instruction during literacy blocks, I began to develop several significant concerns regarding reading instruction. It seemed that in many classrooms, teachers had been asked to discard effective instructional practices such as guided oral reading and discussion of text and to replace them with new, often less effective practices, including reading to students and focusing primarily on fluency. Also, I noted that many teachers were struggling to feel confident about their instructional planning, regardless of whether their school utilized a specific reading program, a basal or anthology, novels, or leveled readers. I believed that much of this uncertainty could be due to frequent changes in literacy approaches and programs.

These concerns motivated me to focus my doctoral dissertation on teachers' beliefs and perceptions about several essential components of reading instruction (vocabulary, comprehension, fluency, and independent reading) and how these related to their classroom practices. In short, I discovered that most elementary and secondary reading and ELA teachers had a reasonably sound knowledge base regarding effective strategies for teaching reading, but they were not reflecting this in their instruction. Therefore, in some classrooms, high-quality literacy instruction seemed to be lacking, which has definitively impacted student learning.

The Hechinger Report (https://hechingerreport.org) found that even before the pandemic of 2020–2022, nearly two-thirds of U.S. students were unable to read at grade level. In the spring of 2021, students in each grade level "scored three to six percentile points lower on a widely used test, the Measures of Academic Progress or MAP, than they did in 2019" (Barshay et al., 2021).

As a result, I became highly motivated to assist educators in developing their understanding about research-based literacy instruction based on the science of reading and how to implement these best practices in the classroom. This book addresses the problem of disorganized and ineffective literacy instruction by offering a primer in the most current research-based literacy practices and providing actionable, effective classroom strategies for educators.

In today's schools, there are highly diverse populations of students, including students with learning disabilities, students for whom English is not their first language, and students living in poverty. All students deserve the opportunity to receive quality instruction using a grade-appropriate text that addresses state literacy standards. When students who face these challenges are included in rich instruction, they will learn and experience success. The literacy instruction model described in this book can be effective in raising reading proficiency for all students.

Evidence From Literacy Assessments and Classroom Observation

In addition to concerns based on my research and observations and declining MAP scores, the National Assessment of Educational Progress (NAEP) has indicated a decline, or plateau, in reading achievement on the national level.

In 2019, the NAEP scores for reading showed that 35 percent of fourth-grade students scored at or above the proficient range, which was slightly lower than in 2017 (National Center for Education Statistics [NCES], 2019). More and more schools are being identified as needing targeted or comprehensive support, or labeled as persistently low-achieving schools, based on the rating scales of the Every Student Succeeds Act (ESSA) (U.S. Department of Education, 2015).

ESSA statistics for 2019 show that some states have identified up to 20 percent of their schools as needing comprehensive support and up to 47 percent of the schools as in need of targeted assistance (U.S. Department of Education, 2019).

Many schools are also seeing stagnant or declining reading scores on standardized tests, such as the Iowa Statewide Assessment of Student Progress (ISASP) (formerly known as Iowa Test of Basic Skills and Iowa Assessments). In comparing students' ISASP scores from 2021 to 2022, averages were similar across both years; however, scores decreased in grades 4, 5, 6, and 8 (Pearson Education, 2018).

Reading achievement is a concern on the international level, as well. One of the most extensive cross-national tests is the Programme for International Student Assessment (PISA), "which every three years measures reading ability, math and science literacy, and other essential skills among 15-year-olds in dozens of developed and developing countries" (DeSilver, 2017).

In 2015, the United States placed twenty-fourth when compared to the other countries that participated in PISA. It is significant that PISA scores in reading showed very little change from 2000 to 2018. In 2018, 14 percent of fourth-grade students in the United States scored in the top levels (5 or 6), and only 4 percent of socioeconomically disadvantaged students scored at levels 5 or 6. In addition, PISA results from 2018 indicated that reading scores for students in the United States fell significantly below those in countries such as China, Hong Kong, Finland, Canada, and New Zealand. On the 2022 PISA assessments, the United States was ranked eighteenth when compared to other countries.

Since the mid-1990s, literacy instruction in many elementary and middle school classrooms has included a model that incorporates (1) short whole-group minilessons, (2) small-group *guided* reading, and (3) literacy stations, rotations, or daily menus of literacy activities, as exemplified by figure I.1. These activities are often disconnected and do not provide comprehensive reading instruction to help students become successful, strategic readers. This type of format for reading instruction allows students to have a limited amount of direct instruction from the teacher, typically just fifteen to twenty minutes in small group and fifteen to thirty minutes in whole group per day.

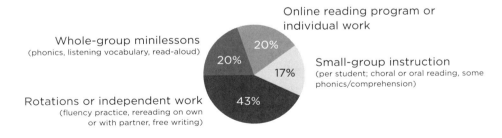

Figure I.1: Common format for literacy instruction.

Along with this frequently practiced model for literacy instruction, many states use the FastBridge assessments to determine students' proficiency levels in reading and identify students who may need interventions (Illuminate Education, 2019). FastBridge literacy assessments are curriculum-based measures (CBM) used to screen students, identify skill gaps, and provide diagnostic information to guide reading instruction and interventions.

To accurately assess students' reading proficiency, the areas of phonics, vocabulary, fluency, and comprehension should all be included in the assessment process. However, most of the schools using the FastBridge assessments report on students' fluency levels, not students' vocabulary or reading and comprehension achievement. Thus, in many classrooms, reading instruction is focused around developing fluency through an emphasis on decoding and increasing students' reading rates (measured in words per minute, or WPM). The ultimate goal of reading instruction is to teach students to comprehend text at high levels; therefore, comprehension should be the major focus of instruction and assessment. Emphasis on decoding or fluency, without including quality instruction in vocabulary and comprehension, creates instruction that addresses only some of the essential components in the science of reading.

The emphasis on fluency takes away from the time available for reading comprehension and vocabulary instruction, which is detrimental in regard to students developing into strategic readers who can create meaning from text. Reading efficiently and accurately is important for reading proficiency; however, it is not sufficient. Fluent reading will "allow readers to attend to the meaning of texts, but fluency alone does not indicate good comprehension" (Literacy Teaching Toolkit, 2023).

Comprehensive literacy instruction directly focuses on all components of the science of reading, including phonemic awareness, phonics, fluency, vocabulary, and comprehension. Each of these components is important and necessary for students to develop reading proficiency; therefore, educators should provide adequate time for quality instruction in each component. While for nearly two decades a major focus of reading instruction has been on fluency, since 2020, some schools are now perhaps overemphasizing phonemic awareness, phonics, and decoding, leaving little time for actual reading, discussion of text, and instruction in vocabulary and comprehension strategies.

Continuous changes in philosophies or approaches to reading instruction and frequent changes in programs, texts, and models used for literacy instruction have played a role in the decline of students' reading proficiency. The reading pendulum has been swinging back and forth since the 1970s because we have not thoroughly understood the best practices for literacy instruction, which has clearly impacted students' reading proficiency, as noted by state and national reading assessments.

The Right to Read Project posited that "evidence available to us since the 90s could have ended the reading wars, but rather than embrace 'settled science,' we allowed publishers and educational gurus to swing us back towards ineffective practices" (Goldberg, 2019).

It is time to change our paradigms regarding reading instruction. We can no longer be satisfied with 20–35 percent of students being nonproficient in reading. Maintaining the status quo will mean that more students will struggle in high school and postsecondary education, and our nation will struggle to compete on a global scale. We need to think again about reading instruction and remove the barriers preventing our students from becoming proficient readers, our schools from meeting their school improvement goals, and our nation from once again being a global leader in education.

Purpose and Goals of This Book

The reading instructional practices described in *Solving the Literacy Puzzle* are based on the knowledge gained through the author's professional experiences and through longitudinal reviews of research by experts such as Stephanie Harvey and Ann Goudvis, Isabel Beck, Robert Marzano, John Hattie, Timothy Shanahan, and the Center for the Improvement of Early Reading Achievement (CIERA). Many, if not most, of the strategies discussed in this book are not new, and teachers may have at least some prior knowledge about them; however, this book consolidates what extensive research conducted over time says about effective literacy instruction and provides a clear model of how to design effective reading instruction that integrates the science of reading and evidence-based strategies.

One diverse school in the midwestern United States implemented the instructional model described in this book after using a small-group balanced literacy format for a number of years. Figure I.2 (page 6) provides evidence of the effectiveness of implementing the framework and instructional strategies in *Solving the Literacy Puzzle* in this school district over time. Years 1 and 2 indicate the percentage of students who scored at or above the *proficient* level on a statewide assessment while the school was using a balanced literacy format. Years 3 and 4 show the percentage of students who scored at or above the *proficient* level when the *Solving the Literacy Puzzle* framework was implemented. This literacy model positively impacted *all* students, and significantly impacted English learner (EL) students and students with individualized education plan (IEP) goals and low socioeconomic levels.

Group	Year 1	Year 2	Year 3	Year 4	Growth
Grade 5 All	49.2	54.3	58.6	70.4	21.2%
Grade 5 IEPs	12.5	16.7	13.6	35.7	23.2%
Grade 5 ELs	35	49.2	48.4	66.7	31.7%
Grade 5 Low SES	41.8	40.7	47.3	62.7	20.9%

Figure I.2: Impact of implementation of *Solving the Literacy Puzzle* in one diverse and lower socioeconomic school district (fully implemented in years 3 and 4).

Literacy instruction that is based on having high expectations and providing access to a universal and rigorous curriculum for all students will be discussed in detail. The use of academic learning time during literacy blocks will also be discussed at length, with the ultimate goal of increasing students' levels of reading proficiency regardless of the use of online reading programs, novels, guided reading books, or trade books.

Solving the Literacy Puzzle begins with information about general principles for research-based literacy instruction, a description of the components of the science of reading, and explanations of how to connect sound practices based on evidence to instruction in all of these components.

- **Chapter 1: Literacy Instruction and Why It Matters**—This chapter reviews the recent history of literacy instruction, how nationwide U.S policy has affected it, and the current obstacles that keep educators from effectively teaching students to read. With a comprehensive overview of the science of reading, this chapter will lay out the research-backed principles upon which the following chapters are based.

- **Chapter 2: Text Selection and Instructional Grouping**—This chapter focuses on how to intentionally select an appropriate text for reading instruction that supports the essential elements and curricular goals for all students. Different formats for grouping students during literacy instruction are discussed in some detail, as well as recommendations, based on research, for grouping students during literacy instruction.

Chapters 3 through 10 will address specific components of literacy instruction aligned with the science of reading. Each chapter will (1) review the current reality based on observations, (2) discuss research-based recommendations for literacy instruction for that specific component, and (3) provide templates, examples, and other resources to support implementation within any reading model or program.

- **Chapter 3: Vocabulary Instruction and Word Retention**—This chapter provides an overview of research in regard to effective vocabulary instruction and its relationship to academic success, reading comprehension, and independent reading. Best practices in selecting vocabulary words for instruction and direct instruction in vocabulary and word-learning strategies, as well as ways to actively engage students in interacting with vocabulary words, are described.

- **Chapter 4: Phonemic Awareness and Language Arts Within Vocabulary Instruction**—The focus of this chapter is on best practices based on research related to phonemic awareness, explicit instruction in phonics, word study, and language arts skills. How to incorporate phonics, word-busting, and language arts skills *through vocabulary instruction* in a way that is integrated and meaningful is described in detail.

- **Chapter 5: Comprehension as the Heart and Goal of Reading**—This chapter includes descriptions of the *universal*, or essential, comprehension strategies that students need to understand and be able to apply while reading, including (1) connecting, (2) predicting, (3) visualizing, (4) main ideas and details, (5) monitoring, (6) summarizing, (7) questioning, and (8) inference. Recommendations for teaching comprehension strategies such as direct instruction and modeling of strategies, think-alouds, and reciprocal teaching are discussed.

- **Chapter 6: Text Discussion and Questioning**—In this chapter, a brief overview of current literacy practices in many elementary classrooms is provided, followed by a brief explanation of research supporting the preplanning of *thinking questions* and providing opportunities for students to interact with text. The value of utilizing discussion protocols is discussed, and a template for designing questions and discussions around text to support and enhance students' comprehension is included.

- **Chapter 7: Fluency and Reading Proficiency**—This chapter begins with the current reality and common practices related to fluency found in many elementary classrooms, along with a discussion about the discrepancy between research on fluency and the emphasis and time spent on fluency development. Next, evidence-based fluency instruction and development is discussed including the importance of students reading text independently and practicing fluency in meaningful ways using the grade-appropriate instructional text.

- **Chapter 8: The Role and Impact of Independent Reading**—Common practices used in today's classrooms often include extensive periods of independent reading of student-selected texts, with limited expectations for students' accountability for their reading. In this chapter, factors related to independent reading of student-selected texts and teacher-selected instructional texts are provided, along with recommendations for meaningful independent reading.

- **Chapter 9: Literacy Development Through Writing**—The current reality regarding writing instruction includes engagement in student-selected writing tasks at a *station*, or as one of the daily *rotations*, with little guidance and accountability for students' writing. In this chapter, recommendations from research on the connections between reading and writing are discussed including shared writing, modeling, integration of vocabulary and language arts skills, and writing in response to literature.

- **Chapter 10: Whole-Group, Small-Group, and Independent Work**— This chapter discusses maximizing academic learning time through whole-group and small-group instruction and ensuring that all students have equity of opportunity in being involved in grade-level instruction. Best practices related to computer-assisted literacy learning are also addressed, and recommendations for engaging students in meaningful independent and partner work that directly supports the various components of reading are included.

The book's conclusion provides additional recommendations for the implementation of this comprehensive research-based literacy instruction and guidance in using *Solving the Literacy Puzzle* for professional learning and to facilitate changes in your school's literacy practices. The appendices contains various activities, examples, graphic organizers, and templates for use in implementing the *Solving the Literacy Puzzle* framework.

Please note that Chapters 1–10 include some reflection questions regarding readers' current instructional practices in literacy. It will be beneficial for readers to respond candidly to these questions before and again after reading each chapter.

Audience for This Book

Solving the Literacy Puzzle aims to provide a model for K–12 reading instruction based on what extensive research has identified as best practices for literacy instruction in the areas of phonics and decoding, vocabulary, comprehension, fluency, independent reading, and writing, with the ultimate goal of increasing students' levels of reading proficiency. This book is intended to serve as a guide for K–12 reading and ELA teachers, Title I teachers, literacy strategists, lead teachers, curriculum directors, and administrators in how to plan and implement effective, comprehensive, research-based instruction that incorporates all components of the science of reading. *Solving the Literacy Puzzle* is set up so that it can readily be utilized for professional development for professional learning communities (PLCs), grade-level teams, and book study groups.

Change and Growth Through Cognitive Dissonance

When human beings are confronted with information that differs from, or contradicts, their current belief systems or their current realities regarding pedagogy, it is common for them to experience *cognitive dissonance*. The *Merriam-Webster* online dictionary defines cognitive dissonance (n.d.) as "psychological conflict resulting from incongruous beliefs and attitudes held simultaneously." Cognitive dissonance is uncomfortable and may cause feelings of frustration, confusion, defensiveness, and even anger. However, cognitive dissonance can also lead people to modify their thoughts or behaviors and to adjust their paradigms to resolve the conflicting thoughts.

The research presented in this book may well contradict some of the beliefs readers have about effective reading instruction and may go against their current pedagogies. Rather than allowing the feelings caused by cognitive dissonance to impact your potential for professional growth, I ask you as readers to open your minds to this information and consider the recommendations included in the comprehensive, research-based reading instruction described in the upcoming chapters. Use figure I.3 as a visual guide. Readers are encouraged to allow cognitive dissonance to occur as this can lead to enhanced learning and positive change.

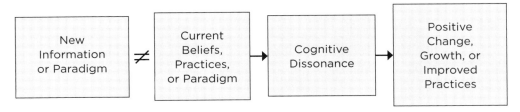

Figure I.3: How to avoid cognitive dissonance.

To begin your journey through this book, complete the "Reading Practices Self-Assessment" (page 10). I recommend you then revisit the assessment periodically while reading and after you finish each chapter. Reviewing your initial responses will help you determine goals and priorities for change based on what you learn in this book.

Reading Practices Self-Assessment

Please candidly complete the following self-assessment about your own or your school district's current reading instructional practices before continuing to read. This self-assessment may be used for instructional planning and professional development.

1. Do **all** your students receive high-quality, whole-group instruction on the grade-level curriculum?

   Always   Often   Sometimes   Rarely

2. Do **all** your students have opportunities to read grade-level-appropriate texts independently, as well as with guidance?

   Always   Often   Sometimes   Rarely

3. Do **all** your students have an adequate amount of teacher contact time during your reading block each day?

   Always   Often   Sometimes   Rarely

4. Do **all** your students have the opportunity to learn and practice research-based comprehension strategies?

   Always   Often   Sometimes   Rarely

5. Is there explicit instruction and modeling of comprehension strategies by the teacher?

   Always   Often   Sometimes   Rarely

6. Do **all** your students have adequate time for guided and independent practice applying the comprehension strategies to a grade-level or age-appropriate text?

   Always   Often   Sometimes   Rarely

7. Do you preplan higher-order questions and engage students in rich discussion about literature?

   Always   Often   Sometimes   Rarely

8. Are strategies used to help students be successful in reading grade-level texts?

   Always   Often   Sometimes   Rarely

page 1 of 2

Solving the Literacy Puzzle © 2024 Solution Tree Press • SolutionTree.com
Visit **go.SolutionTree.com/literacy** to download this free reproducible.

9. Are 6–10 relevant, high-utility, grade-level or age-appropriate vocabulary words explicitly taught each week?

    Always   Often   Sometimes   Rarely

10. Do you provide student-friendly definitions and visuals for vocabulary words?

    Always   Often   Sometimes   Rarely

11. Do you model word-busting strategies and the use of context clues to determine word meanings?

    Always   Often   Sometimes   Rarely

12. Do students create their own definitions and visuals for vocabulary words?

    Always   Often   Sometimes   Rarely

13. Are students given multiple opportunities to use, engage, and interact with vocabulary words?

    Always   Often   Sometimes   Rarely

14. How often do you explicitly model writing for your students?

    Always   Often   Sometimes   Rarely

15. Are students given opportunities to write in response to literature and for other authentic purposes and held accountable for their writing?

    Always   Often   Sometimes   Rarely

16. Do you involve students in independent reading for 15–20 minutes at least three times a week?

    Always   Often   Sometimes   Rarely

Chapter 1

Literacy Instruction and Why It Matters

There are many little ways to enlarge your child's world.
Love of books is the best of all.

—JACQUELINE KENNEDY

Formal reading instruction was born when Samuel Wood wrote the first graded readers in the late 1800s (Barr, 1989). Reading instruction from the early 1800s through the middle of the 20th century consisted of covering one reading book per grade level, such as the McGuffey readers (McGuffey, 1836). In the mid-1950s, basal readers, such as Scott Foresman's *Sally, Dick, and Jane* readers (Smith, 1965), arrived on the scene. These basal readers, and others of their kind, accounted for the entire reading curriculum used in most schools for over thirty years.

Since the 1970s, reading instruction has become a constantly changing entity. During the 1960s, basal programs came under attack because of the perceived lack of systematic instruction in phonics and the quest to use authentic literature. By the mid-1980s, a literature-based approach became the instructional method of choice, followed closely by the whole-language philosophy.

The mid-1990s brought guided reading into the mix, allowing students to receive instruction in small groups based on their levels of development and reading abilities. More recently, a balanced approach to reading instruction, which includes the combination of literature-based instruction with a traditional basal reader, along with the use of other texts, has shown to be useful in some school settings.

Since the late 1990s, the Daily CAFE model (Boushey & Moser, 2006), in which students spend time each day in rotations that include *reading to self*, *reading to someone*, *working on writing*, *word work*, and *listening to reading*, has become widely used in many elementary schools.

It is no surprise that these pendulum swings, along with changes in philosophies, pedagogies, and methodologies, have led new and experienced teachers alike to be uncertain about what effective reading instruction should really look like. In this chapter, we review the history of literacy in the United States from legislation to research trends and use this background to assess the remaining obstacles and challenges to effective literacy instruction.

Legislation Addressing Reading Achievement

The Soviet Union's launch of Sputnik, the first satellite, in 1957 spurred political interest in finding the best methods of teaching reading in order to produce U.S. citizens with high levels of intellectual abilities and to compete technologically and economically with Russia and other countries. In 1964, the Coleman Report was mandated by the Civil Rights Act and looked at the inequalities of educational opportunities in elementary and secondary education based on race, ethnicity, and socioeconomic factors across the United States (Coleman et al., 1966; Hill, 2017). Since the mid-1960s, legislation has been enacted by the federal government to address concerns about student achievement and to help ensure that our nation is competitive on a global scale. Table 1.1 is a recap of the legislation related to literacy that has been put into place since 1964 and its intents and purposes.

Table 1.1: U.S. Literacy Legislation Since 1964

Year	President	Legislation or Program	Intent or Purpose
1964	Lyndon Johnson	Economic Opportunity Act	Programs to combat poverty and improve academic performance.
1965	Lyndon Johnson	Elementary and Secondary Education Act (ESEA)	Established Title I and Head Start programs to improve the performance of students from low socioeconomic and racial or ethnic minority groups.
1967–1977	Lyndon Johnson	Public Law 90-92 (Project Follow Through)	Authorized the most extensive federally funded educational study, which was designed to identify effective methods for teaching disadvantaged students.

1983	National Commission on Excellence in Education	*A Nation at Risk*	Focused public attention even more acutely on low student achievement and led to an increase in federal efforts under ESEA to address quality education for all students.
2002	George W. Bush	No Child Left Behind (NCLB)	Intended to ensure that all schools made adequate yearly progress (AYP) toward the goal of *all* students demonstrating proficiency in reading by 2014. Failure to show AYP resulted in specific consequences for schools.
2002	George W. Bush	Reading First	Intended to improve reading achievement by adopting teaching practices based on scientific research. Provided teachers with knowledge about how reading/ELA time should be used and strategies for teaching young learners to read.
2007	George W. Bush	Re-enactment of NCLB	Required placing schools on academic alert status if they fail to make AYP for one year, and schools must develop school improvement plans for immediate implementation if such failure continues the following year. Makes students eligible for supplemental educational services when their schools are identified as needing improvement after a second consecutive year of AYP failure.
2015	Barack Obama	Every Student Succeeds Act (ESSA)	Placed more of the decision-making and accountability factors for reading proficiency on the shoulders of the states, rather than on the federal government. ESSA requires that more than test scores be reviewed when evaluating schools. States must use four academic factors that are included in the law.

As indicated in table 1.1, since the mid-1960s legislation ranging from ESEA in 1965 to ESSA in 2015, as well as public pressure, has placed reading instruction in schools increasingly under scrutiny by the public, school administrators, and policymakers. Many factors contribute to the increased concerns about reading achievement, including the perception that poor readers may become unproductive citizens who are ill-prepared to succeed in a global society. Studies have indicated that in fourth grade, 80 percent of students from low-income backgrounds are reading below grade level. Falling behind their peers early on affects their classroom performance and can "impact their social skills, health, and economic status later in life. This problem extends to our broader society and economy" (Garcia, 2017).

Despite state and federal legislation and the focus on school accountability, the level of proficiency of our students continues to remain stable, or to decline, in many school districts. Average reading scores in fourth and eighth grades decreased by three points from 2019 to 2022 (NAEP, 2022). In addition to legislation and holding schools accountable, quality, research-based literacy instruction that addresses all the components of the science of reading must be provided for all students to truly impact the level of reading proficiency for our students. Unfortunately, several obstacles have, perhaps, deterred us from providing high-quality literacy instruction.

Obstacles and Challenges to Effective Literacy Instruction

Public concern and the various legislation that has been enacted since 1964 to address the quality of education in the United States has not *fixed* reading instruction nor had the desired impact on students' reading proficiency. Early legislation was focused on addressing poverty and providing services, such as Head Start, for disadvantaged students, which led to positive outcomes but did not improve overall reading achievement. Beginning in 1983, the focus of legislation was on holding schools accountable for providing a quality education as indicated by standardized test scores, which also failed to increase students' reading proficiency. The only legislation that directly focused on reading achievement and the use of research-based instructional strategies was Reading First (2002), which was almost entirely discontinued after less than a decade. Despite good intentions, better funding, and increased data collection, legislation on the national level has failed to create a quality system of literacy instruction that leads to high levels of proficiency for all students.

James F. Baumann, James V. Hoffman, Ann M. Duffy-Hester, and Jennifer Moon Ro (2000) examined reading instruction's status and identified significant concerns regarding the number of students who were not reading up to their potential. Baumann and colleagues' (2000) studies concluded that "when comparing our findings to those of more than a generation ago, one might be tempted to invoke the attitude that, 'the more things change, the more they remain the same'" (p. 359). This may well be the result of the proverbial and constant swinging of the pendulum regarding reading methodologies, philosophies, and pedagogies.

During the time that I spent observing reading instruction, it became apparent that this swinging pendulum has caused many teachers to feel confused about what effective reading instruction really is. Even highly effective veteran teachers have begun questioning their reading instructional practices and grasping at straws to develop what they hope is good literacy instruction. Unfortunately, some teachers are not knowledgeable about, or are not aligning their reading instruction with, effective research-based practices (Miller, 2006).

Many teachers believe, or have been told, that the basal program they may have depended on previously as a guide for their reading curriculum is now a four-letter word, and they have left behind the use of basals, or anthologies, altogether. In 1987, a commission of the National Council of Teachers of English urged schools to "break the strong grip basal readers have on reading instruction and allow teachers to *put real children's books by real writers* into the heart of the curriculum" (Rothman, 1987). In addition, some teachers and administrators believed that "basal reading programs limit or control teachers' instructional decision making through a process referred to as deskilling" (Baumann & Heubach, 1996, p. 1). Thus, teachers are trying to develop reading curricula based on their own expertise or lack of expertise and without the guidance of a basal reading program. Teachers also believe, or have been told, that whole-group instruction and round-robin reading are wrong or ineffective; thus, they are trying to juggle three to five reading groups each day within a limited time frame to meet each group's unique needs. In addition, whole-group instruction has been abandoned, or restricted to 15–30 minutes in many schools, which makes it difficult for teachers to effectively teach all components of the science of reading to *all* students.

The result of all this upheaval is disconnected instruction that involves tossing out the old ways (even though some aspects are still effective) and replacing them with new (sometimes less-effective) strategies, as well as a state of overall dysfunction in reading instruction. Figure 1.1 illustrates some of the major factors that create the confusion and ineffectiveness present in literacy instruction today.

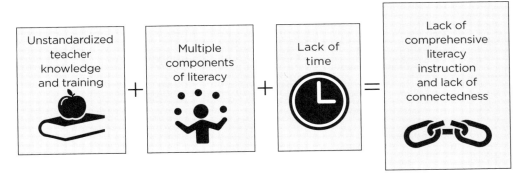

Figure 1.1: Major factors that affect literacy instruction.

It is not surprising that teachers lack confidence in their literacy instruction. Research regarding reading instruction has been unclear and even contradictory, and no one method can be considered *the best*. Virtually every proponent of any method, material, or program can find some sort of evidence that what it has to offer works somewhere, for some students, some of the time (Roe, Smith, & Burns, 2005).

Carol M. Connor and colleagues (2007) of Florida State University concluded through their research that "there is no one *best* method for teaching children to read" and "the efficacy of any particular instructional practice may depend on the skill level of the student" (p. 330). The effectiveness of literacy instruction is dependent on a variety of teacher factors, student factors, and the instructional methods that are implemented.

General Principles of Reading Instruction Supported by Research

Even though reading instructional approaches vary significantly and studies have been unable to identify a particular best method of reading instruction, research over the past several decades provides us with evidence-based recommendations and indicates some commonalities regarding best practices for literacy instruction. Table 1.2 summarizes major research findings since 2000 regarding the essential, or critical, components of effective literacy instruction and related recommendations for instruction.

Table 1.2: Major Research Findings in Literacy 2000–2020

Researcher	Critical Components	Recommendations
National Reading Panel (2000)	Phonemic Awareness, Phonics, Fluency, Vocabulary, Comprehension	Literacy blocks of at least 90 minutes per day; focus on the 5 critical components
Marzano, Pickering, & Pollock (2001)	Construct meaning through prior knowledge and connections between reading and writing	Activate prior knowledge; reading and writing involve social interactions; help students develop metacognition; connect prior knowledge with new knowledge
Schmoker (2011)	Wide reading of both fiction and nonfiction texts	Focus on reading, writing, discussion, and thinking; "involve students in discussion of text at least three times a week and formal writing at least once a month" (Schmoker, 2011, p. 142)
Foorman et al. (2016); Graham et al. (2012)	Oral language, phonological awareness, phonics, spelling, syntax, fluency, vocabulary, comprehension, and the writing process	Provide direct instruction in the content and pedagogical practices that effectively help students develop their reading and writing abilities

Researcher	Critical Components	Recommendations
Hattie & Yates (2013)	High impact/high effect size: vocabulary (0.60); direct instruction (0.60); phonics (0.70); repeated reading (0.75); summarizing (0.79); classroom discussion (0.82); and integrating prior knowledge (0.93) [*Note:* A large effect size (over 0.6) means that the factor has a significant impact on learning.]	Effective instruction should include these high-impact components and should involve activating prior knowledge, explicit instruction, repeated readings, and classroom discussions about text
Heinemann Publishing (2016), a meta-analysis of studies	Direct teaching of comprehension strategies; read aloud to students; silent reading time; monitoring students' understanding during reading; daily opportunities to talk about their reading	Focus on meaning; provide silent reading time; offer regular opportunities to interact with print; balance the teaching of phonics with other important reading activities; teach and model how to use specific cognitive strategies; frontload comprehension strategies; monitor understanding during reading; connect reading to writing
Reutzel & Cooter (2018)	High volumes of reading and writing; use various media and technologies to increase world knowledge; directly teach and model reading and writing strategies	"Engage students in high volumes of reading and writing; explicitly teach reading and writing strategies; encourage students to use strategies to interact with and process text; make connections between literature and content areas" (Reutzel & Cooter, 2018, p. 3)
Shanahan (2019a)	Complex texts support development of reading proficiency; application of vocabulary strategies; using strategies to create meaning	Use complex texts for reading instruction; use grade-level texts; provide opportunities for students to apply vocabulary strategies and to use comprehension strategies to create meaning from the text
Fisher & Frey (2020)	Oral language, phonemic awareness, phonics, vocabulary, fluency, and comprehension (summarizing, asking questions, making inferences)	"Explicit teaching of comprehension strategies including self-monitoring of their own understanding; teach students to apply fix-up strategies including rereading" (Fisher & Frey, 2020, p. 369)

This research indicates solid support for instructing students in all elements of the science of reading from phonemic awareness and phonics to fluency, vocabulary knowledge, and comprehension of text. The research also shows the importance of explicit instruction in vocabulary and comprehension strategies and in providing regular opportunities for students to interact with and discuss text.

The Reading League (2022) describes the science of reading as "a vast, interdisciplinary body of scientifically based research about reading and issues related to reading and writing" (Brady, 2020). This research is based on thousands of studies conducted since the 1970s in multiple countries around the world. The science of reading research recognizes five main components of literacy instruction: phonemic awareness, phonics, fluency, vocabulary, and comprehension.

Cindy Jiban (2022) explains key aspects of literacy instruction based on the science of reading as follows:

- Decoding skills and phonics taught clearly and sequentially
- Reading and writing practice that applies those skills purposefully
- Use of a rich, complex text for all the students in the class
- Multiple readings of the same text "beginning with teacher modeling and moving to student practice" and repeated readings to develop fluency
- Ensuring "the voices of students and the teacher [are heard] in high-quality conversations about the text that focus on language, structure, and deepened understanding"

Jill Staake (2022) reiterates that a science of reading classroom usually follows a structured sequential curriculum that emphasizes phonics. Students spend a significant amount of time learning sounds, blends, and phonemes in order to quickly decode any word they come across (Staake, 2022). Students see fluent reading modeled for them, then practice on their own. They read one text multiple times, focusing on different elements including decoding, vocabulary, and comprehension or determining the meaning of the text (Staake, 2022).

Why Quality Literacy Instruction Matters

NAEP found that students in the United States who live near or below the poverty level indicate lower performance on standardized reading tests than their higher-socioeconomic peers. NCES (2019) indicated that reading scores for both fourth- and eighth-grade students in 2019 were lower than in 2017 and cited factors including parents' levels of education, language constraints, and mobility to be some of the major challenges for urban school settings.

Despite NCLB (U.S. Department of Education, Office of Elementary and Secondary Education, 2002) and the expectations of the ESSA legislation, some struggling students are still not achieving. ESSA statistics for 2019 show that some states have identified up to 20 percent of their schools as needing comprehensive support and up to 47 percent of the schools as in need of targeted assistance.

Students who learn to read well in the early school years are more likely to be engaged in school and experience academic success. On the other hand, a deficiency in reading skills impacts achievement in all other areas of education (Jones, 2006). The Children's Reading Foundation posited that "without a strong foundation in reading, children may lag in every class, year after year, because more than 85 percent of the curriculum is taught through reading and by the end of third grade, 74 percent of struggling readers won't ever catch up" (Jacoby & Lesaux, 2017).

The Carol Pufahl Literacy Foundation (n.d.) found that 43 percent of people with the lowest literacy skills live in poverty, with up to 47 percent receiving food stamps and 70 percent having no job or a part-time job. More than 65 percent of all state and federal correctional system inmates have low literacy levels, with an average literacy level of fourth grade, and 85 percent of juvenile offenders have difficulty reading (Council for Advancement of Adult Literacy, 2008).

By fourth grade, 80 percent of low-income students show that they are reading below grade level. The effects of low literacy proficiency cost the United States $225 billion or more each year in nonproductivity in the workforce, crime, and tax revenue loss, due to unemployment (www.literacyforallfund.org). In *Hot Topics in Education*, the authors posited that our students' literacy achievement significantly impacts our nation's political, economic, and social decisions, as well as our nation's prosperity (Study.com, 2011).

Students with the lowest literacy scores are 16 times more likely, as adults, to have received public financial aid in the past year than students who read proficiently. These adults are also more likely to be in the lowest wage group, earning about 35 percent less than literate people (Gunn, 2018). Lack of success in reading is a major factor in whether adolescents graduate from high school, and approximately 17 percent, or about 1.2 million teens, drop out each year. In addition, 85 percent of youth who are involved in the juvenile court system fall into the category of functionally illiterate (Renaissance Learning, 2019).

Conclusion

National and international studies indicate that U.S. students are not making adequate or even consistent progress in levels of reading proficiency. We must not continue to do what has not been working. This overview of what effective reading instruction should look like, based on research, should lead the reader to conclude that there is no one perfect way to teach reading. However, certain practices positively impact students' literacy development based on studies from a variety of researchers over time.

Research clearly indicates the need for and importance of including instruction in all the components of the science of reading—providing explicit instruction, modeling, and practice in phonemic awareness, phonics, fluency, vocabulary, and comprehension—and making sure that all students engage in the grade-level curriculum. Despite the evidence that there is no magic bullet or best model or program for teaching reading, the recommendations for literacy instruction discussed in this chapter serve as the major focus of *Solving the Literacy Puzzle* and provide teachers with a guide for research-based, comprehensive reading instruction based on tried-and-true best practices. When teachers implement these practices, they can feel confident that their reading instruction is sound, is based on research, and will help all students develop reading proficiency and meet their full potential.

Chapter 2 (page 25) will address selecting the text to use for reading instruction, making decisions about grouping students, and determining the format for literacy instruction. Chapters 3–10 (pages 43, 65, 83, 111, 129, 143, 157, 167, respectively) will provide information about the essential components of the science of reading, including a brief review of research related to the component, strategies for incorporating the component into your reading instruction, and templates for research-based instructional planning.

Reflection Questions for Chapter 1:
Literacy Instruction and Why It Matters

Thinking back over the years, what literacy practices have you continued using due to their positive impact on students' reading proficiency?

Are there some reading instructional practices that you have discontinued using, although they were effective? Why do you think this has occurred?

Are there issues regarding literacy instruction that confuse or frustrate you?

Chapter 2

Text Selection and Instructional Grouping

To learn to read is to light a fire; every syllable that is spelled out is a spark.

—VICTOR HUGO

Universal, or core, instruction occurs when educators teach the whole class a lesson. Whole-group lessons are based on specific grade-level standards and are appropriate for students at their grade level (Colorado Department of Education, 2022). In effective universal, or core, instruction, each student receives high-quality, research-based, differentiated instruction from a general education teacher in a general education (classroom) setting (Iowa Department of Education, 2018). Universal instruction includes the curriculum, instruction, and assessments that all students are guaranteed to participate in at that grade level. Universal, or core, instruction typically focuses on state grade-level standards. All components of the science of reading are included in universal instruction. Instruction may be based on a selected reading model, drawn from a commercially available program, or created by the teachers or school district.

Universal, or core, instruction "should meet the needs of approximately 80% of the students when instructional programming is scientific and evidence-based and delivered by a highly knowledgeable classroom teacher" (Brown, Fabiano, & Pechacek, 2022).

To provide quality core instruction, it is essential to select a text for reading instruction with several considerations in mind and with the ultimate goal of supporting the development of students' reading comprehension. Teachers should utilize various genres so that multiple types of text, both informational and literary, are used for instruction. Perhaps most importantly, teachers need to intentionally choose texts that will support their instructional goals. In this chapter, we'll review the structure and benefits of student grouping for literacy instruction, literacy interventions, and some strategies for developing literacy using grade-level texts and activities.

Literacy Using Grade-Level Texts

Educators strive for all students to be successful in reading grade-level texts and performing well on high-stakes assessments, which test students at their grade level. Unfortunately, in many schools teachers do not use grade-level texts for reading instruction because they seem too difficult for the students, which should be a red flag to educators. The RAND Corporation surveyed thousands of teachers and determined that many students are assigned books that are below grade level—sometimes, far below. The RAND study found that "elementary ELA teachers reported spending the majority of in- and out-of-class reading time on leveled texts" rather than grade-level reading (Stack, 2017, p. 33). Another study by TPNT (formerly The New Teacher Project) Teaching Fellows found that students were only asked to meet grade-level expectations a mere 17 percent of the time (Schmidt, 2020). Suppose, due to leveled literacy instruction, many or even most of the students in our classrooms cannot successfully handle grade-level text. If these students continue to be instructed using below-grade-level texts, when will they catch up? If we ensure that all students leave the classroom at the end of each school year showing proficiency on grade-level text and standards, teachers in subsequent grades will also be able to utilize grade-level text and hold grade-appropriate expectations for students.

All students should have the opportunity to be involved in quality core literacy instruction, focused on grade-level standards, utilizing a grade-appropriate text. When steps are taken to activate prior knowledge, introduce new vocabulary words, and engage in prereading activities, most students will be able to successfully read grade-appropriate text. The Mid-continent Research for Education and Learning's (McREL, 2016) response to intervention (RTI) triangle indicates that 80–90 percent of students will be successful when they receive effective core instruction.

Current reading instructional practices, such as ability grouping (small-group instruction using leveled texts) and students being pulled out of the classroom for reading interventions, often provided by a Title I teacher or an interventionist, mean that some students do not have the opportunity to participate in universal, or core, reading instruction that utilizes a grade-level text. There's actually "scant evidence that leveled reading is an effective strategy, experts say, and mounting concern that it may hurt the weakest readers in the long run" (D'Souza, 2022). Asking students to read below-grade-level texts can cause students to be reading below their peers for so long that they become discouraged, or they may lack self-esteem. Young learners can feel stigmatized by reading low-level books, while their peers are reading chapter books. That can become a self-fulfilling prophecy, widening the achievement gap (D'Souza, 2022). We need to be mindful about the importance of ensuring *all* students have the chance to learn essential ELA standards through core instruction in grade-appropriate texts.

Extensive research has identified multiple benefits of using grade-level texts for literacy instruction for all students. Choosing the right book can have a significant impact on students' enjoyment of reading and their overall development. Age-appropriate texts are typically of higher interest to students; therefore, they motivate students to want to read more. Texts should be selected that will engage and challenge students, while also being age-appropriate. Age-appropriate books will facilitate students' natural development and ensure that they find reading more enjoyable (Busheri et al., 2022). Grade-level texts require students to apply the word-busting and comprehension skills they have been taught and prepare students to do well on grade-level assessments.

Despite concerns about the potential frustration levels of struggling students when reading grade-level texts, studies find the difficulty of a text is typically not detrimental to the students' motivation to read the texts. The interest level and the complexity, or challenge, of the text are factors that may positively impact students' motivation to read (Shanahan, 2022). Stack (2017) posited that "giving all students grade-level (and sometimes, even above grade-level) texts built knowledge and motivated readers with interesting, relevant content" and held students to high expectations, while providing plenty of support.

Teachers need to select the grade-level instructional text based on the learning targets, or standards, that they want to address. Nell K. Duke (2010) recommended that teachers ask, "What am I trying to teach here, and what text is going to facilitate that best?" Edward S. Shapiro (n.d.) determined that high-quality grade-appropriate core reading instruction should be provided to all students and delivered in the general education classroom. Renowned educational researcher Timothy Shanahan (2020b) stated:

> I do support the idea of teaching reading with grade level texts. . . . Studies of the instructional level find that it at best makes no difference—that is, kids learn as much from grade level text as they do from instructional level ones. And, in the worst cases, the studies show that those easier text placements actually hold kids back and severely limit their learning.

Table 2.1 (page 28) explains the effects of using grade-level texts compared to using ability-level texts for literacy instruction.

Table 2.1: The Effects of Using Grade-Level Texts Versus Ability-Level Texts

Teaching With Grade-Level Texts		Teaching With Ability-Level Texts
Students are challenged to apply reading strategies to access and understand the text.	**vs.**	Students read less-complex texts and have less opportunity to access and understand grade-level text.
Grade-level texts are more interesting to the students, which leads to higher levels of motivation to read.	**vs.**	Below-grade-level texts are often less interesting and less age-appropriate.
All students have the chance to learn essential grade-level ELA standards.	**vs.**	Below-grade-level groups may focus on lower-level or fewer standards.
Grade-level texts teach students as much as, or more than, ability-level texts.	**vs.**	Students may learn less compared to students who have access to grade-level texts.
Grade-level texts require students to apply word-busting and comprehension skills.	**vs.**	Less complex text requires less application of reading strategies.
Reading grade-level texts prepares students to do well on grade-level assessments.	**vs.**	Some students are taught to read below-grade-level texts; therefore, they are ill prepared to take grade-level assessments.
More students will be reading on grade level and prepared for the next level.	**vs.**	Students continue to read below grade level as they progress to the next grade.

Matching students with books at their "level" is a practice that many educators and school leaders use; however, this isn't working, as nearly two-thirds of fourth graders and eighth graders are not proficient readers, according to the 2019 NAEP results.

Brown, Mohr, Wilcox, and Barrett (2018) determined that using grade-level or complex text with scaffolding can support the reading growth of older struggling readers. Jiban (2020) went as far as stating, "You deny students the right to improve their reading comprehension if you don't grant them access every day to some meaty grade-level text." Jiban (2020) determined that "students develop their comprehension . . . by working with written texts full of challenging words and syntax."

Using below-level texts, as often occurs in small-group or guided reading, can actually hinder students' reading proficiency. When all students are involved in high-quality, grade-level core literacy instruction, we will be able to increase proficiency levels and create successful, strategic readers.

It is important to intentionally select a text for literacy instruction that meets the following criteria.

- Is somewhat challenging, as this encourages students to work hard on their comprehension skills and apply effective reading comprehension strategies.

- Will be of potentially high interest to students and engage them with the text. Using texts that are more interesting to the students leads to higher motivation and more application of reading comprehension strategies (Duke, 2010).

- Is selected based on the learning targets, or standards, that the teacher wants to address. Duke (2010) recommends that teachers ask, "What am I trying to teach here, and what text is going to facilitate that best?"

- Will directly support the teaching, modeling, and application of a specific comprehension strategy. Duke (2010) reiterates that "it's all about picking the kind of text that's going to be the best vehicle for your comprehension instruction" (Duke, 2010).

- Will provide opportunities for students of all ability levels to engage in rich conversations centered on the grade-level text.

The rubric in figure 2.1 (page 30) may be beneficial to utilize when selecting instructional texts to ensure they adhere to the previous criteria.

After rating various texts using these criteria and this rubric, select an instructional text for which all, or the majority, of the criteria scored *likely* or *very likely*. It's fine to have a rating or two of *unsure*; however, you may decide not to utilize a text that has a number of *unsure* or *not very likely* ratings. Lower ratings often indicate that the book may not support the standards and the goals you are hoping to achieve during literacy instruction.

Text is somewhat challenging and will encourage students to work hard on decoding and context clues skills and apply effective reading comprehension strategies.	Not Very Likely	Unsure	Likely	Very Likely
Text will be engaging, of potentially high interest to students, and will motivate them to continue reading.	Not Very Likely	Unsure	Likely	Very Likely
Text will directly support the learning targets, or standards, that the teacher wants to address.	Not Very Likely	Unsure	Likely	Very Likely
Text will directly support the teaching, modeling, and application of a specific comprehension strategy.	Not Very Likely	Unsure	Likely	Very Likely
Text will provide opportunities for students of all ability levels to engage in rich conversations centered on the grade-level text.	Not Very Likely	Unsure	Likely	Very Likely
Text is considered on grade level and age appropriate.	Not Very Likely	Unsure	Likely	Very Likely

Figure 2.1: Rubric for selecting an appropriate text for effective literacy instruction.

Visit **go.SolutionTree.com/literacy** *for a free reproducible version of this figure.*

Student Groups for Literacy Instruction

Along with choosing a grade-level-appropriate text that is well suited to students' interests and the instructional goals, teachers must make important decisions regarding which setting will provide the most effective instruction. We must carefully consider the format for reading instruction, including the grouping of students. As discussed earlier in this chapter, all students must have the opportunity to participate in the core, grade-level curriculum, based on state standards. Therefore, whole-group instruction should make up the majority of academic time during reading periods or literacy blocks. Unfortunately, since the early 2000s, most schools have greatly reduced, or even eliminated, whole-group instruction and have implemented ability, or leveled, grouping for reading instruction as the daily format for all students, rather than using temporary, flexible small groups to provide additional support for students on specific skills and standards. Ability grouping, also referred to as *tracking*, has been found to have a limited positive impact on students' reading proficiency, and can have some unintended negative consequences.

Ability Grouping or Grouping by Reading Levels

Using small-group instruction for the specific purpose of closing achievement gaps was introduced as *RTI* in 2004, which led to many schools incorporating the use of small-group literacy instruction based on students' proficiency. This typically meant placing students in small groups based on their perceived reading levels. The use of *guided reading* practices including literacy stations or daily rotations became common practice in a large number of schools.

Beginning readers benefit most from being taught explicit skills during intensive small-group instruction. Educators believed the small-group, differentiated reading model allowed teachers the opportunity to reteach and provide additional practice that some students needed on specific skills (Wilson, Nabors, Berg, Simpson, & Timme, 2012).

However, research over time has shown small-group instruction based on ability to have a minimal impact on student learning. Larrijsen and colleagues (2022) determined grouping students in distinct classes according to ability might have little overall benefit. Meta-analyses of studies related to the use of small groups for reading instruction indicated lower effect sizes than for other content areas (only 0.13; Shanahan, 2018).

Studies have shown that in-class grouping for literacy instruction using texts that are matched to the perceived instructional levels of students may have the following consequences.

- The students "most likely to end up in the below grade level groups are racial or linguistic minorities, kids with disabilities, and high poverty kids" (Hallinan & Sorenson, 1983, cited by Shanahan, 2020b).

- Ability grouping can worsen reading gaps over time. Students in high reading groups in early grades had higher reading test scores, while those assigned to low reading groups had lower scores over the years. These differences grew with every year students were grouped in reading (Sparks, 2022).

- Students are being taught to and expected to read below-grade-level texts, yet they are assessed using grade-level materials. The NAEP for reading measures reading comprehension by asking students to read selected grade-appropriate materials and answer questions based on what they have read (NCES, 2019).

- Teachers often have lower expectations for students due to perceived levels of ability. Students who have a history of academic struggles, behavior issues, living in poverty, or transience are often ostracized and separated into small groups based on perceived ability where expectations are lowered (Wilson, 2019).

- "Ability grouping can exacerbate achievement gaps and even slow reading growth for some children, unless the groups are fluid and focused on skills, rather than overall achievement" (Sparks, 2018).

Several studies have corroborated that ability grouping appeared to have no advantages regarding students' growth in reading proficiency. Anthony Buttaro Jr. and Sophia Catsambis (2019) find that rather than reducing gaps in achievement, "students' ability group placements in the early grades evolved into divergent educational paths that grow further apart with multiple years of grouping" (p. 45). A study by Sönke Hendrik Matthewes (2021) explores students' achievement before and after tracking and before and after whole-group comprehensive instruction and finds evidence of positive effects of engagement in whole-group comprehensive instruction on reading scores over time, as compared to students in leveled, or tracked, groups.

In addition to the limited positive impact on student achievement, using a small-group approach to literacy instruction is labor-intensive for teachers and causes teachers to teach skills and strategies multiple times, while struggling to engage students who are not in the small group in meaningful instructional activities. Another drawback to using a small-group format for reading instruction is the limited time available for oral reading, modeling and application of comprehension strategies, and discussion of text within a heterogeneous, whole-group setting. In *The Science of Reading Explained*, Jiban (2022) states:

> We should stop seeing comprehension taught via leveled reading groups, where each group visits the teacher for round-robin reading through a new text "at the right level." Instead, we should see use of a rich, complex text for all the students in a class. We should hear multiple reads of the same text, beginning with teacher modeling and moving to student practice. We should see partnering for repeated readings to develop fluency. We should hear the voices of students and the teacher in high-quality conversations about the text that focus on language, structure, and deepened understanding.

Small-group, leveled instruction severely limits the opportunity for rich discussions of text to support the development of comprehension due to time restraints and the lack of a common text to guide discussions. All students should have the opportunity to receive instruction in a grade-appropriate text and to be engaged in meaningful discussions about text to improve their comprehension skills.

Universal Core Instruction for All Students

In 2015, ESSA brought into focus the importance of all students being engaged in research-based, universal instruction to ensure equity in learning opportunities. ESSA supports a three-tier approach to instruction with the emphasis on quality core instruction for every student. This, in turn, should encourage teachers to include more whole-group instruction during their literacy blocks.

Therefore, when planning reading instruction, it is important to ensure that all students receive high-quality instruction in a heterogeneous, whole-group setting for 45–60 minutes of the literacy block. Universal instruction means that *all* students receive instruction within an evidence-based, core program, typically within the whole-group setting. If the universal, standards-based program is implemented with a high degree of integrity, then most of the students receiving this instruction will indicate a level of proficiency on grade-level assessments (Shapiro, n.d.).

Using a whole-group setting to introduce concepts and strategies allows the teacher to present the basic material to all students at one time. When whole-group instruction is effective and engaging, most students will pick up the new concepts and skills. Strategies, resources, and templates will be provided in subsequent chapters to foster high levels of student engagement for each component of the science of reading.

Trying to introduce a new concept in various small-group settings is both cumbersome and repetitive (Meador, 2023). Whole-group instruction is time-efficient and ensures that every student is exposed to key grade-level concepts.

Whole-group instructional time allows all students to receive explicit instruction in grade-appropriate texts, skills, and strategies. It provides teachers time to model strategies and allows all students, including ELs and students with IEPs, to be included in research-based, quality instruction. Instruction in the content areas, including literacy, should be designed to be comprehensive, while also developing academic language proficiency. Core instruction for ELs can be supported through the use of a number of instructional models, including the Sheltered Instruction Observation Protocol (SIOP) Model (Hermann, n.d.). The SIOP is an instructional model, based on evidence, that has been shown to be effective in addressing the academic needs of ELs (SIOP.com, n.d.).

Students with IEPs can flourish by participating in whole-group instruction in classrooms that integrate effective co-teaching models where students with and without disabilities can access specially designed instruction (Rodriguez & Novak, 2013). Co-teaching involves general education and special education teachers working together to plan lessons, teach, monitor student progress, and manage the class (Morin, n.d.). In addition, all students will benefit through engagement with like and unlike peers in rich discussions of grade-appropriate text. Giving all students opportunities to learn grade-level skills and read grade-appropriate text supports equity and high expectations.

Small-Group Instruction Based on Specific Student Needs

Along with whole-group instruction, *Solving the Literacy Puzzle* recommends small-group instruction (that supports universal instruction) be included as part of the reading block. Rather than students being placed in groups based on their perceived abilities and remaining in these groups for a significant period of time, groups need to be flexible and should include instructional activities based on students' specific needs. Small groups should provide students with different levels of scaffolded support along with *like* peers, or peers with similar learning needs.

Instruction in small groups should support the standards being taught in the whole group during core instruction. Homogeneous small-group instruction can directly target skill gaps, provide more guided practice, and provide more opportunities for immediate feedback (University of Oregon, n.d.). For example, after core instruction using grade-level text, some students may receive reteaching or additional support in understanding the vocabulary words or applying the focused comprehension strategy. This can foster their success with the grade-level text and standards.

It is most effective when small-group instruction is directly connected to whole-group instruction. For example, if summarizing text is the comprehension strategy being taught and modeled during core instruction, the teacher might provide additional modeling and guided practice in summarizing text in a small group for students in need of more support. Small-group instruction usually follows whole-group instruction to reinforce or reteach specific skills and concepts and provides a reduced student-teacher ratio (Van Zant & Volpe, 2018).

Students should receive additional support, reteaching, and practice in phonics, vocabulary, comprehension, fluency, and writing based on the core instruction. Students who are high-achieving should engage in instructional tasks that are cognitively challenging and allow them to apply their learning in creative ways. This can occur through small-group instruction, partner work, or independent projects.

Activities for cooperative learning, including literature circles, discussion groups, and reciprocal teaching, should also be integrated into the small-group component of reading instruction. Literature circles and discussion protocols engage students in meaningful discussions about the text, with all students actively involved through having a clear *role* that they must fill. Reciprocal teaching involves students in *being the teachers*. For example, each small group or pair of students might be *in charge of* sharing a new vocabulary word, providing its meaning, using it in a sentence, creating a visual for the word, and presenting this to the class.

Strategies to Help All Students Succeed With Grade-Level Text

Using grade-level text for literacy instruction can seem overwhelming, especially if students have been taught using leveled books or small-group guided reading. However, there are several steps teachers can take to help all students read grade-level texts. Students who struggle with whole-group instruction using an on-grade-level text may need to have various types of support to be successful. The following are some strategies that can be used to provide different types and levels of support for students who need additional help while reading grade-level texts. These strategies are effective when used from the beginning of the school year or at any time during the school year.

1. Discuss Tricky Words Before Students Read

One effective practice is to carefully peruse the text to identify words that may be difficult for students to decode or to understand. Preteaching these words can be very helpful for students in reading a challenging text. Characters' names, names of places, academic vocabulary words, and rarely used, or unusual, words might need to be addressed prior to reading the text. Following the steps below can be beneficial for many students.

- Before the lesson, read the text. Make a list of words that you anticipate students will struggle with, including characters' names and proper nouns.

- Teach these words to students in context, providing explicit instruction on words that are important in understanding the text.

- Using a sentence, paragraph, or passage from the instructional text, model how you use word-busting skills to figure out words that you do not know.

- Model the use of context clues within the sentence, paragraph, or passage to determine what the word is and what it might mean.

- Have students read the words together preferably several times in isolation or within the sentence, paragraph, or passage. Figure 2.2 (page 36) provides an example from *Charlotte's Web* (White, 1952) of how to teach tricky words while modeling decoding strategies, use of context clues to determine meaning, and language arts skills. Note the use of passages from the text and use of characters' names as this assists students in being better prepared to read the text.

Vocabulary Word	Word-Busting Skills to Model	Context Clues to Determine the Word and Its Meaning	Other Skills to Integrate
sedentary	sed-en-tar-y (break into word parts)	"I'm glad that I'm **sedentary**," said Charlotte. "There's no need to hurry about all day, using up my energy" (p. 80).	Review short *e*, /ar/, and *y* (long *e*)
leftovers	left/overs	"Inside it were **leftovers** from somebody's lunch: a deviled ham sandwich, a piece of Swiss cheese, part of a hard-boiled egg, and the core of a wormy apple" (p. 182).	Compound word
untenable	un-ten-able	"But, my friends," said Wilbur, "if that ancient egg ever breaks, this barn will be **untenable**" (p. 61).	Prefix *un-* and suffix *-able*

Figure 2.2: Example of strategy 1 using Charlotte's Web (White, 1952).

2. Pull Out a Few Challenging Sentences From the Text to Have Students Practice Before Reading the Text Independently

It is important to read through the text carefully from the viewpoint of your students to determine which words and phrases (places, character names, complex or multisyllable words, an unfamiliar context, and so on) students may struggle with. Prior to students reading the text independently or with a partner, modeling how to read these words and phrases fluently and providing guided practice by having the students read along can prevent students from being tripped up when they come to these more challenging portions of the text. This strategy can be a valuable portion of your regular preparation before reading, whether you are using a basal story, an article, or chapters of a novel.

- Choose 2–4 challenging or confusing sentences in the text. These sentences may be longer than other sentences in the text, contain tricky words, or include important vocabulary words.

- Write them on sentence strips or display on the large screen. (You can also just highlight or use a sticky note to mark them directly in the texts that students will use.)

- Model reading these sentences and have students read them with you a couple of times.

An example of a complex sentence from *Charlotte's Web* (White, 1952) is:

> "I am sure," Charlotte said, "that every one of us here will be glad to learn that after four weeks of **unremitting** effort and patience on the part of our friend the goose, she now has something to show for it, as the babies have arrived." (p. 58)

Reading and discussing this sentence prior to students' reading the story or chapter independently will be beneficial to students' reading fluency and their comprehension of the text.

3. Provide Background Information on the Content of the Text

When the instructional text is related to a complex concept or a unique setting, culture, or time period, it is vital to help students activate prior knowledge they may already have, or to learn about the concept, setting, culture, or time period prior to reading the text. For example, if the story is about ancient Greece, you need to help students identify what they already know and to develop some understanding of this context and time period. The more the reader knows about the topic, the easier it is for them to comprehend the text. The following are some strategies to help spark or develop prior knowledge.

- Show a short video clip that relates to the text.
- Read students a different, related book or story to build background knowledge.
- Complete the "K" (What I *Know*) and "W" (What I *Want* to Know) parts of a KWL chart.
- Ask students with some prior knowledge or experiences to teach the class about this topic.

4. During the First Read, Read Part of the Text With Students

If we want students to feel comfortable and prepared to read grade-level text on their own, in addition to teaching unfamiliar words, phrases, and concepts and developing prior knowledge, it is important to get students off on the right foot by reading the first part of the text aloud.

- Model reading the first portion of the text fluently to students.
- Ask students to follow along as you read.

- Assign the students to continue reading the rest of the text on their own or with a partner.

- If you still think that students will struggle—or you have them start reading and discover that they're really struggling—you can provide more support.

- Try *choral reading*, where you and the students read the text aloud together. After the choral reading is finished, students should go back and read the text entirely on their own.

- You might also ask students to whisper read the text to you so that you can provide support along the way.

Note: For students in kindergarten and early first grade, you may wish to read the entire text to them and then read the text altogether, before asking them to read the text independently.

5. With a Longer Text, Break It Up Into Smaller Chunks

Effective teachers understand that long, or complex, texts may seem overwhelming and even frustrating for students. You can almost see students thinking, "Do we have to read all of this?" Reassuring students that they will be reading only a portion of the text at one time is helpful. Making decisions about how much text your students can handle in one day or one literacy block is important. We want students to understand and enjoy the text in manageable *chunks.*

- Thoughtfully decide the best way to read the text based on its length and complexity. Determine how much to read each day.

- If a text is challenging for students, consider asking them to read just a manageable portion or section.

- Read the text, or portions of the text, aloud and discuss the text to build comprehension.

- Stretch the reading out over several days.

6. Have Students Read the Text Multiple Times

Students in the early grades (K–2) should read books and stories more than once. At these grade levels, reading a book or story at least three times helps to build fluency and comprehension. In grades 3 and beyond, rereading at least once can be valuable. After students read the text on their own or with a partner, it is important to read parts of the story or book orally as a class, guided by the teacher, so that students can engage in discussions of the most critical portions of the text.

- Intentionally decide which parts of the text are the most important or interesting in regard to comprehending the story or book.

- Some of the rereads can take place in the whole group with the teacher and students taking turns reading aloud.

- Rereads can also take place in small groups and during independent reading, rotations, or partner reading times.

- For students who still experience difficulty with the text, have them read with a peer or to an adult, with support as needed.

- In the early grades, students should read and reread the story or book for 3–5 days. Older students should read a text at least twice, with an emphasis on engaging with the text through discussions.

7. Support Students Through Interventions

Despite implementing the previous six strategies, some students may still need additional support to read grade-level text with fluency and understanding. These students may benefit from reading the text with adult assistance, engaging in additional rereads of the text, and being provided with preteaching or reteaching of vocabulary, comprehension, and other skills and strategies. Recommendations for supporting struggling students include:

- Additional interventions based on formative, diagnostic assessments, such as FastBridge (CBMreading and aReading) or other assessments (DIBELS [Dynamic Indicators of Basic Early Literacy Skills] and others), should be provided.

- Small-group or individual interventions should be available for students with more serious learning delays based on students' specific needs (ELs, students with learning disabilities or dyslexia).

- Interventions should directly address students' learning gaps in all components of the science of reading—phonics, comprehension, vocabulary, fluency, and writing.

Conclusion

This chapter has addressed the first phase of literacy instructional planning using *Solving the Literacy Puzzle*, which includes choosing an appropriate text that aligns with the identified standards or learning targets and determining the instructional format that will be best matched to the learning targets. Please see the reproducible on page 41 for a template for the first phase of planning for research-based literacy instruction.

Chapter 3 (page 43) will address research-based vocabulary instruction and methods to select words for instruction, how to explicitly teach new words, and ways to engage students in repeated exposures and practice in recognizing and using vocabulary words.

Part 1: Selection of Text and Grouping Format Instructional Template

Instructional text for whole-group instruction (use rubric):

District and essential standards or learning targets:

Instructional groupings:

Additional texts (if needed):

Note: If a set reading program is being utilized, the literacy standards or learning outcomes may already be identified. If no formal program is used for reading instruction, it is recommended that the teacher use the Common Core ELA standards and the school's identified outcomes and objectives as references to determine the learning outcomes and align the standards and learning targets to the instructional text.

Reflection Questions for Chapter 2: Text Selection and Instructional Grouping

How often do *all* your students receive high-quality, whole-group instruction in the grade-level curriculum?

How often do *all* your students have opportunities to read grade-level-appropriate text?

What changes in your current literacy instructional practices, related to instructional text and the grouping of students, might you consider based on chapter 2 (page 25)?

Chapter 3

Vocabulary Instruction and Word Retention

I never teach my pupils. I only attempt to provide the conditions in which they can learn.

—**ALBERT EINSTEIN**

As one of the five core components of the science of reading, quality vocabulary instruction is essential in teaching students how to read. Vocabulary development helps students to activate prior knowledge, express their ideas clearly, and communicate effectively. Vocabulary instruction is important at all levels because there is a clear relationship between vocabulary knowledge and reading comprehension (Olson, 2021). Teaching young students to be word conscious helps them develop useful habits for vocabulary development.

Observations in classrooms and research studies have shown that there is limited time allocated for vocabulary instruction in many of today's classrooms. Jeffrey Lawrence McQuillan (2019) finds that teachers in upper elementary and middle school spent on average only 6 percent of classroom time on vocabulary instruction. The Texas Center for Learning Disabilities determined that typically, only 5 to 10 percent of instructional time is spent on vocabulary instruction (TCLD, 2023). Direct vocabulary instruction in words and in word-learning strategies influences reading comprehension (Strasser & Rio, 2013). Vocabulary instruction should be taught beginning in kindergarten, and it should focus on the use of strategies, such as structural analysis and context clues, and multiple exposures to words and their meanings (Strasser & Rio, 2013).

Observations have indicated that if time is dedicated to vocabulary teaching, the vocabulary words are frequently unrelated to the texts that the students are reading. Words for instruction are often selected randomly, or as part of a vocabulary program, such as *Word Journeys* (Ganske, 2000), rather than words that the students need to know to understand the text they will be reading.

Classroom observations also indicate that it is common for there to be little explicit instruction in vocabulary words and even less modeling of word-learning strategies, such as structural analysis and use of context clues. In addition, vocabulary activities frequently focus on the students' listening or receptive vocabulary, not their reading vocabulary. Fisher and Frey (2014) reiterate the importance of teachers modeling their own word-solving strategies within vocabulary instruction, yet Elizabeth Swanson and colleagues (2015) finds that only two out of nine teachers provide instruction in text-reading practices, such as use of context clues.

Observations also indicate that there is little opportunity for students to develop *deep* understandings of words and to practice word-learning strategies. It is the norm in many classrooms to provide limited activities for repeated exposure to vocabulary or multiple interactions with words. Additionally, independent reading, rather than vocabulary instruction, is commonly relied upon for vocabulary learning, a practice that is not consistently supported by research.

In this chapter, the emphasis will be on current research-based practices to build vocabulary knowledge, enhance word retention, and design effective, engaging vocabulary instruction. This chapter will review why vocabulary knowledge is important and how to select vocabulary words for instruction, as well as describing explicit vocabulary instruction strategies and graphic organizers for use in the classroom. Finally, ways to integrate context clues and word analysis into your vocabulary instruction will be discussed.

The Importance of Vocabulary Knowledge

Since the earliest studies of reading comprehension, researchers have found that knowledge of word meanings has a strong relationship to reading comprehension (Merriam-Webster, n.d.). Isabel L. Beck (clinical professor emerita of education at the University of Pittsburgh), Margaret G. McKeown, and Linda Kucan (2002) determine that vocabulary knowledge is strongly related to achievement in general, as well as to reading proficiency. James F. Baumann, Elizabeth Carr Edwards, Eileen M. Boland, Stephen Olejnik, and Edward J. Kame'enui (2003) conclude, "If words power our language and are important to understanding the text we read, then teaching students lots of words should be a first-order strategy for understanding text" (p. 449).

Yang Dong, Yi Tang, Bonnie Wing-Yin Chow, Weisha Wang, and Wei-Yang Dong (2020) conclude that vocabulary knowledge has a positive impact on text comprehension and that more complex skills like inference can be improved through expanding students' vocabulary knowledge.

Elfrieda H. Hiebert (2020), a doctor of educational psychology from the University of Wisconsin–Madison, determines that deep knowledge of core vocabulary is gained through guided conversations and minilessons in which shared and unique features of words are discussed, as well as from extensive reading. Engaging students in discussions that incorporate the use of vocabulary words leads to a greater understanding of the meanings of the words and how the words can be utilized. Words need to be understood receptively through listening and reading; however, using vocabulary words productively through speaking and writing supports more holistic learning and use of the words (Webb & Nation, 2017). Sonia Q. Cabell, Laura M. Justice, Anita S. McGinty, Jamie DeCoster, and Lindsay D. Forston (2015) determine that teacher-student conversations are positively associated with students' vocabulary gains. Minilessons that include introducing new words in context, determining the words' meanings from context, and providing student-friendly definitions and examples of how to correctly use the words also build students' word knowledge. These experiences are essential for all students if they are to acquire the vocabulary knowledge required for literacy proficiency (Hiebert, 2020).

Selecting Vocabulary Words for Explicit Instruction

Vocabulary instruction should initially focus on the most frequently used words in written English. These 300 words account for 65 percent of the total words in text (Cox, 2023). Visit englishyourway.com.br/vocabulary-the-300-most-commonly-used -english-words to view the 300 most commonly used English words.

Practicing these words individually, as well as in the context of sight word phrases, is important for developing automaticity in recalling common words during reading. Demonstrating automaticity in word recognition means that the student immediately recognizes the words and does not need to use decoding or context clues to read the words.

Beyond basic sight words and high-frequency words, students need intentional and direct instruction in key words that may hinder their fluency and comprehension of the selected text. Teachers should consider vocabulary words that are essential to understanding the text, as well as words that are of high utility, when selecting instructional vocabulary words.

Beck and colleagues' (2002) research provides guidance for educators in choosing which vocabulary words to teach explicitly. Words chosen for instruction should be words that are important for understanding the specific reading selection or concept. When selecting vocabulary words for instruction, Beck and colleagues (2002) suggest that teachers keep the following in mind:

- How generally useful the word is, particularly in understanding the text

- If the word is likely to be seen in other contexts

- What "role the word plays in communicating the meaning of the context in which it is used" (Beck et al., 2002, p. 29)

- If the word is likely to be encountered with some frequency in their reading of a variety of texts

- Including process words like *analyze* and *evaluate* that students will run into on many standardized tests and that are also used in everyday life

Hiebert (2020) corroborates Beck and colleagues' (2002) recommendations by stating that words with moderate to high frequency make up 90 percent or more of the words in school texts; therefore, focusing on words that are often encountered, particularly in more than one context, is valuable. Explicit instruction and practice in word-busting skills, such as decoding and using context clues, should play a significant role in vocabulary instruction to assist students in learning new words that may not be as frequently encountered. Modeling morphemic analysis during vocabulary instruction will help them engage in independent word study (Texas Center for Learning Disabilities, n.d.). Teaching students to recognize that many words are derived from, or related to, high-frequency words also supports students' ability to learn new words as they read.

Explicit Instruction in Vocabulary

After intentionally selecting words for vocabulary instruction, careful planning for explicit instruction in the words should be the next step. Most students need to have intentional and direct vocabulary instruction (Osborn, Lehr, & Hiebert, 2004). Word choice and meaning experts Marieke Tomesen and Cor Aarnoutse (1998) indicate that intentional, direct teaching of words and word-learning strategies can add to students' vocabularies and increase reading comprehension. Leanne Zimmermann, an educator and doctor of special education at the University of Iowa College of Education, and Deborah Reed, director of the Tennessee Reading Research Center, reiterate that "effective vocabulary instruction (1) provides students with both definitional and contextual information about a word, (2) offers multiple exposures to the word, and (3) engages students in active practice that fosters deep processing about a word's meaning and how to use the word" (Zimmerman & Reed, 2017).

Research has shown that effective, meaningful vocabulary instruction includes the following steps (Beck et al., 2002; Marzano, 2020).

1. **Introducing the words in context:** Use sentences or passages from the instructional text, projected on a screen so all students can see them, and model reading the sentence and pronouncing the new words, while also modeling decoding strategies.

2. **Providing or creating visual representations for the word:** Provide pictures that represent the words and what they mean. These can be online pictures or drawings or photos on picture cards.

3. **Explaining or defining the word in "student-friendly" terms:** Put the meaning of the new words in terms that students can relate to and understand.

4. **Providing examples of the word used in different contexts:** Give written or oral examples of using the words in sentences. You may need to use several sentences if it is a multimeaning word.

5. **Contextualizing the word (determining how it is used in the text):** While introducing the words in the context of a sentence or passage, identify the clues in the text that help the reader figure out what the word means. Highlighting or underlining the context clues can be beneficial.

6. **Multiple exposures and repeated practice with the word:** Make sure that students see and read the vocabulary words several times when they are introduced and on several subsequent days. Engage students in games and activities in which they need to use or interact with the vocabulary words.

Graphic Organizers for Whole-Group, Small-Group, or Independent Work

Robert J. Marzano, Debra J. Pickering, and Jane E. Pollock (2001) and Marzano (2020) conclude that concept mapping and semantic mapping, grouping and labeling words, using visuals and graphic organizers, and generating examples and non-examples of words are effective techniques for increasing vocabulary word learning and retention.

The following vocabulary graphic organizers support the learning of vocabulary words during and following explicit instruction. After the teacher has introduced the word and explained its meaning, it is valuable for students to write the word and their own student-friendly definition of the word. Asking students to come up with synonyms, antonyms, people who might use the word, and examples of how the word can be used helps students to develop a deeper understanding of the word. Graphic organizers also encourage students to make connections to other words that they may already know. It works well to have each student, or pairs of students, select one of the new vocabulary words, complete the graphic organizer, then show and explain their completed graphic organizer to the class to help *teach* the new word. Students may complete these graphic organizers, or parts of them, while the teacher explicitly teaches the words, with support during small group, or as independent work. See figure 3.1, figure 3.2, and figure 3.3.

Word Map		
Word:		
Define it in your own words:		
Synonyms	**Antonyms**	**Parts of Speech**

Figure 3.1: Word map.

*Visit **go.SolutionTree.com/literacy** for a free reproducible version of this figure.*

Word Storm

Word #1:

People who might use the word:

Other ways to say the same thing:

Make up a sentence so it shows what the word means:

Word #2:

People who might use the word:

Other ways to say the same thing:

Make up a sentence so it shows what the word means:

Word #3:

People who might use the word:

Other ways to say the same thing:

Make up a sentence so it shows what the word means:

Figure 3.2: Word storm.

*Visit **go.SolutionTree.com/literacy** for a free reproducible version of this figure.*

Word Breakdown

Word:

Visual Image:

Synonyms	My Definition

Word:

Visual Image:

Synonyms	My Definition

Word:

Visual Image:

Synonyms	My Definition

Figure 3.3: Word breakdown.

*Visit **go.SolutionTree.com/literacy** for a free reproducible version of this figure.*

Vocabulary Instruction Recommendations

A major focus in this book is the explicit, robust instruction in vocabulary words needed to read and comprehend the grade-appropriate instructional text and words that are high-utility, frequently encountered, and found in multiple contexts. In addition, teaching and modeling word-busting strategies, like structural analysis, locating base words, identifying prefixes and suffixes, and looking for smaller words within the word, are essential for students to become skilled in dealing with new vocabulary words that they encounter in text. Instruction in word recognition should include sound-letter correspondence, sight words, syllabication (breaking words into syllables), and morphology (breaking words into meaningful parts; Learning First Alliance, 2004). Emphasis is also placed on teaching and modeling the use of context clues to determine word meaning.

Research-based vocabulary instruction utilizes the format of whole-group instruction in intentionally selected vocabulary words, followed by small-group guided practice and support and regular opportunities for students to interact with words. Steps in planning vocabulary instruction should include preplanning, followed by designing whole-group instruction, partner or small-group instruction, and independent work.

Preplanning

Designing research-based vocabulary instruction takes time and planning. Several steps are beneficial to follow when deciding on which vocabulary words to teach, how you will introduce them, and what skills you wish to model related to the words. Preplanning should include the following:

- Determining six to twelve vocabulary words each week for instruction (words that are essential to comprehension of the text)
- Identifying or creating sentences or passages for introduction of the vocabulary words in context
- Determining the word study focus relating to the vocabulary words (decoding, structural analysis, or use of context clues)

Whole-Group Instruction

During universal, core literacy instruction, time should be allocated regularly for explicit instruction in vocabulary words that are directly related to the text that students will be reading. The following instructional tasks should occur during whole-group time so all students have access to learning grade-level vocabulary words. These tasks may happen on days 1 and 2 of the new text or chapter and be reviewed throughout the week.

- Introduction of the vocabulary words in context with teacher modeling of structural analysis and use of context clues to determine word meaning

- Teacher provides an explanation or examples for each vocabulary word
- Teacher provides a visual representation for each vocabulary word
- Whole-group activity or game for interaction with vocabulary words

Partner, Small-Group, and Guided Practice

In addition to whole-group core instruction in vocabulary, some students will benefit from small-group vocabulary work that includes the following activities to provide extra teaching, support, and practice.

- Review of vocabulary words in context, meanings, and visual representations
- Word study minilessons relating to the selected vocabulary words
- Completing a word log or graphic organizer and creating student-friendly definitions and their own visual representations for each word
- Activity or game for interaction with vocabulary words

Independent Work

Following whole-group core vocabulary instruction that includes guided practice, it is helpful for students to work with the vocabulary words with a partner or individually. Repeated practice and multiple exposures to the words will lead to deeper understanding and better retention. Students might complete a word log or graphic organizer and create student-friendly definitions and their own visual representations for each word and engage in additional partner or small-group activities for repeated exposure and active interaction with vocabulary words.

Integration of Context Clues and Word Analysis During Vocabulary Instruction

Students need both sound vocabulary knowledge and the ability to use various strategies to establish the meaning of new words when they encounter them (Osborn et al., 2004). Direct instruction should include teaching specific words, word meanings, and word-learning strategies, such as the use of context clues and morphological analysis. Students must be explicitly taught and given opportunities to apply context clues to determine the meaning of words and phrases. Tonia Bauer and Hengtao Tang (2022) confirm the "importance of teaching students explicit contextual analysis strategies, such as using different types of context clues, to infer the meanings of unfamiliar words" (p. 96).

Jean Osborn and colleagues (2004) conclude that effective word-learning strategies, including using morphological analysis (or word part information) to decode words, can strengthen students' reading skills. Studies show that 80 percent of words with prefixes and suffixes can be inferred from their root words, which indicates there is value in instruction and practice in morphological analysis. The ability to identify and understand smaller word parts, such as prefixes and suffixes, can support the development of students' reading comprehension (Memis, 2019).

Prior to instruction, the vocabulary words for the text should be selected based on importance and relevance to comprehending the text. Sentences or passages from the text to use for introducing the words should be chosen. The sentences need to be projected on a screen so all students see them clearly. The teacher reads each sentence, modeling how to use word-busting skills to figure out what the word is. Word-busting or word-learning skills to model include decoding new words, breaking words into recognizable parts, and making connections to similar words that students might be familiar with. Next, the meaning of the word is identified using the context clues in the sentences. It is helpful to highlight or underline the context clues within the sentences.

Figure 3.4 is an example of explicit instruction in vocabulary words for an instructional text called *The Scavenger Hunt* by Ajit Narra (2019), using sentences from the text and modeling use of word-busting and context clue strategies. Selected vocabulary words for instruction are in bold, and context clues are underlined.

Note: As you read each sentence, model the use of structural analysis to decode the vocabulary words and highlight or underline the context clues that help to determine the meaning of the words. Details about teacher modeling are included.

1. "A game!" says Lajjo, **brightening** up. [Model looking at the root word *bright* and adding *en* and *ing* to decode the new word.]
2. "Yes! It's a **scavenger** [model decoding this word by syllables] **hunt.** You have to find all the items on this list," says Daddu. [Use underlined words as context clues to figure out what *scavenger hunt* means.]
3. The **banks** of the river break. In just a few minutes, the village is flooded with muddy water from the river. [Discuss different ways the word *banks* can be used and model using the underlined words as context clues to what *banks* means in this sentence.]
4. "Lajjo, I'm **thirsty**. Do you have some water?" asks her friend, Prateek. [Model how to decode the new word, reviewing /th/ and /st/ and the long *e* made by the letter *y*.]
5. "Why did you do that?" Lajjo asks, **puzzled**. [Model how to decode the new word using short *u* and taking off the *d*. Model using the underlined context clues to determine the word's meaning.]
6. The army comes in boats laden with supplies for the flood **survivors**. Lajjo's family is **relieved**. [Model how to decode the two new words and use the underlined context clues to determine the meaning of *survivors*. Discuss what the word *relieved* might mean based on the context.]

Figure 3.4: Example of teaching vocabulary words in context.

Independent Reading and Vocabulary Development

Vocabulary development can occur through independent reading. In fact, a significant body of research indicates that the answer to learning words is through independent or incidental learning. However, studies indicate limited learning of new vocabulary words through independent reading alone and the importance of purposeful reading and student accountability. For example, Douglas W. Carnine, Jerry Silbert, Edward J. Karme'enui, and Sara G. Tarver (2004) find that only 5 to 15 percent of unfamiliar words are learned through independent reading. It was determined that independent reading has more impact on student learning of vocabulary when teachers provide intentional instruction, assign related tasks, and hold students accountable for demonstrating their learning (Reutzel, Fawson, & Smith, 2008). Vocabulary can be developed incidentally when students read extensively on their own. However, "specific word instruction is one way to explicitly teach individual vocabulary words that are important, useful, and difficult for students to learn" (National Center on Improving Literacy, 2023). This topic is addressed further in chapter 8 (page 143).

Interaction and Application of Vocabulary Instruction

Effective vocabulary teachers use instructional strategies that teach valuable word-learning behaviors, as well as teaching vocabulary words. Word-learning strategies include decoding words by applying phonics, breaking words into recognizable parts, identifying similarities among words to help determine their meanings, making connections to where the words may have been seen before, and using context clues to determine word meanings. Rich vocabulary instruction goes beyond definitional information and involves students actively in using and thinking about word meanings and creating lots of associations among words (Blachowicz & Fisher, 2006).

In a pivotal study that includes a meta-analysis of the effects of vocabulary instruction, Steven A. Stahl and Marilyn M. Fairbanks (1986) find that vocabulary methods that provided only definitional information about words do not positively affect comprehension. Gustafson (2019) posits that "we do a disservice to students when we devalue vocabulary instruction to a level of copying definitions and matching exercises." Students need frequent encounters with vocabulary words, over a period of three to five days, and regular reviews of words and their meanings. Timothy Shanahan (2022) determines that "it is not enough that kids study word meanings, but they have to learn to use these words in their reading, writing, speaking, and listening." Drill and practice methods and providing only one or two exposures to the words are also not effective ways to enhance vocabulary knowledge. One study finds that fifth graders could use vocabulary words accurately in sentences only 25 percent of the time when they had limited exposure to the words and their meanings.

Active engagement with vocabulary words is vital in helping students develop a deeper understanding of the words and retain the words as part of their reading, speaking, and listening vocabularies. Engaging students with vocabulary words through interaction, communication, and active learning is essential for application and retention of words. Recommended activities for involving students in thinking about vocabulary words, their meanings, and using them include the following.

1. Through the use of word journals, graphic organizers, and other tasks, ask students to design visuals and definitions in their own words.

2. Have students make connections between words and to their own experiences.

3. Teach word families.

4. Use drama, such as tableaus, to model word meanings.

5. Engage students in semantic and concept mappings using words.

6. Provide opportunities for repeated readings of text.

Involving students in word sorts, games, writing tasks, and other ways to use words leads to multiple exposures to and deeper understanding of vocabulary words, as well as encouraging students to apply the vocabulary words orally or in writing.

Games and Activities for Engagement With Vocabulary

Osborn and colleagues (2004) conclude that "extensive independent reading alone cannot ensure that students develop the skills and strategies they need to become independent word learners" (p. 19). Students must be involved in other activities to learn vocabulary words (Osborn et al., 2004). Instructional games can foster friendly competition, motivation, and a relaxed atmosphere in the classroom so students can more readily learn and retain vocabulary words (Cheng & Su, 2012). "Vocabulary games help teachers to create contexts in which the target words are useful and meaningful; they also bring fun for students" (Derakhshan & Khatir, 2015, p. 40).

The following activities and word games can be used in both whole-group and small-group settings. They are interactive and engaging, as well as providing the necessary repeated exposures students need to know words well. Many of the games involve friendly competition and active involvement from students. Some also include *roles* and steps that foster active participation from all students. Students typically enjoy these types of activities, particularly those that include races, relays, and mysteries, which allow all students to be involved and challenge them in a fun and interactive manner.

Vocabulary Card Game

Involving students in interactive games using vocabulary words helps to provide repeated exposures to words and encourages working with vocabulary words through friendly competition. This card game is simple and can be used when limited time is available.

1. Put students in groups of four.

2. Give each group of four a set of vocabulary cards and a set of student-friendly definitions (to match the vocabulary words).

3. Mix the two sets of cards and deal out an equal number to each player in the group.

4. Put the extras (if any) in the middle.

5. The first player says and lays down one of the words or definitions in their hand.

6. The player who has the matching word or definition lays their card down to make the match.

7. Then that player repeats step 5.

8. If no one has the match, the person should draw a card from the pile and see if it matches, then call on someone else to have a turn. Play until all the matches have been made.

Figure 3.5 (page 56) contains examples of vocabulary and student-friendly definition cards.

Flyswatter

This vocabulary activity involves students in physical movement, as well as friendly competition between teams. Using a manipulative, such as a flyswatter, adds motivation and enthusiasm to practicing word recognition.

1. Place vocabulary words in a vertical row on the whiteboard.

2. Put the students in two teams (the color of the flyswatters).

3. Have one person from each team come stand in the middle facing the whiteboard.

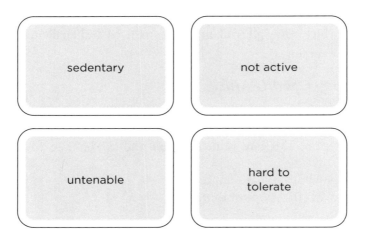

Figure 3.5: Sample vocabulary card game cards.

4. Say a vocabulary word meaning or give another clue.

5. The first person to swat the word gets a point for their team.

6. Leave all the words there throughout the game.

7. Play until all words have been swatted or all students have had a turn.

Magnetic Letters Relay

This is another interactive activity that students enjoy and helps them develop word recognition skills. Magnetic letters are readily available in many classrooms or can be inexpensive to purchase. In addition to word recognition, students apply the skill of spelling to the vocabulary words.

1. Put two sets of magnetic letters on the left and right sides of the whiteboard.

2. Separate the students into two teams.

3. Give clues for the vocabulary words.

4. Have one student from each team make the word with the magnetic letters.

5. The first student done gets a point for their team.

Mystery Word

Students are typically very engaged when they are challenged to solve a mystery. This activity can be almost completely student-led, which adds to students' motivation and makes this game a fun way to practice vocabulary words.

1. Place three clues for each vocabulary word on index cards in envelopes.

2. Call on a student to come up and choose an envelope and read the clues.

3. Clues should go from vague (this is a noun) to more and more specific.

4. The student who guesses the word first comes up and reads the next clue card.

5. After playing a time or two, have the students write the three clues for the words.

6. Incorporate parts of speech, antonyms, synonyms, root words, and meanings.

See figure 3.6 for a sample mystery word clue set. Remember, students will have the vocabulary words in front of them.

Clue #1: This word is a noun.

Clue #2: This word is a compound word.

Clue #3: You might find this word used in reference to a golf course or garden.

Figure 3.6: Example of mystery word clues for the word *caretaker.*

Definition Race

Another way to use friendly competition is to play Definition Race. Students tend to be highly engaged in races, and this game supports repeated exposures and practice with vocabulary words.

1. Prepare by writing each vocabulary word on two index cards.

2. Put the words into two stacks, one for each team.

3. Each student on the teams should have a card or word.

4. When you call a word, the two students with that word should stand up, go to the whiteboard, and write a short definition.

5. The first one with a readable and correct definition gets a team point.

"And the Answer Is . . ."

"And the answer is . . ." is similar to the game *Jeopardy!* in that students must respond to the vocabulary word clues with a question.

1. Put definitions, synonyms, or examples for vocabulary words on slips of paper or index cards.

2. Place them in a container.

3. Pull out a card or slip of paper and read it orally.

4. Call on a student (the first to hold their hand up) to provide the answer in question format (like on *Jeopardy!*): "What is _____ ?"

5. If they are correct, the student comes up, chooses the next card, reads it, and calls on another student.

6. If the answer is wrong or not in a question format, call on another student.

7. Have vocabulary words in a portable chart and point to the word for repeated exposure and practice.

Vocabulary Roundabout

Vocabulary Roundabout involves students in physical movement and challenges them to complete a cloze activity using vocabulary words. Students are motivated to move to the next desk and to tally up their scores.

1. Prepare slips of paper or index cards with cloze sentences (sentences leaving out the vocabulary word that will fit or make sense). Prepare enough for each student in the class. Place one of these on each student's desk.

2. Pass out the answer sheets.

3. Have the vocabulary words in a pocket chart.

4. Students should answer the cloze sentence on their desk (being careful to put their answer by the correct number on the answer sheet).

5. After about 10–15 seconds, say "Roundabout," and students go to the desk with the next number and cloze sentence to complete.

6. Repeat this until all students have been at every desk and are back to their own.

7. Go over answers using word cards and have students score their papers.

Four Corners

Another simple and time-efficient activity to foster interaction with vocabulary words is called Four Corners, and it involves physical movement, as well as development of students' vocabulary knowledge.

1. Have a large die (with sides labeled 1, 2, 3, and 4) and prepare tasks like identifying a synonym or antonym for the word, using the word in a sentence, telling what the word means in your own words, and so on.

2. Pass out scorecards.

3. Have students take their scorecard and a pencil to one of the four corners in the room.

4. Roll the die (1, 2, 3, or 4). The group in the area of the number rolled must answer the question you read orally.

5. If they are correct, they get to circle the number of points on their scorecard that matches the die rolled.

6. Say "Four Corners," and students move to another spot.

7. Repeat.

Word Sorts and Beat the Teacher

Word Sorts are easy to do and beneficial for repeated exposure to vocabulary words. They also provide opportunities to review and apply a wide range of word-building and language arts skills. Beat the Teacher is basically the same as Word Sorts with the added feature of trying to identify the correct word or words before the teacher says or displays the words.

1. Give each student a set of vocabulary word cards (for the week or prior weeks).

2. Ask students to lay the word cards out on their desks or tables.

3. Give a clue (see clues below) and ask students to point to or hold up the correct cards.

4. As a variation, do the same as above but ask students to *beat the teacher* by holding up or pointing to the correct cards before you hold them up or write the words on the whiteboard.

When preparing for Word Sorts and interactive games such as Beat the Teacher, it is essential to preplan the vocabulary words you want to practice and the clues you will give to the students. It is valuable to begin with the following sentence starters and use the various clues provided.

Note the integration of a wide variety of vocabulary and language arts skills through the following word clues.

I'm thinking of . . .

I want you to find . . .

I'm looking for . . .

*a word that is a synonym for
_____ [give a synonym
for the vocabulary word you want
students to find]

* a word with a prefix that means

_____

*a word that is an antonym for
_____ [give an
antonym for the vocabulary word you
want students to find]

* a word with the suffix meaning

_____

*a word that is an example of

_____

*a word that means _____

* a word that is a noun (verb,
pronoun)

*a word that is a compound word

* a word that is an adjective (adverb)

* a word with a silent letter

*a word that has two different
meanings (multimeaning word)

* a word with a short vowel

*a word with a suffix

*a word that is a proper noun

*a word with a prefix

*a word with two or three syllables

*a word that is a homonym

*a word with a long vowel

Vocabulary Word Tableaus

A tableau is a still-life model of something. Asking students to create still-lifes or "statues" that represent vocabulary words is an engaging and interactive way to practice vocabulary words and illustrate their meanings.

1. Organize the students into groups of two to four.

2. Tell them to pick a word from the list that they are going to analyze, or assign groups a specific vocabulary word.

3. Students should think of a group picture (a frozen image or statue) that they can create based on the definition of the word, within a preset amount of time (1–2 minutes).

4. Have each group show the other groups their tableau while the other groups guess which vocabulary word is represented.

5. The group then has a chance to explain why it chose each person's position and the relationship of the position to the definition of the word.

Sometimes, you might assign multiple groups the same word and compare the different tableaus. Make sure to have students explain their positions, or how they demonstrated the meaning with their chosen tableau.

The following is an example of a weekly plan for core, whole-group vocabulary instruction, small-group intervention, and independent practice with vocabulary. This example is generic and may be edited for teachers' use.

Figure 3.7 is a template for instructional planning for vocabulary instruction (part 2). Note that this template is replicated at the end of chapter 4 (page 65) with the addition of language arts skills (part 3 of planning template).

Day 1	Day 2	Days 3 and 4	Day 5
Whole group: Introduction of 4–6 vocabulary words in context with teacher modeling of structural analysis and use of context clues to determine word meanings. Teacher provides explanations and/or examples and visual representations for each word. **Language arts skills are integrated into vocabulary instruction**.	**Whole group:** Introduction of 4–6 vocabulary words in context with teacher modeling of structural analysis and use of context clues to determine word meanings. Teacher provides explanations and/or examples and visual representations.	**Whole group:** Review vocabulary words and minilesson on word study related to the vocabulary words. **Language arts skills are integrated into vocabulary instruction.**	**Whole group:** Game or activity for reinforcement of vocabulary words and meanings. **Small group or partner work:** Share out from word logs or graphic organizers, demonstrate through reciprocal teaching, and do other activities for practice and interaction with words.
Small-group interventions: Reteach/review vocabulary. Assist with vocabulary graphic organizer/ task.	**Small-group interventions:** Reteach/review vocabulary. Assist with vocabulary graphic organizer/task.	**Small-group interventions:** Complete graphic organizer. Prepare for reciprocal teaching, game, or activity using vocabulary words.	
Independent work and rotations: Students write words in word logs, write in their journals, or work on vocabulary graphic organizers.	**Independent work and rotations:** Students write words in word logs, journals, or work on vocabulary graphic organizers.	**Independent work and rotations:** Students complete word logs, journals, or graphic organizer with words, student-friendly definitions, visual representations, and examples for each word. Practice vocabulary and sight words with word cards and other activities.	

Figure 3.7: Sample of instructional sequence (5 days) for vocabulary instruction.

Conclusion

This chapter has provided a detailed discussion about vocabulary instruction using instructional text, including selection of words for instruction, the importance of and steps in explicit instruction, and the value of modeling word analysis and the use of context clues. Ways to engage students with vocabulary words through graphic organizers, active learning, and games were also provided. The information and examples in this chapter provide support for whole-group core vocabulary instruction and opportunities for students to work with words throughout the week.

Chapter 4 (page 65) will explain ways to integrate phonics and language arts skills within core vocabulary instruction, which supports making connections and using time efficiently during literacy academic time.

Part 2: Vocabulary Instructional Template

In your literacy planning template for chapter 2 (page 25), the instructional text was selected, as well as considerations for how instruction will be presented. Using the selected text, plan what parts will be covered this week. For primary students, this could be one book used throughout the week. For older students, this might be several chapters of a book or novel. Then, plan your core vocabulary instruction by identifying the following.

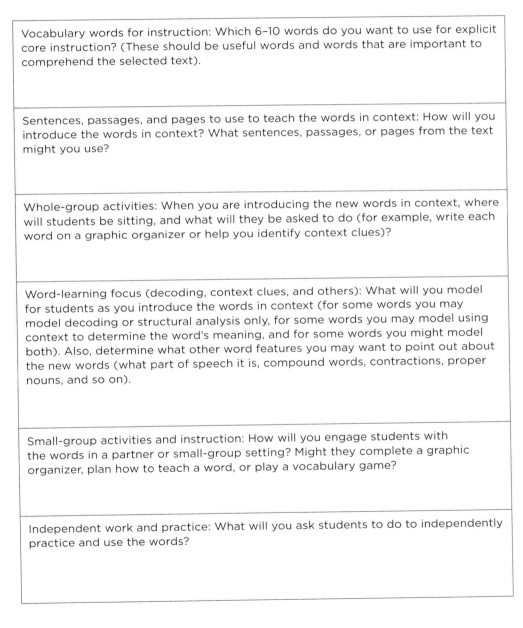

Vocabulary words for instruction: Which 6–10 words do you want to use for explicit core instruction? (These should be useful words and words that are important to comprehend the selected text).

Sentences, passages, and pages to use to teach the words in context: How will you introduce the words in context? What sentences, passages, or pages from the text might you use?

Whole-group activities: When you are introducing the new words in context, where will students be sitting, and what will they be asked to do (for example, write each word on a graphic organizer or help you identify context clues)?

Word-learning focus (decoding, context clues, and others): What will you model for students as you introduce the words in context (for some words you may model decoding or structural analysis only, for some words you may model using context to determine the word's meaning, and for some words you might model both). Also, determine what other word features you may want to point out about the new words (what part of speech it is, compound words, contractions, proper nouns, and so on).

Small-group activities and instruction: How will you engage students with the words in a partner or small-group setting? Might they complete a graphic organizer, plan how to teach a word, or play a vocabulary game?

Independent work and practice: What will you ask students to do to independently practice and use the words?

Reflection Questions for Chapter 3:
Vocabulary Instruction and Word Retention

How often are students provided with explicit instruction in vocabulary and opportunities to create student-friendly definitions and visuals for vocabulary words?

How often do you model word-busting strategies and the use of context clues to determine word meaning?

How frequently are students given opportunities to use, engage, and interact with the vocabulary words?

What changes might you incorporate into your vocabulary instruction based on chapter 3 (page 43)?

Chapter 4

Phonemic Awareness and Language Arts Within Vocabulary Instruction

The more that you read, the more things you will know.

—DR. SEUSS

Chapter 4 will present an overview of research related to phonemic awareness, phonics, and language arts skills. Phonemic and phonological awareness should be a strong instructional focus in preschool through early first grade, and phonics instruction is essential from kindergarten through at least fifth grade. Language arts skills should be taught, reviewed, and practiced throughout K–12. This chapter on phonemic awareness, phonics, and language arts follows the previous chapter on vocabulary instruction (page 43), as it is effective to teach phonics and language arts skills in the context of vocabulary instruction, rather than as stand-alone skills.

One of the components of reading instruction that has been abandoned in some schools during the past decade or more is phonemic awareness and, to a lesser degree, phonics instruction. Phonemic awareness has been shown to be an essential component of reading instruction based on the National Reading Panel (2000) report and research on the science of reading. Phonemic awareness focuses on students being able to both hear and manipulate individual sounds, and to understand that words are made up of sequences of speech sounds. Phonological awareness is the ability to distinguish word parts, such as syllables, and is an aspect of phonemic awareness. Kay MacPhee (2018) finds that "students who were able to identify phonemes rapidly were able to read more fluently because of this rapid processing." Observations in kindergarten and first-grade classrooms indicate that in many classrooms little time and emphasis has been placed on phonemic awareness since 2015.

NCLB (U.S. Department of Education, n.d.) and ESSA (U.S. Department of Education, 2015) placed an urgency on improving our nation's reading proficiency by teaching letter sounds, words, and other reading skills earlier and at a quicker pace. The reading curriculum previously used for first grade is now typically taught in kindergarten classrooms. Due to this push to increase reading skills, many pre-school, kindergarten, and first-grade teachers have discontinued instruction in pho-nemic awareness and, to a lesser extent, phonics. Decades of research have shown that students' phonemic awareness skills are vital to their reading success, from the early grades through the later elementary years. Many studies confirm that phone-mic awareness is a crucial skill that predicts future reading proficiency (Del Campo, Buchanan, Abbott, & Berninger, 2015).

Phonemic awareness (PA) is the ability to detect and manipulate sound segments auditorily, or from spoken words (Pufpaff, 2009). PA includes identifying, isolat-ing, substituting, segmenting, blending, and deleting individual letter sounds, or *phonemes*. Phonemic awareness differs from phonics in that PA focuses on the letter sounds as heard and manipulated orally, while phonics focuses on recognizing written letters and their sounds. Phonemic awareness is the awareness of sounds, not letters. Kelli D. Cummings, Ruth A. Kaminski, Roland H. Good III, and Maya O'Neil (2011) state that PA is not about how letters and sounds correspond or how to sound out letters to create words; it is about hearing, thinking, and manipulating individual sounds with spoken words.

Multiple studies have shown that many early childhood teachers lack an ade-quate understanding of what phonemic awareness is and how to teach it. Elaine A. Cheesman, Joan M. McGuire, Donald Shankweiler, and Michael Coyne (2009) examine the knowledge of phonemic awareness instruction of 223 first-year special education, early childhood education, and elementary education teachers. Results of this study show that a good number of beginning special and general education teachers seem to be inadequately prepared to effectively deliver phonemic aware-ness instruction. The teachers had "limited knowledge of PA, confused PA with phonics, and were generally unable to select task-appropriate materials or activities" (Cheesman et al., 2009, p. 270). Washburn finds that the definition and concepts included in phonemic awareness are often misunderstood by educators (Washburn, Joshi, & Cantrell, 2011a, 2011b).

An analysis of data by researchers Emad M. Alghazo and Yasser A. Al-Hilawani (2010) reveals significant gaps between teachers' phonemic awareness knowledge and skills and their instructional practices. It was found that participants did not, in real-ity, practice significant proportions of their PA knowledge and skills during teaching.

Observations that I have performed in early childhood classrooms in many diverse types of schools indicate that in a good number of preschool, prekindergarten, and kindergarten programs, phonemic awareness is not a focus of literacy instruction and is even nonexistent in some schools. Instead, instruction moves quickly to visual recognition of letters, matching letters to their sounds, and writing letters and words. However, in the past few years, some schools have begun implementing phonemic awareness programs, such as the Heggerty Phonemic Awareness Curriculum, which provides clear, sequential scripting for teachers to use for phonemic awareness lessons; the Best for All: Sounds First program, which includes lessons based on the Orton-Gillingham method; and the Intensive Phonological Awareness (IPA) Program, which supports systematic phonological awareness instruction for students in grades K–2 (Schuele & Murphy (2014). These programs are sequential and address all elements of phonemic awareness efficiently. The Heggerty and Best for All: Sounds First programs are typically used for whole-group minilessons, while the IPA Program is geared to be used for small-group interventions.

This book recommends that instructional time be allocated for phonemic awareness in preschool through kindergarten and early first grade and for systematic instruction in phonics from first through fifth grade.

The Importance of Phonemic Awareness

The National Reading Panel (2000) indicated that the core components for literacy instruction include phonemic awareness and phonics. Before students learn to recognize letters and match letters to their sounds, they should receive intentional instruction and practice in phonemic awareness skills. Phonemic awareness instruction helps students understand how sounds represent oral language and see connections between the sounds and the letters representing them (Bell, 2010). In addition, multiple studies have shown how important phonemic awareness is to students during their early childhood years and as they move forward in school.

Meghan Pendergast, Gary Bingham, and Nicole Patton-Terry (2015) conclude that phonemic awareness is critical in reading development. Phonemic awareness is essential for reading development because written words correspond to spoken words, and this understanding of the speech sounds that letters and letter combinations represent helps students to move on from a printed word to making meaning of the word while reading (Moats, 2019). Awareness of auditory sounds is required to learn letter-sound correspondences and then blend sounds together to decode a word (Kilpatrick, 2015).

Intentional classroom instruction in phonemic awareness is necessary for all pre-school and kindergarten students and provides a foundation to build additional reading skills (Callaghan & Madelaine, 2012).

Table 4.1 is a recap of significant findings regarding the value of helping young learners develop strong skills in phonemic awareness.

Table 4.1: Supported Findings in Favor of Helping Young Students Develop Phonemic Awareness

Researchers	Findings
Alcock, Ngorosho, Deus, & Jukes (2010)	In addition to building their confidence, phonemic awareness helps students become proficient in reading.
Carson, Gillon, & Boustead (2012)	Phonemic awareness is an early literacy skill that predicts reading acquisition and future success in reading.
Kjeldsen, Kärnä, Niemi, Olofsson, & Witting (2014)	Developing phonemic awareness skills in kindergarten predicted students' reading comprehension abilities through grade 9.
Pendergast, Bingham, & Patton-Terry (2015)	Students who display weak phonological skills at the end of first grade continue to have reading difficulties in subsequent years, unless steps are taken for remediation.
Suggate (2016)	Previous meta-analyses suggest that phonemic awareness and phonics interventions are particularly helpful for younger students.
Brady (2020)	The beginner must first become aware of individual phonemes in spoken words to subsequently learn that those phonemes are represented by letters. Fostering phoneme awareness before introducing letters is advised because it allows students to focus on the spoken form of phonemes, avoiding confusion with visual letters or letter names.

PA focuses on several specific skills that require explicit instruction and practice. PA skill areas include the ability to hear words that rhyme ("*cat, bat*") and alliteration, or words that begin or end with the same sound ("*red, rabbit*" and "*toad, lad*"). A third PA skill is being able to break a word into its separate sounds, or phonemes, and combine individual sounds into words ("*map . . . m-a-p*"). Hearing and counting the parts or syllables in words (*um-brel-la*) and then being able to blend and segment syllables ("*af-ter . . . after,*" "*chicken . . . chick-en*") is another vital PA skill for students to develop. Students also need to be able to identify and manipulate the sounds in words. For example, "Say *pig*. Now change the last sound to a /t/. What word do you hear now? *Pit*." The development of these specific phonemic awareness skills prepares students to connect this learning to the written letters and words.

The information in table 4.2 describes all the phonemic awareness skill areas, a suggested sequence for instruction, and examples of practicing these skills.

Table 4.2: Phonemic Awareness Skills Sequence

Phonemic Awareness Skill	Application or Instruction for Practice
Syllable	How many syllables do you hear in *baby*? In *carnival*? Clap them.
Segmentation	How can we break the word *rabbit* into its parts? (*rab-bit*)
Syllable blending	What word do you hear when I say *bird house* (*birdhouse*)? How about *rain drop* (*raindrop*)?
Rhyming	Do *mad* and *Dad* rhyme? Which word rhymes with *hat*: *lap*, *tab*, or *mat*? Name a word that rhymes with *box*.
Phoneme isolation	What sound do you hear at the beginning of each word: *fun*, *rat*, and *now*? Do you hear the /s/ sound at the beginning or end of the word *sad*? How about *lass*?
Initial alliteration	Which word begins with the /t/ sound: *top* or *boat*? Name a word that begins with the /t/ sound.
Final alliteration	Which word ends with the /s/ sound: *bag* or *less*? Name a word that ends with the /s/ sound.
Sound blending	What do you hear when I say /c/ /u/ /t/ (*cut*)? How about when I say /w/ /e/ /b/ (*web*)?
Sound deletion	What is the word *bat* without the /b/ (*at*)? What is the word *map* without the /p/ (*ma*)?
Sound substitution	Change the /m/ in *map* to the /n/ sound. What is the word (*nap*)? Change the /p/ in *sap* to the /d/ sound. What is the word (*sad*)?

It works well to focus on one skill for some time, then add another skill. Repetition of all the PA skills regularly is also important. Phonemic awareness should be taught, reviewed, and practiced throughout the school year in preschool and kindergarten. Spending a few weeks on each skill, then having brief review and practice sessions on the previously learned skills throughout the school year, helps to solidify students' PA learning. By first grade, typically reviewing PA skills during the first nine weeks should be adequate for most students. In second and third grade, students should be screened for phoneme awareness to determine students who have not mastered

PA skills and to provide additional instruction for these students (Kilpatrick, 2015). Students who struggle with the skills may need one-to-one or small-group interventions on specific phonemic awareness skills. Once students master these PA skills, instruction can move forward to matching letter sounds with the actual written letters.

The Benefits of Explicit Instruction in Phonics

Phonics is another area of reading instruction that has been given little attention in some schools due to the whole-language, language experience, and even guided reading philosophies. Direct instruction in phonics, including letter sounds, blends, digraphs, and other phonetic skills, has been very limited. The focus of instructional time during literacy blocks has been on developing fluency or reading accurately and at a targeted pace. Phonics, vocabulary, and comprehension have all been considered of lesser importance than fluency in many schools.

Many school districts still may not be using explicit, systematic phonics programs. Instead, they use a balanced literacy framework, which typically consists of five segments that students engage in with partners or independently including read-aloud, guided reading, shared reading, independent reading, and word study (Lorimer-Eisely & Reed, 2019). This framework involves a balance between teacher-led reading and writing instruction and independent learning. However, balanced literacy often does not include explicit phonics instruction (Professional Learning Board, 2023).

Within the balanced literacy framework, students are taught techniques such as guessing, looking at pictures, and decoding. In theory, this sounds good; however, we must be cautious about utilizing unscientific practices for reading instruction. The balanced literacy approach may not include phonics, and it lacks the structured, explicit instruction and content needed to help all students learn to read with proficiency. Lexia (2023) concludes that "most students need explicit and direct instruction in foundational reading skills." Without additional intervention, balanced literacy will only help 30 percent of students become successful readers, while literacy instruction based on the science of reading can help up to 95 percent of students become successful readers (Lexia, 2023).

Fortunately, more importance has been placed upon, and more time has been allocated for, phonics instruction over the past decade, particularly for students who struggle with decoding and fluency. Stanislas Dehaene, a neuroscientist and author of *Reading in the Brain* (2010), explains that even expert readers use the phonological pathway to read and understand words. However, our ability to read is so automatic that we hardly realize that we are using phonics knowledge (Dehaene, 2010). Teachers have the immense task of ensuring that each student possesses a solid foundation in phonics and a range of reading strategies to learn how to read. We can teach these essential early reading skills through explicit and systematic phonics instruction.

Explicit phonics instruction should occur regularly during core instruction and typically will take 5–15 minutes of core instructional time. Phonics instruction should begin by stating what students will be learning about and practicing. Instruction may involve teaching consonant sounds, short vowel sounds, long vowel sounds (made with two vowels together or with silent *e*), digraphs (*th, sh, ch, wh*, and so on), and other phonics skills that are appropriate to the students' grade level.

Following the introduction of the learning target, the letters and sounds should be displayed and modeled. The teacher should teach the letters and sounds and give examples. Providing visuals for each sound can be very helpful, as can focusing on sounds through shared reading of various texts, like big books and poetry. Students need to be involved in identifying the letters and sounds and using them to decode and spell words. Interactive games, physical movement, songs, and other resources should be used for guided practice, followed by independent practice to check students' understanding.

Generally, the sequence for teaching phonics skills (once students have gained skills in phonemic awareness) is (1) consonant sounds, beginning with the most common (*s, t, p, n, r*) and moving on to the other consonants; (2) short vowel sounds (putting them together with consonants to make consonant-vowel-consonant (CVC) words like *cat, man, sit*, and *mop*); (3) long vowel sounds (using two vowels together and silent *e*, like *pain | pane* and *tail | tale*); (4) digraphs, which are two consonants that together make one sound (*sh, th, wh, ng, ch*, and so on); (5) common irregular word parts like *-ough, -ight*, and *-ould*); and (6) other phonics skills that are generalizable and useful for decoding and spelling new words.

The following is a script you can use to lead a minilesson on consonant-vowel-*e* (CVE) words and silent *e*.

Today we are going to review the short vowel sounds and learn about Magic E!

When I hold up a picture card, tell me what vowel sound you hear in the word. **Hold up pictures and ask students to make the short vowel sound they hear in each word.**

You're doing really well remembering the short vowel sounds! Now let's practice reading some words with short vowel sounds. **Point**

to each CVC word on the board/screen and ask students to read or decode them: hop, pin, pet, tub, mad, and so on.

Now I'm going to introduce you to a special letter! Its name is Magic E! It looks the same as the e in the middle of a word, but when we put e on the end of a word, it can do magic! **Point to the word hop.** As you told me before, this is the word hop, and the o says its short sound in this word. **Put an e on the end of hop.**

Now this word is hope. What happened to the short o sound? That's right; now the o is saying the long sound. The e at the end of the word doesn't make a sound of its own; it's "silent," but it does magic by turning the vowel from its short sound to its long sound!

Let's try Magic E with these other words. **Model adding e to each of the other short vowel words on the board/screen: pin, pine; pet, Pete; tub, tube; mad, made; and cod, code.**

Next you're going to try using Magic E. **Place CVC words on the easel/chart and ask students what the word is. Then, ask various students to come up and add Magic E to the end of the words. Ask students what the new words are (for example, pan, pane; Tim, time; hug, huge; bod, bode; and met, mete.)**

You all did great using Magic E! When you see a word that has an e on the end, see if you can figure out the word by trying the long vowel sound. We'll practice using Magic E again tomorrow.

Developing students' phonemic awareness and phonics skills has been shown to positively connect to reading; therefore, teaching explicit and systematic phonics plays a vital role in teaching students how to read (Emmitt, Hornsby, & Wilson, 2013). Phonics instruction teaches students to understand sound-symbol correlations. With phonics and sight word instruction, students learn to read confidently and are better able to read more difficult texts with new content they may encounter later.

Word Study and Language Arts Skills Integration

Explicit instruction and practice in phonics will help students develop their vocabulary knowledge, as well as skills in decoding new words that they encounter in text. Along with word recognition and decoding, core instruction should include language arts skills and word study to foster deeper understandings of words and their proper usage in speaking and writing. It is highly effective to integrate word study and language arts skills into vocabulary instruction during whole-group lessons.

In this section, readers will develop a clear understanding of the value of teaching word consciousness and language arts skills, best practices for teaching these skills, and examples of ways to engage students in learning and applying the skills.

If a teacher uses a basal program for reading instruction, they may include language arts instruction within the literacy block; however, language arts skills, such as grammar, usage, syntax, and punctuation, are often neglected in the classroom due to time constraints. If a teacher utilizes leveled readers or has developed their own curriculum for reading instruction, language arts skills are unlikely to play a significant role in their instruction. Language arts skills may be integrated into oral reading practice, writing, and vocabulary instruction and must be included in our literacy instruction for the following reasons.

- Language arts skills constitute an individual's ability to comprehend, construct, and communicate meaning through critical reading, thinking, writing, and speaking in many different forms.

- Marilyn Eisenberg (2013) posits that language study helps students control their lives by becoming more effective thinkers. They must practice language skills and receive frequent feedback across all areas of study to improve. According to Eisenberg (2013), "language arts form the foundation for all effective communication. They constitute an individual's ability to comprehend, construct and communicate meaning through critical reading, thinking, writing and speaking."

- ELA skills enable students to think more critically and even abstractly about oral and written information. Teaching students to be competent in grammar enables them to better understand the meaning of the written word, therefore supporting reading comprehension and thinking skills (Mometrix Academy, 2022).

- Critical thinking and communication through class discussion or in an essay teach valuable life skills. ELA "continues to be an essential aspect of every curriculum and each individual's educational process" (Schoolyard SchoolSpecialty.com, 2017).

- Knowledge of syntax helps readers understand how written components are joined together to make meaning. Teaching students to be competent in grammar enables them to better understand the meaning of the written word, therefore supporting reading comprehension (Mometrix Academy, 2022).

The Common Core State Standards Initiative provides clear guidance regarding essential language arts skills (National Governors Association Center for Best Practices & Council of Chief State School Officers, 2010). States and school districts also have grade-level standards and learning outcomes for language arts. These include skills related to grammar, parts of speech, word choice and usage, writing complete sentences, using correct punctuation, and other reading, writing, listening, and speaking skills. More complex language arts skills include similes, metaphors, synonyms and antonyms, idioms, and understanding figurative language. A complete language arts curriculum should include grammar, spelling, handwriting, vocabulary, composition, and speaking. For students in kindergarten through middle school, reading, spelling, handwriting, and basic grammar and vocabulary skills should be taught to support students' reading and writing development (Homeschool Compass, 2021). Shanahan, as cited by Bernard (2022), determined:

> There is a lot of evidence showing the importance of grammar in reading comprehension. Studies over the years have shown a clear relationship between syntactic or grammatical sophistication and reading comprehension; that is, as students learn to employ more complex sentences in their oral and written language, their ability to make sense of what they read increases, too.

Instruction in language arts skills is essential for students to develop into proficient readers and writers. As you continue reading, strategies for teaching phonemic awareness, phonics, word study, and language arts skills will be described. Ways to engage students through activities that include reading, writing, speaking, and listening will be provided.

Instructional Strategies for Phonemic Awareness, Phonics, and Language Arts

The planning of core instruction in phonemic awareness, phonics, and language arts skills should include (1) determining a phonemic awareness or phonics skill to focus on, (2) planning how you might integrate this skill during vocabulary instruction, (3) choosing the grade-level language arts skills you want to address, and (4) planning how can you integrate these skills during vocabulary instruction. In addition, plans for active learning of the skills during whole-group instruction, how students will practice and apply the skills with partners or in small groups, and what students will do independently to practice the skills should be determined.

Phonemic awareness can be taught and practiced in short sessions, often taking 3–10 minutes of academic learning time. These skills can also be reinforced through quick games (while lining up for recess or going home, while washing hands for lunch, and so on). For example, "Name a word that starts with the /l/ sound" or "Say a word that rhymes with _____ ."

Phonics instruction should also be provided in 5- to 15-minute segments of time. Minilessons (see example on page 71) work well for teaching phonics skills, and students may practice the skills independently or with partners during the independent work time of the literacy block. Phonics skills should be reinforced during vocabulary instruction and through games and activities as well.

Language arts skills may be taught as minilessons during vocabulary instruction and during writing instruction, modeling, and shared writing. The following are examples of interactive games and activities for teaching language arts skills. A plethora of websites, such as www.splashlearn.com, www.phonicsbloom.com, and www.education.com, provide grammar games as well.

Mystery Grammar Game

(parts of speech, vocabulary development, speaking, listening)

Without looking at the card, students will put a word card on their foreheads so that their partners can see the word. That student then describes the word on the card to the person wearing the card without saying the actual word. The clues should include what part of speech the word is. For example, "This word means _____ , it is a noun, and it rhymes with _____ ."

Grandpa's Dog

(adjectives, word usage, speaking, listening)

Students will practice using adjectives in this game. The first player says the sentence "My grandpa's dog is _____ ," filling in the blank with an adjective that begins with *a*. The next student repeats the sentence using an adjective that begins with *b*, and so on. This game could be changed up to use the sentence "My grandpa's dog likes to _____ ," with students filling in the blank with verbs.

Shared Writing Paragraph

(writing complete sentences and paragraphs, speaking)

Place students in groups of six, then have each student write a complete sentence on a sentence strip about any topic they choose. The object of the game is for the group to then arrange all of the sentences together into a paragraph (which will be unusual and, perhaps, funny). Students will need to add conjunctions to help the sentences flow and to try to get them to make sense when put together. When the groups are finished, students should read their paragraphs aloud. A discussion about why the paragraphs are unusual or unclear should follow.

Simon Says With Grammar

(parts of speech, listening, speaking)

Before playing, decide upon some simple movements or signals that will be used to identify different parts of speech. For example, if students think the word is a noun, they might touch their nose. If they hear a verb, they might clap their hands, and so on. Have students practice a few times, then start naming actual nouns, verbs, adjectives, and other parts of speech. If the student makes the right movement or signal, they stay in the game. If not, they should sit down.

Word Sorts

(may include a wide variety of phonics and language arts skills)

As described in chapter 3 (page 43), Word Sorts are an excellent way to integrate and practice phonics and language arts skills. In addition, having students apply specific language arts skills in their writing tasks is an efficient way to practice these skills and formatively assess their knowledge.

Word Detectives

(helps students develop word consciousness and reinforces identification of parts of speech, word origins, suffixes and prefixes, and relationships between words)

This strategy is also sometimes called Word Watchers. Word Detectives is a simple and easily integrated strategy for incorporating phonics and language arts skills within vocabulary instruction. This strategy involves creating a concise list of language arts skills (grade-level standards) and providing brief minilessons on the skills as you teach vocabulary words in context. After modeling how you identify the specific skills while you teach the vocabulary sentences, students can begin to do the same. For example, a student might say, "I see two adjectives in this sentence" or "This sentence is a question because . . ."

Please see figure 4.1 for an example of a second-grade Word Detectives or Word Watchers chart.

Nouns	Apostrophes in possessives (*girl's, girls'*)
Verbs	
Collective nouns (*group*)	Context clues to determine the meaning of a word or phrase
Irregular **plural nouns** (*feet, children, teeth, mice, fish*)	Prefixes: Determine meaning when prefix is added to a known word (*happy* or *unhappy, tell* or *retell*)
Reflexive pronouns (*myself, ourselves*)	
Past tense of irregular verbs (*sat, hid, told*)	**Root words** as clues to the meaning of an unknown word (*addition, additional*)
Adjectives	Compound words (*birdhouse, lighthouse, housefly, bookshelf*)
Adverbs	
Capitalize first word of a sentence	Distinguish shades of meaning among closely related words
Capitalize people's names, holidays, product names, and geographic names	**Multimeaning Words**
Punctuation at the end of a sentence	
Use of commas	
Apostrophes to form **contractions** (*doesn't* or *can't*)	

Figure 4.1: Example of a second-grade Word Detectives or Word Watchers chart.

Application During Reading

During explicit instruction in vocabulary where the teacher reads the sentences and models the use of decoding skills and context clues, ask questions to incorporate ELA standards (see the example of explicit instruction that follows). Then, during guided oral reading of the text, ask students to locate sentences and words that connect to the language arts skills. For example, "Raise your hand when you see an adjective on this page" and "What clues do you have that this event is fictional?"

Examples of Teaching Vocabulary Words in Context, Phonics Integration, and Language Arts Skills

The following is an example of how to integrate phonics and language arts skills into explicit vocabulary instruction. These are the same sentences from *The Scavenger Hunt* (Narra, 2019) vocabulary instruction example shared earlier (page 52); however, now phonics and language arts skills have been added. The words are introduced in bold print in the context of sentences taken directly from the instructional text, and the italicized sentences indicate the questions the teacher could ask that focus on the specific skills. As a note, the ELA standards for grade 2 that are integrated into this this lesson are bolded in figure 4.1 (page 77; you can also find them here: www.education.com/common-core/second-grade/ela).

Introduce the vocabulary words in the context of sentences from the text, modeling decoding and structural analysis of the new words and use of context clues to determine word meaning. In addition, use questions like the italicized ones that follow to integrate phonics and language arts skills.

1. "A game!" says Lajjo, brightening up. "Yes! It's a **scavenger** hunt. You have to find all the items on this list," says Daddu. *[Which words have a long vowel sound? Do any words have a "magic" e? Let's underline all the nouns.]* Skills: long vowels, silent *e*, nouns

2. The **banks** of the river break. In just a few minutes, the village is **flooded** with muddy water from the river. *[Can you find a word that is plural? Are there any multimeaning words (banks)? Find two words that have suffixes. Why is there a comma after "In just a few minutes"?]* Skills: plural words, multimeaning words, suffixes, commas

3. "Lajjo, I'm **thirsty.** Do you have some water?" asks her friend, Prateek. *[Can you see a contraction in this sentence? Why is there a question mark at the end of the second sentence? What are two proper nouns in this sentence?]* Skills: contractions, question marks, proper nouns

4. "Why did you do that?" Lajjo asks, **puzzled**. *[How did you know Lajjo was asking a question (why, ?, asks)? Is there a word that can have two meanings in this sentence?]* Skills: clues that a sentence is a question, multimeaning words

5. The army comes in boats laden with supplies for the flood **survivors**. Lajjo's family is relieved. *[What is the root word of supplies? What are two adjectives in this sentence?]* Skills: root words, adjectives

Language arts skills from the list of grade-level standards can also be reinforced during teacher-guided oral reading of the instructional text, during writing minilessons, and during shared writing.

Figure 4.2 is a generic example of a weekly instructional plan for phonemic awareness, phonics, and language arts skills being integrated into vocabulary and writing instruction. This template may be edited for teacher use.

Days 1 and 2	Days 3 and 4	Day 5
Whole group: **Phonics Instruction or Minilesson and Practice** Introduction of 4–6 vocabulary words in context with teacher modeling of structural analysis and use of context clues to determine word meanings. Teacher provides explanations or examples and visual representations for each word. **Language arts skills and phonics skills integrated** **Small-group interventions:** Reteach or review vocabulary. Assist with vocabulary graphic organizer or task. **Review language arts skill.** Independent work or rotations: Students write words in word logs, write in journals, or work on vocabulary graphic organizers.	**Whole group:** Review vocabulary words and minilesson on word study related to the vocabulary words. Language arts skills are integrated into vocabulary instruction. Small-group interventions: Complete graphic organizer, prepare for reciprocal teaching, and play a game or do an activity using vocabulary words. **Review language arts skill.** **Independent work or rotations:** Students finish vocabulary graphic organizer and **complete task for application of language arts skills**. Practice vocabulary and sight words with word cards and other activities. **Task for application of phonics/language arts skills.**	**Whole group:** **Phonics Instruction and Practice or Assessment** Play a game or do an activity for reinforcement of vocabulary words and meanings. **Small-group or partner work:** Share out from word logs or graphic organizers, demonstrate through reciprocal teaching, and do other activities for practice and interaction with words.

Figure 4.2: Example of instructional sequence (five days) for phonemic awareness and phonics, and vocabulary instruction with integration of language arts skills.

Conclusion

All teachers face time constraints that impact their instruction; however, research has clearly shown the importance and necessity of teaching phonemic awareness, phonics, word study, and language arts skills. Educators must make it a priority to allocate time for minilessons and practice in phonemic awareness and phonics and to teach language arts skills efficiently within vocabulary instruction, teacher-guided oral reading, and writing. You'll find on page 81 a reproducible template for planning phonemic awareness, phonics, and vocabulary, with the inclusion of language arts skills, that can be edited for teacher use.

Chapter 5 (page 83) will describe the component of reading comprehension, including what research has shown, why comprehension instruction is so important, evidence-based strategies, and examples and resources for teaching students to apply effective comprehension strategies to create meaning from text.

Part 3: Phonemic Awareness, Phonics, and Language Arts Instructional Planning Template

This template will assist you in intentionally planning the integration of phonics and language arts skills within your explicit vocabulary instruction. All components of an effective vocabulary or language arts lesson are included beginning with the phonics and language arts skills you want to focus on while teaching the vocabulary words in context. In addition, you will plan how you will involve students during whole-group, small-group, and independent work to help them learn and apply specific phonics and language arts skills.

Phonemic awareness or phonics practice:
Word-learning focus during vocabulary instruction (decoding, context clues, and so on):
Language arts skills focus during vocabulary instruction:
Whole-group activities:
Independent work:
Small-group activities:

Reflection Questions for Chapter 4: Phonemic Awareness and Language Arts Within Vocabulary Instruction

What emphasis are phonics and language arts skills given in your classroom? How much time is allocated for this instruction?

How often do students engage in games and other interactive tasks to practice and apply phonics and language arts skills?

How often do you integrate instruction in phonics and language arts skills into your vocabulary instruction?

Which tools and examples included in this chapter might you utilize to enhance your phonics and language arts instruction within your teaching of vocabulary words in context?

Chapter 5

Comprehension as the Heart and Goal of Reading

> When you want to teach children to think . . . you begin
> making them readers and thinkers of significant thoughts
> from the beginning.
>
> **—BERTRAND RUSSELL**

A core component of the science of reading and one of the five essential elements of reading recommended by the National Reading Panel (2000) is comprehension. Since the early 2000s, comprehension has often not been given the emphasis or the time that is needed for students to become strategic readers. Dorothy Brandon (2021) determines that just recognizing words on a page but not knowing what the words mean does not support comprehension of text. Reading comprehension happens when words on a page are used to create thoughts. Therefore, adequate direct instruction, modeling, and application of comprehension strategies must be priorities during reading academic blocks. This chapter will address why comprehension instruction is so important, research-based comprehension strategies, explicit instruction in comprehension strategies, and application of comprehension strategies.

The Importance of Knowing Common Practices in Reading Comprehension Instruction

Classroom observations since the late 1970s have indicated that in many classrooms there is minimal time allocated for instruction in comprehension strategies. Two factors seem to have fostered the limited time allocations and lower emphasis on reading comprehension during literacy instruction that has been evident since the early 2000s. These factors include (1) the implementation of reading instruction that is highly focused on phonics and fluency in many classrooms, and (2) the implementation of the balanced literacy or the Daily CAFE model, in which students work in small groups or independently during rotations (Boushey & Behne, 2019). Significantly more time is allotted for fluency and decoding instruction. Also, there is often little explicit instruction in comprehension strategies, other than through think-alouds, with the teacher doing the modeling. Often, students are not given the guided practice necessary for mastery and application of reading comprehension strategies.

Lizbeth M. Brevik's (2019) extensive observational study concludes that 48 percent of the observed reading instruction segments contain no comprehension strategy instruction, and no observed sessions contain explicit and detailed strategy instruction. Camilla G. Magnusson, Astrid Roe, and Marte Blikstad-Bala (2018) report that teachers provide strategy instruction in 25 percent of classroom observations.

Amy M. Elleman and Eric L. Oslund (2019) conclude that "despite decades of reading comprehension research, a limited amount of time is spent using evidence-based methods in classrooms" (p. 3).

We know that reading aloud to students can be an effective way to model fluency and strategic reading. It is beneficial to read high-quality books, including classics, aloud to students of all ages, and some time should be allocated for reading aloud during the school day. However, a major trend in today's classrooms is teachers reading the instructional text (story, novel, content-area textbook) *to* students rather than providing instruction in the tools students need to read successfully on their own. Sarah L. Ulerick (2018) states that "reading is a process of active construction of meaning." When teachers read the text to students, the students are not applying strategies for comprehending the written words. Despite having the best intentions, reading text that has been selected for literacy instruction *to* students allows only the teacher to practice reading, not the students. Think about if you were trying to learn to golf and you only had the opportunity to observe other proficient golfers—how well would you develop your own skills in golfing?

Thinking aloud and modeling reading comprehension strategies is essential; however, the belief that students will apply the strategies they have seen modeled by the teacher on their own or with peer guidance is misguided. Consider the golfing analogy again. One learns to golf by being taught techniques and having guided and independent practice. Likewise, students must practice applying comprehension strategies through guided and independent reading activities.

Another common practice today is to provide students with regular opportunities for independent reading of self-selected texts. During these independent, sustained silent reading (SSR), or read-to-self times, there is often little accountability for students to apply comprehension strategies while they read independently. After explicit instruction and modeling of comprehension strategies, teachers should determine specific strategies for students to apply during independent reading and closely monitor students' progress through informal assessments (Neri & Linde, 2022).

The most important goal of reading instruction is to teach students to comprehend, use, and retain what they have read. In their book *Strategies That Work*, Stephanie Harvey and Anne Goudvis (2000) state, "Comprehension is not just one more thing. When it comes to reading, it is likely the most important thing" (p. 6). Surprisingly, however, in many classrooms little time is spent on direct instruction, modeling, and opportunities for student application of reading comprehension strategies. Teachers often incorporate the think-aloud strategy where they model their own thinking and comprehension; however, students frequently do not have the opportunity to directly learn, practice, and model comprehension strategies on their own. Studies indicate that this has been a trend in some schools since the late 1970s. Table 5.1 (page 86) summarizes some of the research about reading comprehension instruction in elementary schools and how it has stayed much the same over time.

Shanahan (2019a) supports the importance of explicit instruction and practice in reading comprehension. Shanahan determined that some teachers spend disproportionate amounts of time on the foundational skills (phonological and phonemic awareness, phonics, oral reading fluency) as compared to reading comprehension. If teachers are "devoting a large majority of the reading academic time to foundational skills (because those are benchmarked), they may be doing long-term damage; foundational skills are necessary, but insufficient to make students capable readers" (Shanahan, 2019a). Robyn Ewing and Marguerite Maher (2014) define reading as not just decoding or sounding words out but creating meaning from text. Ewing and Maher (2014) posit that during reading instruction "the focus should be on deep understanding and interpretation of ideas and thoughts" (p. 46). Sheila W. Valencia, Karen K. Wixson, and P. David Pearson (2014) iterate that reading comprehension was placed on a "back burner from the mid-1990s to the mid-2000s and it is time it returned to a central role in discussions about reading instruction" (p. 236).

Table 5.1: Reading Comprehension Research Findings

Researcher	Study	Findings
Durkin (1978)	*What Classroom Observations Reveal About Reading Comprehension Instruction*	Teachers offered almost no comprehension instruction, and instead of teaching students how to understand what they read, teachers typically gave assignments that *tested* students on their comprehension.
Taylor, Pearson, Clark, & Walpole (2000)	*Effective Schools and Accomplished Teachers: Lessons About Primary-Grade Reading Instruction in Low-Income Schools*	Comprehension instruction in grades 1–3 was minimal. Teaching comprehension included asking literal questions while students were reading in a small-group or whole-class setting and having students respond to independent reading.
Ness (2011)	*Explicit Reading Comprehension Instruction in Elementary Classrooms: Teacher Use of Reading Comprehension Strategies*	In 3,000 minutes of direct classroom observation in 20 first- through fifth-grade classrooms, a total of 751 minutes (or 25% of instructional time) was allotted for reading comprehension instruction.
Duke, Ward, & Pearson (2021)	*The* Science of Reading *Comprehension Instruction*	A meta-analysis found that comprehension instruction occurred a mean of 8.4 sessions over a mean period of 35 school days (24%). Still, the instruction improved students' reading comprehension performance.

The Components of Comprehension

Although there is a plethora of strategies and skills that may be taught to develop students' reading comprehension, studies over time have identified some *universal* comprehension strategies. Katherine A. Dougherty-Stahl (2004) and others identify several strategies as being essential for developing good comprehension including activating prior knowledge, predicting (before, during, and after reading), visualizing or using sensory imagery, questioning and clarifying, making inferences, and summarizing.

Nell K. Duke, P. David Pearson, Stephanie L. Strachan, and Alison K. Billman (2011) find that setting purposes for reading; previewing and predicting; monitoring, clarifying, and fixing; visualizing; and drawing inferences are strategies that support strategic reading and foster comprehension. Nearly every research-based reading program, or model, supports instruction in connecting, predicting, visualizing, questioning, monitoring and clarifying, inference and drawing conclusions, and summarizing using main ideas and details; therefore, these are considered to be essential strategies for developing comprehension and assisting students in deriving meaning from text and retaining what they have read.

Austin (2022) concurs that the following list includes essential comprehension strategies that should be addressed during literacy instruction through explicit instruction, modeling, and application.

- **Connecting** (or activating prior knowledge)

- **Predicting** (before reading, during reading [check and amend], and after reading [evaluate])

- **Visualizing** (using all five senses to create mental images while reading)

- **Questioning** (developing questions before, during, and after reading)

- **Monitoring and clarifying, or metacognition** (checking understanding and using fix-it strategies as needed)

- **Summarizing** (retelling the key points from the text, using main ideas and details)

- **Inferring and drawing conclusions** (using what you know and evidence from the text)

Direct Instruction in Critical Comprehension Strategies

The explicit instruction, modeling, and application of research-based comprehension strategies are important aspects of *Solving the Literacy Puzzle*. Comprehension instruction occurs in the whole-group setting, in small groups, and through participation in literature circles, book clubs, and discussion groups. Camille Blachowicz and Peter Fisher (2006) find that it is beneficial for teachers to teach and demonstrate comprehension strategies for all students.

Educators know that students need direct, explicit instruction in some aspects of the reading process. Not all students learn to read by being immersed in reading alone. The science of reading has established that explicit instruction in reading strategies is associated with higher learning outcomes for students (Fletcher, Lyon, Fuchs, & Barnes, 2019; Foorman et al., 2016). Explicit instruction includes modeling new skills, allowing students to have ample practice along with feedback, and providing intentional review of the skills.

Good readers can often figure out the secrets to reading for themselves, but this does not always happen with struggling readers. Struggling readers may need additional explicit instruction before they are able to apply strategies to real text (Duffy,

2003). Steps to include in explicit instruction are what the strategy is and why it should be used, followed by scaffolded instruction that provides modeling, guided practice, and independent practice in applying the strategy. Some examples of the steps in explicit instruction are included as follows for the strategy of *connecting*.

Steps in explicit comprehension instruction:

1. **Provide the name or a description of the strategy:** "Today we will be learning about and practicing a strategy called connecting, which means thinking about how what you are reading relates to your own experiences or things you already know."

2. **Inform students why the strategy or skill is important:** "Connecting helps us to better understand what we are reading and to see how the text relates to other things we know or have seen."

3. **Tell students when they should use the strategy:** "We should look for connections to our lives and what we have experienced whenever we are reading and especially if we are confused about what we are reading."

4. **State the objective or expectation for the students' learning:** "After I teach and model for you how to make connections between the text and your lives, you will be practicing making connections as you read our next story."

5. **Model or demonstrate (more than once) the strategy or skill ("I Do"):** Use the think-aloud technique while orally reading an example passage, a page, or a portion of the instructional text. Model aloud for students what connections you can make.

6. **Provide guided practice in application of the strategy ("We Do"):** Use the think-aloud technique while orally reading an example passage or a page or portion of the instructional text and ask students to raise their hands and share connections that they have made.

7. **Allow students (with accountability) to apply the strategy independently ("You Do"):** Give students a graphic organizer or another activity to practice making their own connections while reading.

Brevik (2019) concludes that explicit comprehension strategy instruction is a necessary practice to help students to become strategic readers. Whole-group instruction with a common text allows the teacher to directly teach and demonstrate effective strategies for *all* students. Small-group instruction and independent reading provide opportunities for students to apply the strategies in another context. Shared reading time should be used to reteach and reinforce the strategies taught and modeled through think-alouds. Some educators make the mistake of assuming that students will habituate the strategies modeled through think-alouds and automatically transfer them while reading independently. Instead, these strategies need to be explicitly taught, modeled, and practiced over time.

In addition to whole-group instruction, the teacher should model and provide guided practice in applying the comprehension strategy in flexible small groups. Guided practice in application of strategies may be done using the whole-group instructional text or another text, such as a leveled book. Students should have the opportunity to apply the strategy with like peers, with teacher support, and in various contexts.

As you read on, each essential comprehension strategy will be described along with its research base, and activities and graphic organizers for teaching and practicing each strategy will be provided. There are also examples of scripts that may be used for explicit instruction in the strategies of *visualizing* and *making inferences.*

Connecting

When students connect the texts they read to their lives, they begin to see relationships between what they read and the larger world (Harvey & Goudvis, 2000). Susan R. Goldman, Catherine Snow, and Sharon Vaughn (2016) determine that instruction best supports new learning when prior knowledge is leveraged. These connections help to enhance students' comprehension and the development of higher levels of thinking. Connecting or activating prior knowledge may be taught and practiced by using a KWL (What I *Know*, What I *Want* to Know, and What I *Learned*) chart and discussing what students already know about the topic or concept in the first (*K*) column. A simple semantic map, or web, is another useful tool for recording students' connections. Brainstorming and making a list of what students know and have experienced is another technique to activate prior knowledge and teach students to connect prior learning with new learning. Figure 5.1 (page 90), figure 5.2 (page 90), and figure 5.3 (page 91) are useful in helping students to learn, practice, and apply making connections during reading. These tools may be used for guided or independent practice in whole group, small groups, or during independent work time.

Making Connections During Reading

During reading, or after students have read the instructional text or a self-selected text, ask them to write down three connections that they can make to their personal lives or experiences. These can be any type of connections, or you might ask for a connection to their own lives, a connection to another text or a movie, or a connection to the world.

Connection #1:

_____

_____

Connection #2:

_____

_____

Connection #3:

_____

_____

Figure 5.1: Making connections during reading graphic organizer.

Visit **go.SolutionTree.com/literacy** *for a free reproducible version of this figure.*

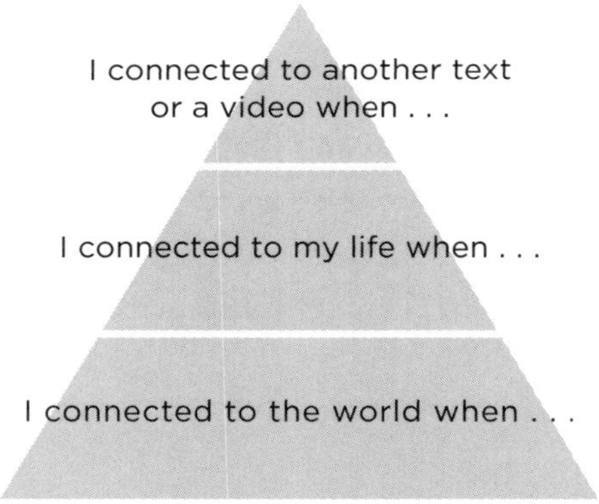

I connected to another text
or a video when . . .

I connected to my life when . . .

I connected to the world when . . .

During reading, or after students have read the instructional text or a self-selected text, ask them to write down a connection to their personal lives or experiences, a connection to another text or movie, and a connection to the world.

Figure 5.2: My pyramid of connections graphic organizer.

Visit **go.SolutionTree.com/literacy** *for a free reproducible version of this figure.*

Students should think about questions that they have about the text before and during reading. Questions should include things they are wondering about and things they may be confused about in regard to comprehending the text. They should also indicate if their questions were answered and what strategies they used to clarify.

What I *Know* . . .	What I *Want* to Know . . .	What I *Learned* . . .
Complete this column before reading to activate prior knowledge and encourage connections with their own experiences.	Complete this column before reading to develop questions students want answered. Add questions during reading.	Complete this column after reading. Have students check to see if they found the answers to their questions.

Figure 5.3: KWL chart.

Visit **go.SolutionTree.com/literacy** *for a free reproducible version of this figure.*

Predicting

Previewing and predicting have been shown to be effective in helping students construct meaning. Good readers make predictions before, during, and after reading. Teaching students to predict before they read, read purposefully to check their predictions, and amend their predictions during reading are important strategies for constructing meaning. Pourhosein-Gilakjani and Sabouri (2016) state that successful readers make predictions about what will occur next and monitor their predictions, changing any predictions that are not supported by the text.

The previewing and predicting technique is a useful tool for teaching and practicing prediction before and during reading. Students take a text walk through the story or chapter and make predictions about what they think will happen or what they think they will learn. While students read the text, they either confirm or discard their predictions and make new predictions.

The graphic organizers and templates included in this section support students' practice and application of the comprehension strategy of predicting. They encourage students to predict and then check and revise their predictions as they read. This process supports engagement with the text and the development of metacognition. Figure 5.4 and figure 5.5 show examples of the process of making predictions before, during, and after reading.

Making Predictions Before, During, and After Reading

Ask students to make at least one prediction about the text they will be reading before they read.

My prediction *before* reading:

After reading the text or a portion of it, students should think about if their prediction was correct and why or why not.

Was I correct? Why or why not?

Ask students to stop reading at a certain point, or at several points, to not only check their first prediction, but also make a new prediction or two.

My prediction *during* reading:

Was I correct? Why or why not?

My next prediction *during* reading:

Was I correct? Why or why not?

After reading the text, ask students to consider if the predictions they made during reading were correct and provide their rationale. Then, have them make predictions about the next chapter or if the story/book were to continue.

My prediction *after* reading:

My next prediction would be . . .

Figure 5.4: Making predictions before, during, and after reading.
Visit **go.SolutionTree.com/literacy** *for a free reproducible version of this figure.*

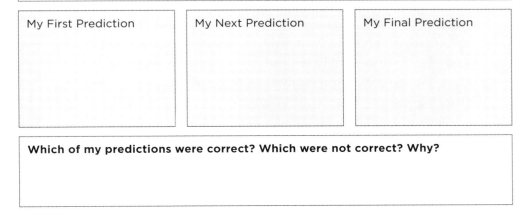

Making and Checking Predictions

The instructions for the previous graphic organizer may be used with this prediction chart as well. The purpose is for the students to make predictions, check them, and make new predictions based on the text.

My First Prediction	My Next Prediction	My Final Prediction

Which of my predictions were correct? Which were not correct? Why?

Figure 5.5: Making and checking predictions.

Visit **go.SolutionTree.com/literacy** *for a free reproducible version of this figure.*

Visualizing

Effective, strategic readers visualize or create mental pictures during and after reading. They use the images to draw conclusions, create interpretations of the text, and recall important details. Good readers have a motion picture running through their minds as they read. Creating mental images aids in developing comprehension and leads to the transfer and retention of information. Readers use images to immerse themselves in details as they read. These details give depth to the reading, engage the reader more deeply, and make the text more memorable (Serafini, 2011). Muzdizal (2019) finds that using mental imaging, or visualizing, while reading led to significant gains in students' comprehension and retellings of text.

Examples of Explicit Instruction in the Visualizing Strategy

As discussed, direct or explicit instruction in comprehension strategies is essential. Using the think-aloud technique can be effective in teaching and modeling the strategies. It is recommended that explicit instruction in each strategy be provided over time, with two or three days of teaching and modeling the strategy, a day or two of guided practice, and some opportunities to apply the strategy with a partner or independently. It is important to continue to review and practice each strategy periodically, as you add new strategies to the students' repertoires. The following is an example of a script for two days of explicit instruction in the visualizing strategy. The components of explicit instruction as described on page 88 are highlighted in the script.

Day 1: Explicit Instruction for Visualizing Strategy

Today we are going to work on a comprehension strategy called visualizing or making pictures in your head. Some of you may have learned about this strategy before, but we need to review it because it is so important. We will be practicing visualizing today, and later you will need to be able to tell and show me what you have visualized. **Introduce and name the strategy, and tell the learning expectations.**

When good readers read, to understand what they read and remember it later, they have a movie running in their heads while they read. This is called visualizing. When we read without visualizing, we don't fully understand what we are reading, and we won't remember it well. **Describe the strategy and why it is important.**

For example, if I read a whole page of a book but get to the end of the page and have no clue about what I have read, it is because I was not visualizing. I was probably thinking about what to get at the grocery store instead! I have to reread the page. Good readers visualize whenever they are reading. **Tell when to use the strategy.**

Let me show you what I mean.

Read a passage aloud, pausing often to think aloud about your own mental images. After you finish, ask students to share out some of the things they heard you visualize. **Model the strategies using the think-aloud technique (I Do).**

Now I'm going to ask you to visualize. I'll be reading you a passage, and I want you to close your eyes and make pictures in your head. Don't stop with one picture—keep a movie of what is happening playing in your mind.

Read passage to students with their eyes closed.

Have students share afterward about what they visualized. Guided practice (We Do)

You will be practicing visualizing during independent work time today. **Independent practice (You Do)**

Day 2: Explicit Instruction for Visualizing Strategy

Review the objective from yesterday **(students will visualize or make mental pictures while they read)**. Review orally some of the things they visualized when you read day 1's passage. Review that good readers visualize whenever they read to better understand and remember what they read. Visualizing is like making a movie in your head while you read.

Yesterday we focused on visualizing only with our sense of sight—what we could "see" in our minds. You can visualize with all your senses—seeing, hearing, smelling, touching, and even tasting.

Read a passage to the students, stopping to think aloud about what you are seeing, hearing, smelling, feeling, and tasting. Ask students to orally recall what they heard you visualize.

Now you will get the chance to practice visualizing with your five senses. **Have students close their eyes and visualize as you read the passage aloud, then share their thoughts.**

Encouraging students to create mental images from the text as they read can be supported by graphic organizers, such as the following templates. It is helpful to begin by guiding students to visualize in whole group or small groups and discuss their mental images. After ample guided practice, students should be able to complete the graphic organizers on their own. It is beneficial to have students share their mental images with the class or other students. Having students complete a *See, Hear, Feel, Taste, Smell* chart as they read gives purpose and accountability to the reading task and encourages students to use all their senses to create imagery as they read. Students may also draw or write down what they visualize as they read and share their visualizations with the class or a small group. See figure 5.6 (page 96) for a *See, Hear, Feel, Taste, Smell* chart.

Visualizing While I Read

After teaching, modeling, and providing guided practice in visualizing, ask students to complete the following chart using each of their senses. What did they see, hear, feel, taste, and smell while reading the text?

When I visualize, I make a movie in my mind, and I can:

See _____ because the book said _____

Hear _____ because the book said _____

Feel _____ because the book said _____

Smell _____ because the book said _____

Taste _____ because the book said _____

While students are reading, have them jot down brief descriptions of what they visualized as they read and main events or important information from the text.

Things I Visualized:

**Things That Are
Important to Remember:**

Figure 5.6: Visualizing while reading.
Visit **go.SolutionTree.com/literacy** *for a free reproducible version of this figure.*

Questioning, Monitoring, and Clarifying

Students also need to learn and practice metacognition (being aware of what they are thinking) and questioning their own comprehension. They need to understand

and practice strategies, such as rereading and reading on, for clarification when they are lost or confused.

Gay Su Pinnell (2000) determines, "As long as the teacher is asking all the questions, students are not responsible for their own comprehension" (p. 23). Students need to learn to ask questions about what they do not understand, what they have learned, how they can connect new learning to their lives, and what else they may want or need to know.

Higher-Order Critical Thinking

To develop higher-order critical thinking, students must formulate their own questions while they are reading. A proficient reader's mind is always alive with questions. Jiban (2022) recommends that we teach students to apply metacognitive strategies like monitoring their own understanding and building inferences while reading. Teaching, modeling, and providing guided practice in *metacognition*, or thinking about your own thinking and understanding, can help students comprehend the text more deeply. Students need to be aware of how well they are understanding the text, what questions they have about the text, and how they might clarify misunderstandings and confusion. Explicit instruction and teacher modeling of metacognition is essential for students to begin to be aware of their own understanding of text.

Graphic Organizers, Activities, and Templates for Monitoring and Questioning

Using the following templates during whole-group instruction will help the teacher to teach and model monitoring and questioning as they read. When teachers model their own thinking, including telling when they are confused, strategies they can use to "fix" their confusion, and questions that they are asking about the text, students will begin to understand and apply metacognition. Then, students will be able to complete these activities and graphic organizers (figures 5.3, 5.7, and 5.8 pages 91, 98, and 99, respectively) with partners or independently.

Providing students with sticky notes and asking them to develop questions to be shared with the class or asked of their peers during reading is an effective way to engage students in questioning. The first column (*K*) on the KWL chart was discussed under *Connecting* (page 89). Now, completing the *W* and *L* sections of a KWL chart is a useful tool for listing students' questions and what they have learned from the text.

Monitoring and Clarifying During Reading

This graphic organizer involves students in monitoring their understanding as they read. It also helps them to apply fix-it strategies like reading on, rereading, and using context clues to clarify their understanding.

Words or events I do not understand or need to know more about:

1. Word, Event, or Action:

    Fix-it strategy used (context, read on, reread, ask someone)

    What I figured out:

2. Word, Event, or Action:

    Fix-it strategy used (context, read on, reread, ask someone)

    What I figured out:

1. Reread the sentence and look for clues to help you figure out the word or section.	2. Reread the sentences before and after the word looking for clues about the word or section.
3. Read on further to see if this helps you to understand better.	4. Use pictures or a friend to help you.

Figure 5.7: Words or events I don't understand chart.

Visit **go.SolutionTree.com/literacy** *for a free reproducible version of this figure.*

This is another graphic organizer for students to develop metacognition through questioning and determining the answers to their questions. While they are reading, students need to think about questions related to what the characters did and why, what the characters said, why a significant event happened, and what a word or section that was confusing meant.

Ask questions about . . .	Your Question	Your Question	What You Found Out
What someone or something did			
What someone or something said			
Why something happened			
What did this word or section mean			

Figure 5.8: Asking questions as I read chart.

Visit **go.SolutionTree.com/literacy** *for a free reproducible version of this figure.*

Summarizing

Lori D. Oczkus (2018) determines that summarizing is important for understanding fiction and nonfiction text and summarization helps students "construct an overall understanding of text" (p. 29). Good readers can recount story elements, text patterns, and important events from the text. Students need modeling and practice in retelling stories and describing characters, settings, conflicts, main events, problems, and solutions.

Students need to be able to synthesize information and express main ideas and the text's overall meaning. Students must practice determining meaning, important concepts, and themes in text as they read, understanding that their thinking evolves in the process. Summarizing helps readers move past the literal meaning of the text to inference and other higher levels of processing (Serafini, 2011).

Techniques such as story maps, which require students to synthesize the story into its main events in sequential order; graphic organizers of story elements; and the herringbone strategy, where students identify the main idea of the text and six supporting details, are useful activities to help students develop summarization skills.

Summarizing involves identifying main ideas and supporting details in the text. It also includes the order of events or the sequencing of the story, recognizing cause and effect, and understanding the conflict and resolution. The graphic organizers in figure 5.9 and figure 5.10 are templates that can guide students to apply summarization skills. Modeling through thinking aloud and providing guided practice in summarizing is needed prior to students working with partners or independently completing these templates.

Making Inferences and Drawing Conclusions

Inferring means being able to take what you know and the information found in the text to *infer* or draw conclusions. Inference is a vital reading comprehension skill, as text frequently does not include direct explanations of events, characters, actions, and other plot elements. To fully comprehend text, readers need to be able to *read between the lines*. To have a deeper understanding of text and the meaning behind it, inference must be applied. Björn B. de Koning, Lisanne T. Bos, Stephanie I. Wassenburg, and Menno van der Schoot (2017) study the impact of direct training in making inferences on reading comprehension and find that students not only increase their reading comprehension scores, but also indicate that they are more motivated to read.

This graphic organizer helps students practice identifying main ideas and events from the text and using these to summarize, or retell, what they have read and learned.

In the top four boxes, write key ideas and main events from the story. In the bottom box, write a summary of the story using the key ideas and main events you have chosen.

1.	2.	3.	4.

Summary:

Figure 5.9: Summarizing using main ideas and events.

Visit **go.SolutionTree.com/literacy** *for a free reproducible version of this figure.*

Key point or main event at the beginning:
Key point or main event in the middle:
Key point or main event at the end:
Summary:

Figure 5.10: Summarizing with the beginning, middle, and end graphic organizer.

Visit **go.SolutionTree.com/literacy** *for a free reproducible version of this figure.*

Explicit Instruction in Inference

Nihat Bayat and Gökhan Cetizkaya's (2020) study finds that inference making should be included within literacy instruction to enhance students' reading comprehension. The following is a script for explicit instruction in inference followed by graphic organizers that will support students' learning and practice in the skill of making inferences based on what they know from their own experiences and clues from the text.

We know that when good readers are reading, they engage or involve themselves in the text they are reading.

A strategy that good readers use is called inferring or "inference." When you infer, you use things you already know and information in the text you are reading to draw conclusions. **Name and describe the strategy.**

When you infer, you draw a conclusion or decide something based on evidence from the text.

Good readers infer throughout the reading process. Inferring helps you to engage in and think deeply about what you are reading, understand it better, and enjoy reading more. **Explain why the strategy is important and when it should be used.**

Think-Aloud Example 1

The men walked down the road to the factory with their heads bent down toward their chests. They hurried on with their caps pulled down almost over their eyes and their scarves tied tightly over their faces.

What was the weather like as the men walked to the factory?

I know when it is cold outside people often walk hunched over and close together. **Highlight this in the first sentence in one color.** In the text it said the men had on caps and scarves to cover their faces. **Highlight this in another color.** From what I know and the information in the text, I can infer that the weather is cold and possibly windy.

Did the paragraph say it was cold and windy? No. Using what I know and some evidence from the paragraph, I was able to draw a conclusion or infer. **Modeling using the strategy through the think-aloud technique (I Do)**

Think-Aloud Example 2

Maggie rushed outside through the open door. "Sadie! Come here, Sadie!" she shouted. Maggie looked all around the yard and up and down the street. Finally, she went back inside and said to her mother in a tearful voice, "Sadie's gone! She's lost! Her leash and collar are on the floor by her water bowl!"

What is happening?

I know that if you rush outside and call out a name, you are probably looking for someone or something. **Highlight in one color the first two sentences.** In the text it says she looked all around. She told her mother Sadie is gone, and it talks about a leash, collar, and water bowl. **Highlight in another color.** Even though the text doesn't say this, I think I can conclude that Maggie's dog got out and is lost and that she is upset and worried.

Inference, then, means using what you know and the clues or evidence from the text to decide or predict something or to draw conclusions. **Modeling the strategy using the think-aloud technique**

Graphic Organizers, Activities, and Templates for Making Inferences

During explicit instruction and guided practice in making inferences, students will understand that inferring means using what we know or have experienced and what we read in the text to infer, or draw conclusions. Students should jot down what they know and what the text says so they can make inferences of their own; they can use figures 5.11 and 5.12 (page 104) to do this. It may be helpful to provide students with a page or section of the text that would lend itself to inferring.

What the Text Says or Shows	+	What I Know	=	Inferences I Can Make
_____		_____		_____
_____		_____		_____
_____		_____		_____
_____		_____		_____

Figure 5.11: Making inferences.

Visit **go.SolutionTree.com/literacy** *for a free reproducible version of this figure.*

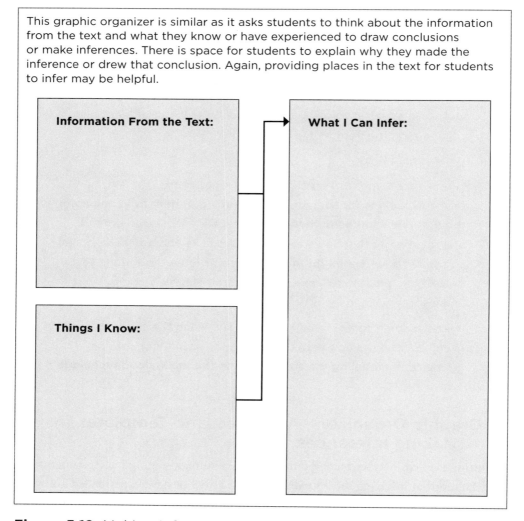

This graphic organizer is similar as it asks students to think about the information from the text and what they know or have experienced to draw conclusions or make inferences. There is space for students to explain why they made the inference or drew that conclusion. Again, providing places in the text for students to infer may be helpful.

Information From the Text:

What I Can Infer:

Things I Know:

Figure 5.12: Making inferences.

Visit **go.SolutionTree.com/literacy** *for a free reproducible version of this figure.*

Think-Alouds for Comprehension Instruction

Since the 1990s, a common practice for many teachers is to use think-alouds as tools for teaching and modeling comprehension strategies. With the think-aloud technique, the teacher models comprehension strategies by verbalizing their thinking process while reading. This helps to make explicit what good readers implicitly do when they are reading. Think-alouds can effectively support instruction in reading fluency, vocabulary strategies such as the use of context clues, and comprehension;

however, if not utilized in an evidence-based manner, these techniques have less of a positive impact on students in becoming proficient, strategic readers.

In today's classrooms, it is common for teachers to use leveled books or the instructional text to implement think-alouds. Unfortunately, this can lead to teachers reading the instructional text aloud *to* students, rather than allowing them to read the text independently. Think-alouds can be highly effective if used to model strategies within portions of the instructional text or by using examples or passages from other texts.

Students *must* be challenged to read text on their own and to apply vocabulary and comprehension strategies to construct meaning out of text. This does not typically happen if the text has already been read aloud to the students. Therefore, the passages selected for reading aloud should not include the entire text that students are being asked to read.

A major drawback of using the think-aloud technique is that it is common for the teacher to *model only* and not follow up with opportunities for students to engage in guided or independent practice of the modeled skills and strategies, which are essential aspects of sound literacy instruction. Lana Santoro, David J. Chard, Lisa Howard, and Scott K. Baker (2008) conclude that think-alouds must be carefully planned if they are to affect students' comprehension. Think-alouds can promote comprehension and vocabulary development if they include well-planned explicit comprehension instruction and active, engaging discussions about text (Santoro et al., 2008).

Think-alouds are most effective when the teacher uses portions of a text to teach and model what the strategy is and how to apply it while reading, then follows this modeling with opportunities for students to try to use the strategy with guidance. Asking students to apply the strategy and share their ideas is valuable. Rich discussions around the strategy and its application are necessary for a deeper understanding of how to increase comprehension by applying the strategy. Working on the strategy with a partner, or in a small group, for additional guided practice is also important. Finally, it is essential that students engage in independent practice in applying the strategy while reading, through various activities and graphic organizers.

Following explicit instruction and modeling through think-alouds, engaging students in supported practice with comprehension strategies will help them to apply the strategies while reading independently (Victoria Department of Education, 2018). When students are given the opportunity to think aloud, this can be even more powerful. Neny Novridewi, Sri Wachyunni, and Urip Sulistiyo (2023) determine that when students are engaged in reciprocal teaching, such as thinking aloud, reading achievement significantly increases, and students' learning motivation increases.

Recorded Text and Its Effect on Comprehension

Another common aspect of reading instruction that has emerged is using text-to-speech (TTS) technology, where a computer, tablet, or CD player reads the story, chapter, or article aloud to the students. Students typically have the text in front of them, and most programs track the text as it is read. It is important to note that students actually demonstrate their *listening* comprehension much more than their independent reading comprehension when the text is being read to them.

Although TTS technology is widely used in schools, the research related to using TTS technology is inconclusive, and there is a minimal research base on the effects of using TTS to support comprehension. Some key points from studies related to using TTS narration include the following.

- Research indicates mixed results regarding the impact of TTS on comprehension. There is a lack of research concerning the effect of interactive electronic texts on the reading comprehension of students with reading disabilities (Gonzalez, 2014).

- "TTS did not affect students' fluency, comprehension, or task completion time, although social validity interviews revealed that each student valued the independence and efficiency TTS provided" (Meyer & Bouck, 2014, p. 32).

- A meta-analysis on the effects of online read-aloud programs on reading comprehension for students with reading difficulties revealed a modest effect size of 0.35 (Wood, Moxley, Tighe, & Wagner, 2017).

Teachers should use caution when considering having students listen to books electronically. Typically, when students are asked to listen to text, they are practicing their listening comprehension, rather than reading independently and applying strategies to create meaning from the text.

Reading Comprehension Instruction Recommendations

Solving the Literacy Puzzle recommends that the *universal,* or most critical, comprehension strategies, as identified through the research, be the focus of explicit instruction, modeling, and guided practice on a regular basis. These strategies include (1) connecting, (2) visualizing, (3) predicting, (4) questioning, (5) monitoring and clarifying or metacognition, (6) summarizing using main ideas and details, and (7) inferring and drawing conclusions.

In *Solving the Literacy Puzzle*, it is recommended that one comprehension strategy remain the focus of instruction for one to two weeks to provide sufficient opportunities for explicit instruction, modeling, guided practice, independent practice, and application in other contexts. Strategies should be reviewed throughout the year and embedded in discussion groups, literature circles, and other activities. Components of comprehension strategy instruction in *Solving the Literacy Puzzle* include the following.

- **Whole-Group Instruction**
  - Explicit instruction in the comprehension strategy is provided in a whole-group setting (following the steps in explicit instruction).
  - Teacher models specific strategy application through the think-aloud technique, using high-interest literature and the instructional text.

- **Partner or Small-Group Guided Practice**
  - Review of explicit instruction and additional teacher modeling of strategies should occur using the instructional text or leveled texts.
  - Partner or small-group guided practice should occur with examples from the instructional text or leveled texts (students practice think-alouds).

- **Independent Practice**
  - Students engage in independent practice in strategy application using the instructional text, with some form of accountability.
  - Students engage in independent practice in strategy application using other texts.

When planning comprehension instruction, the teacher needs to determine the evidence-based strategy to be taught and practiced and which text is best suited for explicit instruction in that strategy. How the strategy will be modeled through demonstration or think-alouds must also be intentionally planned. Also, planning for scaffolded instruction is important so that students participate in guided practice and, later on, independent application of the comprehension strategy. Figure 5.13 (page 108) is a generic example of planning the comprehension component of core instruction, which may be edited for teachers' use. Following the conclusion of this chapter there is a template that may be used for planning comprehension instruction.

Day 1	Day 2	Days 3 and 4	Day 5
Whole group: Explicit instruction and modeling of comprehension strategy using generic or instructional text (read-aloud or think-aloud) **Small group interventions:** Review and modeling of application of strategy with instructional or ability-level text	**Whole group:** Review of explicit instruction and additional teacher modeling of comprehension strategy using generic or instructional text **Small group interventions:** Additional guided practice of strategy application with instructional or ability-level text **Independent work and rotations:** Work on comprehension task or graphic organizer	**Whole group:** Brief review of comprehension strategy **Small group interventions:** Guided or independent practice of comprehension strategy with generic or instructional text; complete comprehension graphic organizer or another task **Independent work and rotations:** Work on comprehension task or graphic organizer; activity for comprehension strategy application with additional text	**Small group or partner work:** Guided or independent practice with generic or instructional text Activity to apply comprehension strategy **Whole group:** Formative assessment on comprehension strategy

Figure 5.13: Instructional sequence (five days) for comprehension strategies.

Conclusion

Comprehension is the goal of reading, and students need to be taught strategies to enhance their comprehension of a variety of texts. Comprehension strategies are best taught explicitly, modeled by the teacher or students, then applied within a variety of texts including the instructional text and students' self-selected books. Comprehension is also directly supported through having rich discussions about text. Chapter 6 (page 111) addresses effective questioning techniques, the characteristics of quality questions, and engaging students in meaningful discussions about text.

The reproducible "Part 4: Comprehension Instructional Planning Template" (page 109) is useful for planning the comprehension component of comprehensive, core literacy instruction.

Part 4: Comprehension Instructional Planning Template

Research-based comprehension strategy selected:

Text to use for explicit instruction:

Strategies to model with think-aloud during whole-group, core instruction:

Small-group activity for application of strategy:

Independent practice activities for application of strategy:

Solving the Literacy Puzzle © 2024 Solution Tree Press • SolutionTree.com
Visit **go.SolutionTree.com/literacy** to download this free reproducible.

Reflection Questions for Chapter 5: Comprehension as the Heart and Goal of Reading

What research-based comprehension strategies do all students have the opportunity to learn and apply in your classroom?

How often is there explicit instruction and modeling of comprehension strategies by the teacher?

How often do *all* students have adequate time for guided and independent practice in applying the comprehension strategies while reading grade-level or age-appropriate texts?

Chapter 6

Text Discussion and Questioning

The object of teaching a child is to enable him to get along without a teacher.

—**ELBERT HUBBARD**

We understand from research and through classroom observations that reading comprehension must be at the *heart* of literacy instruction for students to become successful, strategic readers. Discussions about text are essential in supporting students' comprehension. Text discussions should be carefully and intentionally planned, with ample time allocated for rich discussions. In this chapter, the importance of asking preplanned higher-order questions and involving students in actively talking about text is addressed. Also, various protocols for discussions are described.

Common Practices in Reading Comprehension Instruction

Classroom observational data, gathered over the past twenty years, indicate that minimal time is spent in many elementary classrooms on students' engagement in whole-group, or even small-group, discussion of text. Due to today's commonly used literacy instructional formats (such as having a short whole-group minilesson and reading some text, followed by small, leveled reading groups—typically 10- to 15-minute sessions), teachers are finding it difficult to hold meaningful discussions about the instructional text.

Bruce B. Frey, Steven W. Lee, Nona Tollefson, Lisa Pass, and Donita Massengill Shaw (2005) note that within a balanced reading model, 18 percent of literacy instructional time is spent on read alouds by the teacher, with *no additional time* specifically allocated for discussion of text with students (as cited by Hebzynski, 2017).

Based on the author's surveys and interviews with teachers since 2006, text discussion is frequently limited to lower-level, spur-of-the-moment questioning by the teacher, with little time for multiple students to respond and to interact with one another. Students have few opportunities to engage in rich discussions about text, guided by higher-order questions from the teacher. Also, students are rarely asked to generate *thick* questions (questions that require higher levels of thinking, such as application, analysis, and evaluation) or given the opportunity to be involved in discussion protocols that engage all students in rich conversation about text.

The Importance of Quality Questioning and Discussion

Questioning is one of the nine research-based strategies presented in *Classroom Instruction That Works* and indicates a significant positive effect on learning (Marzano, Pickering, & Pollock, 2001). Questions need to be *thick* or *thinking* questions that help students develop a deeper understanding of what they have read. For the most part, even with veteran teachers, effective questions do not happen spontaneously and typically need to be intentionally preplanned. Impromptu questioning often results in asking questions that do not require students to use higher levels of thinking. The Illinois Center for Innovation in Teaching and Learning (ICITL, n.d.) concluded that "effective questioning sessions in classroom require advance preparation." The following are characteristics of effective or *quality* questions.

- Clear and concise
- Purposeful (to support the learning of concepts and skills)
- Thoughtfully preplanned
- Higher-order and open-ended
- Unidimensional (focused on one intentional concept or idea)
- Have a clear instructional purpose (Sood, 2019)

Table 6.1 reiterates similar characteristics and illustrates the features of quality questions and how they compare to less-effective questions.

Table 6.1: Comparison of Quality Questions to Lower-Level, Less-Effective Questions

Quality Questions	Why	Lower-Level, Less-Effective Questions
Are higher-order and open-ended	Allow for multiple responses	Are *closed* or may have one correct response
Are focused on concepts and skills	Address standards, learning outcomes	Are random, "just for fun," conversational
Have a clear instructional purpose	Asking the question will lead to higher levels of student learning and/or application	May be enjoyable, but do not support learning and application
Fall above the recall and comprehension levels	Encourage higher levels of thinking	Are lower-level and less complex
Provoke thought and discussion	Lead to rich conversations about text	Include little thought and do not lead to further discussion

Question analysis, based on the characteristics of quality questions and through use of table 6.1, is important when designing preplanned questions for discussion of text. Let's try it! Identify the better, or higher-quality, question for *Charlotte's Web* (White, 1952):

1. How did Wilbur and Charlotte feel about each other?

2. What are three things that Wilbur learned from his friendship with Charlotte?

In addition to determining if the question has the characteristics of a quality question, as indicated in table 6.1, *which question 2 does*, it is helpful to think about how a student might respond to the question. For the first question, a student's response would likely be "They were friends" or "They liked each other a lot." This question is not purposeful and would require thinking only at the basic comprehension level. The second question is at a higher level, and students would need to think more deeply and use more complex language to respond.

The benefits of engaging students in rich discussions of text, based on quality, *thinking* questions, include the following.

*   Text-based discussions are powerful tools for engaging students in higher-level thinking and developing metacognition (Elosúa, García-Madruga, Vila, Gómez-Veiga, & Gil, 2013).

- Discussion of text helps students to develop metacognitive skills and take responsibility for their own learning, which enhances reading proficiency.

- Using quality questioning techniques, such as asking higher-order questions and allowing wait time, improves student outcomes (Walsh & Sattes, 2016).

- Discussion leads students to test new ideas and to access knowledge and insight from other students with diverse points of view. They become connected to a topic and are provided with opportunities to share about their thoughts, their voices, and their experiences. Students are affirmed as co-creators of knowledge and will develop a deeper understanding of the text (Cavanaugh, 2008).

Elosúa and colleagues (2013) determine that text-based discussions are powerful tools for engaging students in higher-level thinking and developing metacognition.

In addition, current research suggests that discussion can (1) increase student learning, (2) motivate students, (3) assist teachers in assessing student thinking, and (4) shift the authority from the teacher (or textbook) to the classroom community. Feifei Han and Robert A. Ellis (2021) conclude that learning through discussions is positively linked to students' attitudes about the value of learning and has a positive impact on academic achievement.

Holding rich discussions related to comprehending text includes many benefits, including the following.

1. Adding interest through higher-order questioning and collaboration
2. Engaging students in thinking and communicating about the text
3. Allowing for teacher and peer feedback
4. Ensuring that all students are involved and contributing to learning
5. Encouraging dialogue among and between students (Hunt, 2020)

Discussion is a strategy that can help teachers understand what students already know and determine what they still need to learn. In this sense, listening to students' ideas during discussions can serve as formative assessments that help teachers make decisions about their instruction (Sela, Davis, & Hulse, 2019).

From TOAD to Prince

A sound process for text discussion is the Teacher-Facilitated, Oral Reading, Application of Strategies, and Discussion (TOAD) format. This protocol assists teachers in being well prepared for rich discussions of text that focus on grade-level standards, as well as helping students learn through discussions using higher-order questions. The components or steps in the TOAD process are illustrated and described in the following text.

Teacher-Facilitated, Oral Reading, Application of Strategies, and Discussion (TOAD)

- Teacher-facilitated
  - Teacher plans the text (whole or parts) to read orally.
  - Teacher preplans "thick" questions.
  - Teacher plans where to stop to "think aloud."
  - Teacher guides the oral reading and discussion.
- Oral reading of grade-appropriate text
  - Read aloud as a group all or portions of a story or novel that students have read independently or with a partner.
  - Teacher and students take turns reading.
  - Teacher modeling and practice assists students in developing fluency skills.
  - Modeling and practice focuses on fluency skills (italicized words, punctuation, expression).
- Application of strategies and skills
  - Teacher models their own "expert" use of strategies through think-alouds.
  - Students apply strategies or think aloud as they read.
  - Demonstrate and encourage students to apply skills (vocabulary in context, compound words, multimeaning words, cause and effect, and so on).
  - Engage students in the text.
  - Provide chances for reciprocal teaching (students being the teachers).
- Discussion
  - Students ask and answer questions that facilitate comprehension (preplanned).
  - Students actively engage in dialogue about the text.

- Students apply various levels of thinking about the text.

- Students share ideas and learn from each other.

- Teacher can assess understanding and strategy application.

- Incorporate literature circles or discussion protocols.

Note: It works well to mark or highlight where you will stop to think aloud, have notes about your modeling, and have the preplanned questions on sticky notes.

The following is an example of a completed TOAD plan for *The Scavenger Hunt* (Narra, 2019) and *After the Flood* (K5 Learning, n.d.).

TOAD Instructional Planning Example for *The Scavenger Hunt* and *After the Flood*

- Text:

  - *The Scavenger Hunt* and *After the Flood*

- Sections, pages, and chapters to be read aloud and discussed:

  - The Scavenger Hunt

    + Day 1: Pages 1–8

    + Day 2: Pages 9–17

    + Day 3: Pages 1–17

  - After the Flood

    + Day 4: First four paragraphs

    + Day 5: All

- Format for reading aloud (round robin, "popcorn," volunteers, choral):

  - *The Scavenger Hunt*

    + Day 1: Teacher modeling pages 1–3; "popcorn" reading pages 4–8

    + Day 2: Teacher modeling pages 9–10; round robin reading pages 11–17

    + Day 3: Volunteer reading pages 1–8; choral reading pages 9–11; volunteer reading pages 12–17

- *After the Flood*
  - + Days 4 and 5: Teacher modeling first four paragraphs; "popcorn" reading for the rest of the passage; rereading rotating girls and boys
- Focus for modeling and practicing fluency:
  - Expression using punctuation and the storyline (putting selves in characters' shoes)
- Focus of each think-aloud (vocabulary skills, comprehension strategies, language arts skills, and so on)
  - Questioning: Asking "I wonder . . ." questions about the events in the text
- Teacher think-alouds (where in the text will you stop and model)
  - Day 1: Page 3—I am wondering if Lajjo's home has gotten flooded before since they live near a river. I am wondering what Lajjo's family can do to get away from the water.
  - Day 2: Page 10—I wonder why Lajjo needs a piece of cloth. I wonder why Mai would give Lajjo a piece of her sari.
  - Day 4: First four paragraphs of *After the Flood*—After paragraph 2, I wonder how Vicky is feeling about all the rain; is it good for the plants, or is it something to be worried about?
  - After paragraph 4, I wonder why Vicky is not supposed to open the door!
- If students will be asked to think aloud, on which pages?
  - After pages 12, 15, and 17 in *The Scavenger Hunt*: Ask students what questions they have and to share these.
  - After paragraphs 9 and 12 and the last paragraph in *After the Flood*: Ask students what questions they have and to share these.
- Preplanned "thick" questions to ask during and after the reading aloud of the text:

- For pages 1–8:

  + Page 3—Why do you think Lajjo is scared? What do you think she is afraid will happen?

  + Page 6—What did Mai mean when she said, "All you care about is a doll?" Why do you think she is angry?

  + Page 8—Why is Lajjo so excited about a game?

  + Page 8—Do you have any ideas about why Daddu is asking Lajjo to find those specific items?

Note: While reading, ask students to share the questions that they generated while they were reading pages 1–8 independently.

- For pages 9–17:

  + Page 9—Why do you think Mai gave Lajjo a piece of her sari? How do you think this made Lajjo feel (remember that Mai was angry with her earlier)?

  + Page 12—How does the carpenter feel about Lajjo playing a game? Why does he feel this way?

  + Page 14—What were you asking yourself or wondering about when Daddu was working with the bucket and other items? (Questioning strategy)

  + Page 16—Why was what Daddu did so important? What are your thoughts about how Daddu knew how to do this? Would Lajjo think getting her doll back was the best thing that could happen?

Note: While reading, ask students to share the questions that they generated while they were reading pages 9–17 independently.

Discussion Protocols

Discussion protocols, or structures, consist of clear steps, or serve as a *recipe* for students to use for reading, discussing, or reporting what they learned from the text. Discussion protocols help to facilitate meaningful and productive discussions. Protocols ensure equal participation and accountability for all students (Sela et al., 2019). When everyone understands the steps, roles, and process procedures of the protocol, students will work more independently, as well as more collaboratively.

Protocols hold *each* student accountable and responsible for building background knowledge about a topic and analyzing what they read. Additionally, Kari Thierer (2019) concludes that protocols offer structured processes to support focused and productive conversations and build collective understanding. Discussion protocols also allow the teacher to assess which students are struggling with the text and may need further support for better comprehension (Sela et al., 2019).

The following are several discussion protocols that are beneficial in supporting whole-class and small-group discussions.

The Final Word

- Put students in groups (4–6 works well).
- Give students the same number of questions to discuss as there are group members (4 members in group = 4 questions).
- Questions need to be "thick" or good thinking questions for discussion or debate (preplanned and written by the teacher *or* the students).
- Determine who will go first, and that student reads question 1 aloud.
- Each person in the group (moving around clockwise) gives a 30- to 60-second response to the question or to other responses (minimum of 30 seconds).
- After all have responded, the person who read the question gets 60 seconds to have the "Final Word." This person can restate their own thoughts or summarize the group's ideas.
- Repeat with the other questions until all have had the chance to read a question and to have the "Final Word."

The First Word

- Put students in groups (4–6 works well).
- Give students the same number of questions to discuss as there are group members (4 members in group = 4 questions).
- Questions need to be "thick" or good thinking questions for discussion or debate (preplanned and written by the teacher *or* the students).
- Determine who reads question 1 aloud. This student has 60 seconds to respond with their own thoughts and opinions.

- Each person in the group (moving around clockwise) gives a 30- to 60-second response to the question or to other responses (minimum of 30 seconds).

- Repeat with the other questions until all have had the chance to read a question and to have the "First Word."

Thumbs Up, Thumbs Down

- Put students in groups of 6–8, or this can be done with the whole class.

- Have preplanned, written "thinking" questions for discussion or debate.

- The teacher or a student reads the first question and gives a 30- to 60-second response.

- The others in the group hold a "thumbs up" if they agree or a "thumbs down" if they disagree *or* have different ideas.

- Each person in the group tells *why* they agree and adds support or tells *why* they disagree.

- Person who read the question summarizes what the group members or class said. Repeat.

Inside-Outside Circle

- Have the class form two circles (an inside circle and an outside circle with equal numbers and have them standing and facing each other).

- Have preplanned, written "thinking" questions (5–8 for inside circle people, 5–8 for outside circle people).

- The inside circle people should ask their outside circle partner the first question. The outside circle people answer the question with a 30-second response.

- The inside circle people should then "coach" or "praise" their outside circle partner.

- The outside circle people move one place to their right and meet up with a new inside circle person.

- The inside circle people read question 2.

- Repeat until all inside circle questions have been asked and answered.

- Now repeat with the outside circle people asking their questions.

"A Penny for Your Thoughts" or "My Two Cents Worth"

- Set up groups of 4–8 members.

- Place the statements or questions from or about the text (on strips or index cards) in the center.

- Place enough pennies in the center for each person to have two (4 people = 8 pennies, and so on).

- Determine the order of play. The first player picks up a statement (if numbered, start with 1) and reads it aloud.

- This player then takes a penny and responds to the statement (must tell "why" or give rationale for answer).

- Taking turns, each person in the group takes a penny and shares their ideas or response and their rationale until all have shared once.

- Continue taking turns sharing until all pennies have been used. Some people may only use one penny and others two or three pennies, as long as all share at least once.

- Return all pennies to the center.

- Go to the next person, who picks a statement or question and repeats the process.

A Hatful of Quotes

- A group member draws a slip of paper with a quote or statement from the text out of the hat.

- This person reads the quote aloud and responds to it for 30–90 seconds (tells why it's important or meaningful, shares an opinion, says why they agree with the quote or disagree with the quote, makes a connection, asks a question, shares an experience, and so on).

- This person asks at least two other group members to respond to the quote *and* to their comments for 30–60 seconds each (agree, disagree, make a connection, ask a question, share an experience, and so on).

- This person states a summary of the comments or responses: "It sounds like we think . . ." or "To summarize what we've said . . ."

- Continue in a clockwise manner until all group members have read at least one quote and all quotes have been responded to.
- Share out the summary statement for each quote with the large group (you may want to jot it down).

Student-Generated Questions and Student-Led Discussions

To make discussion protocols even more rigorous and engaging, students should be taught how to create higher-order questions and use these questions to lead and facilitate their group's discussions. Various researchers, including Miri Barak and Sheizaf Rafaeli (2004) and Fu-Yun Yu (2009) find that student-generated questions and discussions are associated with enhanced learning and improved academic performance. Designing their own questions encourages students to evaluate their own performance on an ongoing basis and employ metacognitive strategies. Beyond these learning benefits, assuming a role as a discussion leader through designing and using their own questions promotes students' sense of ownership and positive attitudes toward learning (Barak & Rafaeli, 2004; Yu, 2009).

Students will require instruction in the qualities of effective, higher-order questions and how to identify these qualities. They will need several opportunities to read, ask, and answer thick questions with teacher guidance. Students will also practice designing their own questions using the characteristics of quality questions criteria. Once students have engaged in these steps, they should generate and use their own questions during discussion protocols.

Megan T. DiSciscio (2022) concludes that discussion protocols engage students in creative discourse and allow students to take ownership of their own learning community. Adding the additional aspect of students generating their own questions increases motivation, engagement, and ownership in discussions of text.

Questioning and Discussion of Text Within *Solving the Literacy Puzzle*

In planning for literacy instruction following the recommendations of *Solving the Literacy Puzzle*, teachers should preplan thick, higher-order questions for use during text discussions and while utilizing discussion protocols. Some questions should be designed to focus on the comprehension strategy being taught in whole group and in small groups. Questions should also require students to make connections and better understand the characters, events, plot, and themes of the text.

In addition to preplanning good questions, teachers need to use *effective questioning techniques* such as the following.

- Enacting wait time 1 (thinking time after the question is posed)

- Enacting wait time 2 (thinking time after a student has responded to the question)

- Responding to students in ways that probe for deeper student responses

- Asking more than one student to respond

- Encouraging students to listen to and evaluate their own and other students' ideas

Discussions should be carefully planned to address the standards and learning targets, as well as fostering the students' enjoyment of reading. Perhaps even more important than the teacher's preplanned questions and questioning techniques is teaching students to write their own thick questions and utilize them in student-led discussions. The ICITL (n.d.) posits that higher-level questions involve the ability to analyze, evaluate, or create, think more deeply, and engage in problem-solving.

Discussion protocols and literature circles should be included in literacy instruction regularly. Time must be allocated and dedicated to holding rich discussions of literature. Discussion protocols, led by students and utilizing student-generated questions, ensure that students are engaged and accountable and that student participation in learning through discussion is *not left to chance*.

Conclusion

To support the development of high levels of reading comprehension, preplanning higher-order questions that intentionally lead students to think more deeply and to engage in meaningful discussions about text is a necessity. The Teacher-Facilitated, Oral Reading, Application of Strategies, and Discussion (TOAD) framework is useful in planning for text talks. Discussion protocols are also useful for high levels of student engagement in discussion of text. The following is a generic planning template for part 5 of *Solving the Literacy Puzzle* for planning questions and discussions around text. In addition, there is a blank planning template that may be used for TOAD.

Chapter 7 (page 129) will focus on the component of fluency, including what it is, current practices, what research has shown, and how to teach fluency effectively. Examples and recommendations for helping students develop into fluent readers will be discussed.

Part 5: Questioning and Discussion Instructional Template

What text will be used?

What parts or sections will be read and discussed?

Preplanned questions (related to comprehension strategy and learning targets):

Format for discussion (whole group, small group, discussion protocol):

Time allocated for discussion:

TOAD Instructional Planning Template

Text:
Sections, pages, and chapters to be read aloud and discussed:
Format for reading aloud (round robin, "popcorn," volunteers, choral):
Focus for modeling and practicing fluency:
Teacher think-alouds (where in the text you will stop and model):
Focus of each think-aloud (vocabulary skills, comprehension strategies, language arts skills, and so on):
If students will be asked to "think-aloud," on which pages?
Preplanned thick questions to ask during and after the reading aloud of the text:
Will a discussion protocol be used?

Note: It works well to mark or highlight where you will stop to think aloud and have notes about your modeling, as well as the preplanned questions, on sticky notes.

Generic Example of Instructional Sequence

Day 1	Day 2	Days 3 and 4	Day 5
Whole Group: Explicit instruction and modeling of comprehension strategy using generic or instructional text (Read-aloud or think-aloud). **Small Group Interventions:** Review and modeling of application of strategy with instructional or ability-level text.	**Whole Group:** Review of explicit instruction and additional teacher modeling of comprehension strategy using generic or instructional text. Use of "thick" preplanned questions to discuss text. **Small Group Interventions:** Additional guided practice of strategy application with instructional or ability-level text. **Independent Work or Rotations:** Work on comprehension task or graphic organizer.	**Whole Group:** Brief review of comprehension strategy. **Small Group Interventions:** Guided or independent practice of comprehension strategy with generic or instructional text. Use of "thick" preplanned questions to discuss text. **Independent Work or Rotations:** Work on preparing for discussion protocol (preparing for their "role" and/or designing "thick" questions they will use.	**Small Group or Partner Work:** Guided or independent practice with generic or instructional text. Engage in discussion protocol or literature circles. **Whole Group:** Formative Assessment on comprehension strategy.

Reflection Questions for Chapter 6: Text Discussion and Questioning

How often do you preplan higher-order thinking questions to use for facilitating discussions about the instructional text?

Do you regularly ask higher-order questions and allow for adequate wait time or thinking time (5 seconds or more)? How can you implement these items into your already existing lesson plans?

How often do you use techniques to ensure engagement of *all* students in responding to higher-order thinking questions?

Chapter 7

Fluency and Reading Proficiency

You know you've read a good book when you turn the last page and feel a little as if you have lost a friend.

—PAUL SWEENEY

As discussed in chapters 3 (page 43) and 5 (page 83), research and classroom observations demonstrate that minimal time is being used for explicit instruction and practice in vocabulary and comprehension; however, significant academic time is allocated to fluency work in many of today's classrooms. Fluent reading includes a variety of aspects including reading rate (WPM), accuracy, word recognition, and prosody, which refers to phrasing, expression, and intonation. While it is important for students to learn and practice commonly used words and sight words and how to apply punctuation, practicing fluency solely for the sake of reading a set number of words correctly per minute should not be a major focus of reading instruction. In many classrooms, the following activities are often used to practice fluency in oral reading.

1. Frequent use of repeated readings of random text (rereading passages or poetry several times to develop accuracy and pace)

2. Practicing Readers' Theater scripts (scripted text with various roles or parts that tells a story, similar to a play)

3. Engaging students in fluency clubs (small groups who meet and practice fluent reading before school or after school and perform scripts or poems for audiences)

4. Buddy or partner reading (a peer is expected to assess and correct another student's reading accuracy)

5. Asking students to do cold and hot readings of passages (cold readings are when a student has not read or had the passage read to them, and hot readings are when a student has practiced the passage at least once, and often several times)

6. Regularly assessing students' fluency (rate of reading, WPM)

These fluency activities often seem to take precedence over providing students with opportunities to learn vocabulary and word-learning strategies and comprehension strategies. In many schools, timed assessments of students' reading rate (WPM) and prosody are frequently administered, and data are collected on a frequent basis. The goal is to meet the benchmarks or cut scores put forth by the FastBridge (Renaissance Learning, 2019), or similar assessments, not to assess students' understanding of text.

William J. Therrien, Katherine Wickstrom, and Kevin Jones (2006) conclude that "the dramatic improvements in reading fluency obtained through repeated reading have not always translated into gains in reading comprehension" (p. 89; see also Schroeder-Van Cleve, 2007). In some classrooms, little focus is placed on assessing comprehension or making meaning from text, which is the ultimate goal of reading.

This focus on fluency (rate and prosody) takes away from the time available to focus on more critical aspects of literacy, such as word-learning techniques and learning to be strategic readers who comprehend text well. It is vital to note that fluency is only problematic if it affects students' comprehension, which is relatively uncommon.

Fluency can readily be practiced through core instruction using a common text while students are reading orally and discussing the text, while rereading the instructional text, and through poetry. Specific strategies for developing fluency through the whole-group instructional text are described later in this chapter.

Fluency interventions are appropriate for students who are accurate in their reading of grade-level texts but lack automaticity and a good pace while reading, which hinders comprehension (Ohio Literacy Advisory Council, 2021). Loewus (2015) determines that approximately 25 percent of students may lack skills in fluency and may benefit from fluency interventions. The time spent on whole-group fluency development could be better spent on explicit instruction and guided practice in vocabulary and comprehension strategies.

Research Related to Fluency and Fluency Instruction

Various studies have determined the importance of being able to read fluently to comprehend text. Word recognition is important in learning to read, and recognizing some words automatically, such as sight words, contributes to reading fluently (McArthur et al., 2013). Accuracy and automaticity in word recognition are the most important aspects of fluency. Students must quickly recall words and decode new words while reading so that comprehension is not hindered (National Reading Panel, 2000). However, using significant amounts of academic learning time to teach, practice, and assess students' fluency is not consistently supported by research, as indicated in table 7.1.

Table 7.1: Student Fluency Statistics

Researcher	Findings
CIERA (2006)	Teaching students to recognize words faster improved fluency; however, in none of the studies did comprehension significantly differ from that of control groups.
Walczyk & Griffith-Ross (2007)	Proficient readers can typically comprehend what they read, which also indicates a connection between oral reading fluency and reading proficiency.
Georgiou, Parrila, Cui, & Papadopoulos (2013)	Fluency and decoding represented one factor, while comprehension was a second. At later developmental periods, reading rate is no longer an adequate measure of reading comprehension.
Wang, Algozzine, Ma, & Porfeli (2011)	Using repeated readings to develop fluency showed a statistically significant increase of 31.41% words read per minute after the repeated reading treatment. However, for reading comprehension, the study found an increase of 5.41%.
Myer (2015)	Though the findings of studies varied, two out of three results supported the importance of teaching fluency and comprehension together.
Torppa, Vasalampi, Eklund, Sulkunen, & Niemi (2020)	Reading comprehension difficulties are often distinct from difficulties in reading fluency. The reason for their poor performance is something other than difficulties in decoding; slow readers can succeed in reading comprehension tasks.

This research clearly indicates that reading fluency does not equate to reading proficiency. Some fluent readers pay little attention to what the text means, thus having difficulty with comprehension, and there are students whose reading fluency may be below expectations; however, they comprehend text well.

Suppose a student is disfluent to the extent that it hinders comprehension. In this case, teachers should use additional interventions such as the Read Naturally program (Read Naturally, Inc., 1999) for intensive assistance. Read Naturally is a commercially developed program that combines three evidence-based intervention strategies for improving fluency skills in struggling readers. Providing opportunities for repeated readings of text can be beneficial for students who need additional support in developing fluency. A common model for repeated readings includes the following steps.

1. Read the text aloud to model what fluency should sound like.

2. Break up the text and read each section one at a time while students repeat each part after you.

3. Read the text together.

4. Have students practice reading the text on their own or with a partner several times.

Fluency is just one aspect of reading proficiency. The most important goal of reading is comprehension of the text, which enhances learning and application of learning.

It is beneficial to provide interventions and additional practice in fluency using these and other tools for students who struggle with fluency, either individually or in a small group. However, extra work and practice specifically focused on fluency is not necessary for all students in the classroom, nor should it take up much time during literacy instruction.

Most Common Words, Sight Words, and High-Frequency Words

To build students' reading fluency, it is critical that teachers, particularly in grades K–3, focus portions of their literacy instruction on the most commonly used words in the English language. The 100 most frequently used words make up over 50 percent of the words found in text (Fry, 2001).

Learning the first 300 most frequently used words, as identified by Edward Fry (1999) addresses 65 percent of words in written text. A majority of these words are not phonetic and must be memorized, which takes repeated practice. Jonathan Solity and Janet Vousden (2009) determine that "children need to learn just 100 words and 61 phonic skills to read the English language and words beyond the key 100 are rarely used" (p. 470), and the core 100 words form 53 percent of the English language. When students learn the 100 most common words in the English language, they can read a variety of texts at a good pace.

High-frequency words can be decoded; however, learning to read them with automaticity will increase students' reading fluency (Joseph, Nation, & Liversedge, 2013).

Sight words do not follow the regular letter-sound correspondences and cannot be decoded (for example, *have, there, of*); therefore, students must recognize them automatically.

When teaching sight words, there are several research-based recommendations to remember (Ayala & Connor, 2013; January, Lovelace, Foster, & Ardoin, 2017). Lists, such as Fry's (1999) 100 words and Edward W. Dolch's (1980) 220 words, guide teachers in considering which words are the highest priorities for instruction. However, words students will encounter in a book or story should also be taught along with words from the sight word lists. Teachers may choose to use online programs like Anki, Memrise, and Rype (https://apps.ankiweb.net, www.memrise.com/en-us, www.rypeapp.com) for brief, online sight word practice.

Fry's 100 Instant Words are available widely on the web and in several of Fry's publications such as *1000 Instant Words* (Fry, 1999) and *The Reading Teacher's Book of Lists* (Fry & Kress, 2006). Visit www.k12reader.com/dolch-word-list to view Dolch's 220 words. Refer to sightwords.com/sight-words/dolch and www.michigan.gov/documents/Dolch_Basic_220_List_105824_7.doc for grade-level sight-word lists and activities.

It can be valuable to have students practice the sight words in phrases, as this promotes automaticity in recognizing sight words and teaches students to read smoothly, rather than word by word. The following are two sets of phrases that contain many of the most common sight words and can be used for sight word practice (Livingston, n.d.).

Group 1

1. the little boy
2. a good boy
3. is about me
4. then you give
5. was to come
6. old and new
7. what we know
8. that old man
9. in and out
10. not up here
11. good for you
12. down at work
13. with his cat
14. it was new
15. work on it
16. can come here

Group 2

1. he is it
2. I can go
3. they are here
4. one by one

5. good and wet	11. up and down
6. came with me	12. her green hat
7. about a dog	13. say and do
8. had a hat	14. when they come
9. if you come	15. so I went
10. some good candy	16. my little house

For young students in preschool or prekindergarten, it is best to choose and focus on one or two sight words at a time (typically per week) from the instructional text that also appear on the first 100 words list (Fry, 1999). Students in grades 1 through 3 can practice six to ten words at a time, and students in fourth grade and beyond most likely can manage practicing ten or more sight words at one time. It is important to continuously review words after they have been learned to make sure students retain them. In addition, whenever possible, some kind of a *hook* should be provided for the students to remember the word (for example, drawing eyes inside the *o*s in the word *look*).

The Iowa Reading Research Center (Reed & Hinzman, 2018) offered the following recommendations regarding teaching sight words.

- Introduce new sight words one at a time (and provide a brief definition or example of how to use the word). Follow this with multiple exposures to the words in books and other texts, as well as providing regular practice with the words.

- Avoid introducing two sight words that are similar or may be easily confused at the same time; for instance, *will* and *well* should be taught at separate times.

- Provide brief (5–10 minutes) sessions on a regular basis over time for reviewing sight words (Reed, Hinzman, & Reed, 2018).

- Practice fluency using sight word phrases.

Fluency Practice and Strategies Using a Common Grade-Level Text

Besides instruction and practice in common sight words, modeling fluent reading for students and practicing reading fluently are essential for students to be proficient and accurate readers. Rather than using a separate text and a significant amount of academic learning time practicing random passages, fluency may be developed through whole-group instruction with a common text, such as a novel or a basal story. It is crucial that students read the text on their own, following vocabulary instruction that is focused on words students need to know to comprehend the text (see chapter 3, page 43, on selecting vocabulary words for instruction) and establishing prior knowledge through various techniques like a text walk.

The teacher might then demonstrate fluent reading while students follow along in the common text for a portion of the story. However, the students must read the text independently, especially beyond the middle of first grade. When the teacher reads the text *to* the students, many of the students are not engaged, and the teacher may be the only one practicing reading fluency. Students who wish to read orally should be given this opportunity. For students who struggle with reading, they may feel comfortable reading aloud to the teacher or another student, rather than the whole class. Giving them a chance to prepare ahead of time to read a page or passage of the text aloud is also good practice. Many of the students who volunteer to read from the common text will be fluent readers who will provide modeling for their peers. Providing opportunities to read the instructional text multiple times both orally and silently, whether this is a story, part of a novel, or an informational passage, allows students to develop fluency.

Braunshausen (n.d.) determines that activities like echo and choral reading give students a chance to practice effective reading skills and allow the teacher to act as a fluency model, while utilizing a grade-level text.

Educators should avoid the one-book-a-day approach and instead spend three to five days on one common text, as this is important for fluency development. It is less useful to have students encounter a new selection daily. A better approach to building fluency is to have them practice reading the same paragraph or page several times until they have reached a predetermined level of fluency (Samuels, 2002).

Having students be the expert readers on a paragraph or page of their choice from the instructional text is an effective strategy for practicing fluency. After selecting or being assigned a section of the story, novel, or article, the student should practice it multiple times until they can read the page or passage fluently. Then, when you read the text aloud in whole group or in small groups, they will be prepared, confident, and able to demonstrate fluency. Research has shown that repeated readings produce statistically significant improvements in reading speed, word recognition, and oral reading expression (Samuels, 2002). Following are the steps included in the expert readers technique.

- Have students select or assign individual students paragraphs or pages from the instructional text for which they want to be an expert reader.

- Have them practice their section multiple times on their own or with a partner until they are able to read it fluently (smoothly, with expression, and with phrasing, or prosody).

- Students should then read their section during oral reading and discussion of the instructional text (story, article, or chapter).

In addition to the whole-group instructional activities, small groups are another avenue for fluency practice. Having students read aloud allows the teacher to diagnose problems with fluency and address them. Shared reading is an excellent opportunity for fluency practice as the class rereads the text for several days and students will read the text on their own during silent reading time. Whisper reading, buddy reading, and students recording and listening to themselves read can be effective ways to practice fluency in small groups.

Using poetry, related to the themes or content you are studying, is also an avenue for fluency development. In poems, text often flows easily and is well suited for repeated reading and fluency practice (A World of Language Learners, 2021). Spending a brief amount of time each day reading and rereading poems provides effective fluency practice. Having a Poetry Corner where students choose a poem, practice the poem until they are fluent, and present it to the class, or another audience, is a motivating and effective way to develop fluency. The following is a routine for repeated reading using poetry and short passages to build fluency.

1. Pass out copies of a poem or passage to all students and display the poem or passage using a projector.

2. Read the poem or passage aloud, highlighting difficult words or words that demonstrate phonics and language arts skill.

3. Read each line or section and have students echo your reading replicating your expression, rate, and phrasing.

4. Engage the students in choral reading of the poem several times, along with the teacher.

5. Ask students to practice the poem or passage multiple times throughout the week individually and with a partner.

6. After several days of practice, have students perform the poem or passage for a small group or the large group (students may sit on a stool with a light shining on them during their performance).

Note that it is beneficial to have poems on a big chart or screen to practice throughout the day or week. Making poetry booklets for students to have in their desks for practice and to take home is also valuable.

Readers' Theater, a script with various roles similar to a skit or play, can be another useful technique for fluency development as it provides students with repeated exposures to text; integrates reading, listening, and speaking; engages and motivates students; builds students' confidence; and provides a real purpose for reading (Cromwell, n.d.).

Readers' Theater is most valuable when the content relates to the instructional text's theme or topic, or the science or social studies standards, and when the script is at the appropriate level for the students. Teachers should also be aware of the amount of academic learning time that is allocated for the Readers' Theater and use this technique in ways that do not take away from other aspects of reading instruction.

Recommendations for Fluency Instruction

Whether the reading task is a page from a common text, a portion of a story, a poem, or a Readers' Theater script, it is important to allow students ample time to practice reading the text and enable them to perform the piece. Fluency activities should be part of the instruction involving the grade-level text, common instructional text, or related texts, not separate practice with an unrelated text.

- Help students to develop automaticity first in the 100 most common words found in text, then in the 300 most common words found in text, as well as district-identified grade-level sight words.

- Model fluency in whole- and small-group settings.

- Teach and practice fluency as part of whole-group and small-group instruction with the instructional text (Expert Readers).

- For students who need additional fluency work because it is hindering comprehension, provide one-to-one or small-group interventions.

- Use research-based fluency practices for fluency interventions (Read Naturally, Inc.)

- Remember that comprehension is the essence and goal of reading, *not* fluency.

- Avoid overemphasis on fluency and timed readings so students do not become word callers who read fluently and accurately but do not focus on making meaning of the text.

Fluency is an important aspect of the science of reading and should be modeled and practiced with all students within whole-group, core instruction using the instructional text. Small-group interventions to build fluency may be beneficial for some students as well.

Table 7.2 is a generic example of planning the reading fluency component of core instruction, which may be edited for teachers' use. At the end of this chapter, there is a template that may be used for planning the fluency component of reading instruction.

Table 7.2: Instructional Sequence for Weekly Fluency Instruction and Practice

Day 1	Day 2	Day 3	Days 4 and 5
Whole group: Sight word teaching and practice. Teacher modeling of reading the first portion of the common text.	**Whole group:** Teacher and students take turns reading portions of the common text from the previous day orally. Students select, or are assigned, a section of the common text to practice being the *expert* reader.	**Whole group:** Sight word review and practice with game or activity. Teacher and students take turns reading portions of the common text from the previous day orally.	**Whole group:** Teacher and students take turns reading portions of the common text from the previous day orally. Some students read aloud their *expert* section.
Small group interventions: Students read the assigned common text aloud with teacher support/modeling.	**Small group interventions:** Students read the assigned common text aloud with teacher support/modeling.	**Small group interventions:** Students read the assigned common text aloud with teacher support/modeling.	**Small group interventions:** Reread portions of the instructional text or work on poem or passage to read chorally.
Independent work and rotations: Students read the assigned common text silently, then with a partner. Practice sight words.	**Independent work and rotations:** Students read the assigned text, and then practice their *expert* reader sections. Practice vocabulary and sight words or phrases.	**Independent work and rotations:** Students read the assigned text, and then practice their *expert* reader sections. Practice sight words.	**Independent work and rotations:** Students read and practice a related poem or a leveled text for additional fluency practice. *Perform* their poem or other text for a small group or the whole group.

Conclusion

Fluency is an important aspect of the science of reading; therefore, the literacy block should include intentional instruction, modeling, and practice in aspects of fluency such as phrasing, pace, and expression. However, this can take place within the reading and discussion of the instructional text and should not take up a major amount of literacy academic time. It is valuable to practice common words, sight words, and sight phrases along with teaching words that students need to know to comprehend the text. Chapter 8 (page 143) will focus on best practices for independent reading of the instructional text and of student-selected texts and ways to make independent reading time more meaningful. In the following pages, you will find a generic example of weekly fluency instructional planning and a template for planning fluency instruction.

Reflection Questions for Chapter 7: Fluency and Reading Proficiency

How often is fluency the focus of your whole-group and small-group instruction?

What percentage of your literacy block time is dedicated to teaching and practicing fluency?

Do fluency activities take time away from reading grade-appropriate text and teaching comprehension and vocabulary strategies?

Part 6: Instructional Planning Template for Fluency

The following is part 6 of the *Solving the Literacy Puzzle* instructional planning template for the fluency component.

Part 6: Fluency
Sight words and words from text to practice:
Common text to use for fluency development:
Teacher actions:
Student activities for fluency practice:

Chapter 8

The Role and Impact of Independent Reading

> If you are going to get anywhere in life you have to read a
> lot of books.
>
> **—ROALD DAHL**

Due to today's commonly used frameworks for literacy blocks, especially the most frequently utilized format known as *balanced literacy*, many students receive a relatively short amount of whole-group explicit instruction in reading strategies. This whole-group instruction is typically 10–30 minutes, and the rest of the reading block is often spent with students in small groups or guided reading groups with the teacher, while the other students engage in stations, rotations, and independent and partner work. The balanced literacy model for literacy instruction often leads to students spending extensive time on unstructured, independent reading. Balanced literacy has become the most commonly used approach in American schools. Lexia (2023) reports that 72 percent of teachers use balanced literacy as their most often used instructional model. Balanced literacy instruction is "focused on shared reading (for example, the teacher reads aloud to students and asks questions about the text), guided reading (students read texts at their current ability level in homogeneous groups), and independent reading (students self-select books to read on their own)" (Lorimor-Easley & Reed, 2019). In this chapter, we will review common practices in independent reading, the deployment of teacher-selected independent reading selections, recommended practices, and several graphic organizers for processing and engaging with text.

Common Practices in Independent Reading (SSR)

When teachers use SSR for reading instruction, students are often expected to engage in independent reading for 20 minutes to 60 minutes per day. Students often self-select their independent reading texts, which leads to students reading books that are too easy, books that are too difficult, or books in which students only look at the pictures. Also, students are usually not held accountable for what they read. In some classrooms, students must maintain a reading log where they record the book title, the author, and the pages they read; however, this is often the only accountability measure. When students are not provided with expectations for accountability when reading independently, many times reading is not really happening.

Classroom observations and studies have indicated that it is common for students to frequently be engaged in *nonreading* activities during SSR or independent reading time. These activities may include (1) pretending to read, (2) scanning and looking at pictures, (3) making multiple trips to select a different text, and (4) other off-task behaviors, such as talking, drawing, sharpening pencils, and using the restroom, all to avoid independent reading. These issues may lead to little time actually spent reading text; therefore, there is little or limited development of reading skills and strategies. It is difficult to achieve higher levels of reading ability and fluency if students were not using the SSR time wisely and without observation or accountability (Manurung, Pardede, & Pruba, 2020).

Several researchers have found that there is a relationship between reading achievement and time spent reading. Correlations are generally positive, but low. Direct benefits appear to reach a peak at relatively low levels of voluntary reading (Topping, Samuels, & Paul, 2007). Osborn and colleagues (2004) conclude that research cannot substantiate whether good readers are good because they read more or whether they choose to read more because they are good readers, a dilemma called the Matthew effect. John T. Guthrie (2008) reminds us, "Reading engagement and reading achievement interact in a spiral. Higher achievers read more, and the more engaged these students become, the higher they achieve. Likewise, lower achievers read less, and the less engaged decline in achievement" (p. 3).

Are good readers good because they read more, or do they choose to read more because they are good readers? This is the perplexing problem related to time spent on independent reading. Studies also indicate uncertainty about how often and how long students need to read to develop reading proficiency. Renaissance Learning (2016) reports that 15 minutes seems to be the "magic number at which students start seeing substantial positive gains in reading achievement."

Several studies conclude that the effect of silent reading practice is pretty small, and if it does result in better reading comprehension, this would likely take a long time. Sherry Sanden (2014) reports that independent reading is a developmental process that occurs more beneficially when under the guidance of an expert adult who can monitor and support students' reading actions and behaviors. Some have estimated that 30 minutes of independent reading per day is the equivalent of 15 school days, and independent reading takes away from the instruction that would happen during these extra days. However, research has not clearly indicated whether having students engage in independent silent reading, with limited amounts of guidance and feedback, improves reading achievement and fluency (National Reading Panel, 2000).

The National Reading Panel (2000) attempted to review studies on the impact of independent reading on students' reading achievement; however, there was a lack of research both in number and in quality. More research is needed to study the impact of independent reading on various aspects of reading development. It is "critical to clarify more definitively the relationship between programs that encourage independent reading and reading development" (National Reading Panel, 2000, pp. 3–4).

Although studies have shown small or no gains as a result of independent silent reading, 10–20 minutes several times each week should be allocated for independent reading to develop students' interest in and enthusiasm for reading and a lifelong love of reading as a leisure activity and a way to seek information. The National Reading Panel (2000) findings determine that students in upper grades may want to spend up to 30 minutes in independent silent reading, but beyond this, students will benefit more from activities that demand application of vocabulary, comprehension, and other skills.

Reutzel and colleagues (2008) find that failing to hold students accountable for their reading may result in students who do not engage during independent reading times. They suggest that teachers provide intentional instruction, assign related literacy tasks, and hold students accountable for their reading and learning. Shanahan (2019a) goes so far as to state that "independent reading at school is not a research-based practice." Shanahan (2019a) suggests using academic time to raise reading achievement and encourage students to choose to read independently. Review the following key considerations about independent reading.

- Be cognizant of the time being allocated for independent reading of student-selected texts (perhaps 15 minutes several times a week is sufficient).

- Monitor students' reading actions and behaviors. (Are the books they are reading at a level that challenges them a bit? Are they actually using the time to read?)

- Hold students accountable for their independent reading by assigning tasks that foster application of literacy skills and strategies.

- Encourage students to apply what they learned in whole-group and small-group instruction when they are reading independently.

Independent Reading of Teacher-Selected Grade-Level Instructional Texts

It is essential to use a grade-level text for reading instruction, particularly during whole-group instruction. Students are assessed using grade-level text; therefore, instruction should focus on age-appropriate text. Using a grade-level-appropriate reading program helps teachers feel confident that they are engaging students in standards-driven instruction that allows them to grow as independent readers and prepares them for successful reading in years to come (Gunderson, D'Silva, & Oto, 2019). Some schools do not purchase a commercial literacy program, and teachers are in charge of developing their literacy instruction on their own or with peers. Determining what text to use for core instruction that will be grade-appropriate and will facilitate independent reading, as well as whole-group reading and discussion of text, can be challenging, especially if teachers must design their own reading curriculum.

While both teacher-created and commercial reading curricula can be effective in providing students with comprehensive literacy instruction, there is more time and labor involved for teachers who create their own curricula. Commercial programs are much less labor intensive, and the text is often more grade-appropriate and aligned with grade-level, district, and state standards. Table 8.1 is a comparison of using teacher-developed literacy instruction and using a commercial literacy program.

Students must read common grade-level instructional text, not have it read *to* them. Think about how you learned to read—most likely, you struggled and persisted until you could read either a book of your own choice or an assigned text. This challenge led to a feeling of accomplishment and motivated you to try more books. Even if your parents, or other adults, read *to* you, you had to read on your own to become a true reader.

Table 8.1: Teacher-Developed Literacy Instruction vs. Commercial Literacy Programs

Teacher-Developed Literacy Instruction	Commercial Literacy Programs
Time-intensive planning	Less time-intensive planning
Lack of confidence in instruction	Instruction is supported by research
Inconsistency in teaching core and grade-level standards	Consistency in alignment of instruction with core and grade-level standards
Difficult and time-consuming to decide upon and locate instructional text	Instructional text is provided and age-appropriate
Challenge of including instruction in all components of the science of reading	Instruction and activities for all components of the science of reading are included
Students may not be reading grade-level text	Grade-level text is provided
Difficult and time-consuming to develop formative and summative assessments	Formative and summative assessments are included with program
Challenging to develop interventions for struggling students and students in need of enrichment	Intervention strategies and resources for students are provided

We can help lower-level readers bridge the gap by having them read challenging texts, including grade-level texts (Learning at the Primary Pond, 2020). Teachers can do many things to prepare students for their independent reading tasks using grade-level text, before instruction, during reading, and after reading.

Planning for Instruction

- Preview the chapter and determine which vocabulary words and concepts are essential.

- Read over the material while thinking about student needs. How much prior knowledge and other tools will the students need to understand the text?

- Ask, "Where are the trouble spots in this chapter?" (Braunshausen, n.d.), and determine how to prepare students for these challenges.

Before Reading the Text

- Discuss and break apart tricky words for or with the students, teaching or reviewing decoding or structural analysis of words (including characters' names).

- Explicitly teach vocabulary that students may struggle with and words that are important to know to read the text fluently and to comprehend the text.

- Provide or build background information on the text.

During Independent Reading of the Text

- If you're working with a longer text, break it up into smaller chunks.

- During the first read, read part of the text for or with the students to set the tone, clarify where needed, and get the students off to a good start.

- Ask students to apply comprehension strategies as they read on their own and think about their understanding of the text.

- Ask questions that focus attention on main ideas and important points in the text.

- Emphasize the parts in a text that require students to make inferences.

- Summarize key sections or events.

- Encourage students to revisit predictions they have made before reading to see if they are confirmed by the text (Texas Education Agency, 2002).

Shanahan (2020) suggests telling students how demanding the instructional texts are going to be. Then, the teacher must provide instruction that helps students to build their skills in the content and the vocabulary. The teacher should *not* read the entire story, chapter, or article *to* the students. Who wants to read something that someone has already read to them? Students need to be motivated and have a purpose for reading. They also need to construct meaning as they read, which requires independent reading of the text. Teachers must make certain that all students have visual access to the text. Students' eyes must be *on the text* for learning to occur. If students are disengaged from the text, the only one getting practice in reading is the teacher.

Students need overt instruction and practice in these before-reading tasks and strategies for those tasks and strategies to become part of their toolbox of study skills. When the teacher takes steps such as those described earlier, students will have the necessary tools to read the instructional text independently (Braunshausen, n.d.). For students who have significant cognitive delays, adults may need to listen to them read and provide ongoing assistance for them to be successful.

After Reading the Text

After students have read the instructional text, the teacher needs to facilitate meaningful discussion of the text. This process may include reading portions of the text or the whole text together orally using various oral reading techniques, like round robin, popcorn, and choral reading. It is also valuable to reread and discuss important parts of the text to deepen comprehension.

This rich discussion of the text during rereading is essential in helping students to develop their skills as strategic readers. Students need opportunities to take leadership in their learning and think and talk about the thought processes they use during reading. This should happen through class discussions when text is being read aloud together in large and small groups (Parrish, 2020).

Recommended Practices Related to Independent Reading of Student-Selected Texts

In addition to opportunities to read grade-level instructional texts, students need the opportunity to read and practice strategies in self-selected texts that they can read (Harvey & Goudvis, 2000).

Students need to select books for independent reading that are on an appropriate level and on a topic of interest to the student. The text should be easy enough that they will be able to read the text independently yet challenging enough to allow students to have the opportunity to apply structural analysis skills and context or picture clues. Regie Routman (2017) determines that almost all students need and benefit from having adults monitor their reading to ensure they comprehend, self-correct, self-direct, set reasonable goals, and enjoy the books they are choosing to read. The teacher also needs to monitor students' behavior during independent reading with self-selected books, ensure that this time is not used for other purposes, and make sure that students are engaged in active reading. It is also important for students to have goals or purposes for their reading, and to be held accountable for what they have read and learned. Reading and thinking logs, graphic organizers, and sticky note activities can be used to encourage students to intentionally read and engage with text.

Instructional Recommendations for Independent Reading of Student-Selected Text

- Provide students with 15–20 minutes of independent reading time at least 3–4 days per week.
- Monitor book choices considering level, content, and quality of literature.
- Monitor level of engagement during independent reading time.

- Challenge students to apply the vocabulary and comprehension strategies from whole-group and small-group instruction.

Instructional Recommendations for Independent Reading of Teacher-Selected Instructional Text

- Use a grade-level common text for whole-group instruction for all students.

- Prepare students to read the instructional text successfully using the methods described earlier (teach vocabulary, build prior knowledge, preteach tricky words and names, and so on).

- After instruction, assign students a portion of the story, novel, or article to read independently (providing support for students with cognitive disabilities).

- Hold students accountable through the use of reading logs, graphic organizers, preparation for discussions, and other techniques.

Recommendations for Word Retention and Avoiding Word Calling

A significant number of students do not engage, apply strategies, or process text while they read. This leads to a habit of *word calling*, or reading quickly without thinking, which can lead to a lack of understanding and poor retention of the text. During independent reading time, students need to apply comprehension strategies that have been taught and practiced during core instruction. It is important to encourage students to stop and process as they read, as well as to regularly monitor their own understanding of the text. The following are some techniques and graphic organizers for holding students accountable for processing text and applying comprehension strategies as they read.

Techniques for Accountability During Independent Reading

- Ask students to jot on sticky notes 3–4 times during the independent reading time (specific skills and strategies directed by the teacher). Examples of things they might record on the sticky notes are as follows.
  - Words, phrases, or figures of speech and what they mean
  - Character traits and how they are demonstrated

- - Questions they have or "I wonder . . ." statements
  - Application of a comprehension strategy (where and which strategy)

- If students are reading from the instructional text or from a small-group text, have them prepare for a discussion protocol or a literature circle (assign a role and ask them to prepare for their part in the discussion).

- Have students engage in a one-to-one reading conference with the teacher to discuss the reading they have been doing.

- Use an interactive anchor chart question of the day. Write a question on the chart paper, such as "What character trait did the main character display and give reasons to support your ideas?" While students read, they will collect evidence to answer the question and write their response on a sticky note, which will go on the chart.

- Ask students to prepare for a Book Talk where they will discuss various parts of their book or story. They might be asked to tell about the characters, the setting, the author, some main events, the problem and solution, and how they felt about the book. The Book Talk can be with small groups or the large group (with 3–4 each day).

- Have students complete a graphic organizer (or part of one) or a processing log during independent reading time (with a goal of having it completed at the end of the week). See examples in figure 8.1 (page 152), figure 8.2 (page 153), and figure 8.3 (page 154).

Graphic Organizers for Processing and Engagement With Text

It works well to ask students to complete parts of these graphic organizers (figures 8.1, page 152, 8.2, page 153, and 8.3, page 154) before or while independently reading the text. We want them to apply strategies and be held accountable, but we do not want to take away their enjoyment of reading; therefore, asking students to complete two or three of the tasks on a graphic organizer each day, over a three- to five-day period, is recommended.

Before Reading New Text

What can you *predict* from the front and back covers and the pictures?

What *connections* can you make to things you've seen, heard, or experienced?

During Reading

What questions do you have, or what are you wondering about?

What have you visualized?

Are there any words, phrases, or passages that you are unclear or confused about?

What is a prediction you can make?

After Reading

Was your *prediction* correct?

Write a one sentence summary.

Figure 8.1: "Processing as we read" template.

Visit **go.SolutionTree.com/literacy** *for a free reproducible version of this figure.*

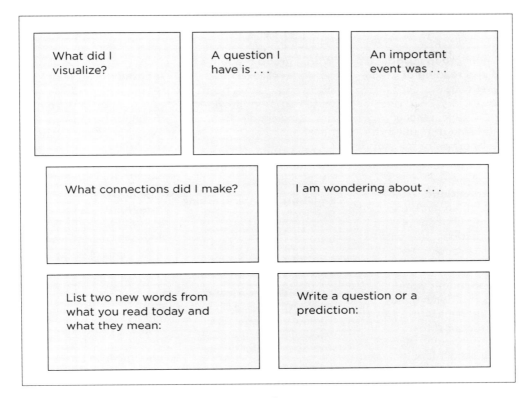

Figure 8.2: Thinking and response log.

Visit **go.SolutionTree.com/literacy** *for a free reproducible version of this figure.*

Figure 8.3 (page 154) is a generic example of planning the independent reading component of core instruction, which may be edited for teachers' use. At the end of this chapter there is a template that may be used for planning the independent reading component of reading instruction.

Day 1	Days 2, 3, and 4	Day 5
Whole group introduction to and reading of grade-level text: Preteach vocabulary, build prior knowledge, teacher modeling of reading the first portion of the story/book. (10–15 minutes)	**Whole group reading of grade-level text:** Read orally and discuss portions, or all text, from previous day using preplanned questions. Prepare students for next chapter or section of text. (15–20 minutes)	**Whole group reading of grade-level text:** Read orally and discuss portions from previous day using preplanned questions or discussion protocol, literature circles, and so on. (10–15 minutes)
Small-group interventions: Review vocabulary and read assigned pages of instructional text with small groups. (30–45 minutes)	**Small-group interventions:** Review vocabulary and read assigned pages of instructional text with small groups. (30–45 minutes)	**Small-group interventions:** Reread text (all or portions), reviewing vocabulary and comprehension strategy. (30–45 minutes)
Independent work and rotations: Read assignment from instructional text independently, then SSR with accountability tasks. (30–45 minutes)	**Independent work and rotations:** Read assignment from instructional text independently, then SSR with accountability tasks. (30–45 minutes)	**Independent work and rotations:** Reread text with a partner or in small groups or engage in literature circle or discussion protocol. (30–45 minutes)

Figure 8.3: Weekly instructional plan for independent reading.

Conclusion

Independent reading or SSR has become a part of literacy instruction in many classrooms, although research is mixed in regard to the impact of SSR on students' reading abilities. Students should read both self-selected texts and grade-level-appropriate instructional texts and should be held accountable for the use of their time and their application of learning. Teachers should follow recommendations as described in chapter 8 (page 143) to enhance the benefits of independent reading. Chapter 9 (page 157) will describe techniques for connecting writing to literacy instruction in relevant ways that support the development of reading and writing proficiency.

Reflection Questions for Chapter 8: The Role and Impact of Independent Reading

How often are your students given more than 20 minutes per day for independent or partner reading, using a text of the students' choice?

How frequently do students read or reread from the grade-level instructional text with your facilitation?

How often do you engage students in tasks or activities that hold them accountable for being productive during independent reading?

Part 7: Instructional Planning Template for Independent Reading

Part 7 of the *Solving the Literacy Puzzle* instructional planning template follows. This part addresses planning for independent reading of the instructional grade-level text, as well as independent reading or SSR.

Part 7: Independent Reading
Common, grade-level text to use for instruction:
Vocabulary and "tricky" words to preteach:
Steps to build prior knowledge:
Other steps to prepare students to read the text:
What part of the text will you model by reading aloud?
What pages or chapters will students be asked to read independently from the grade-level instructional text?
How will students apply vocabulary, comprehension, and other skills from whole-group instruction?
How much time will be allocated for independent reading of student-selected texts?
Will students be held accountable for their independent reading? If so, in what way?

Chapter 9

Literacy Development Through Writing

Reading gives us someplace to go when we have to stay where we are.

—MASON COOLEY

Although the science of reading does not specifically include the component of writing, a language arts component should be integrated into literacy instruction so students become proficient in communicating through written language. As mentioned earlier, the areas of focus for schools change periodically; however, well-rounded literacy instruction includes the five core components of reading: phonemic awareness, phonics, fluency, vocabulary, and comprehension, as well as addressing the common grade-level language arts standards. The purpose of this chapter is to review the importance of language arts, including writing; discuss research-based strategies for writing instruction; and describe instructional methods that integrate writing into other aspects of reading instruction, including writing in response to literature.

Common Practices for Writing Instruction

It is not uncommon in today's classrooms for the major avenue for writing instruction to be *free writing* or *journaling*, which is one of the daily rotations included in the balanced literacy model and Daily 5 model (Boushey & Moser, 2006). Students are often given opportunities for free-choice writing activities during literacy stations, rotations, or independent work times. In addition, little guidance or accountability is required for students' written work, and the writings are often not shared or used for real purposes. Writing in school can be purposeful if the tasks align with the reasons people write in the outside world; if the topic is relevant to students' own lives; and if it can be published and put to real use (WfP Centre, 2021). In fact, it is common for students to create no final products at all or to repeatedly create similar products (little books such as "I like red. I like dogs. I like my mom," and so on). A 2019 survey of more than 600 elementary school teachers by *Education Week* determines that more than two-thirds of elementary teachers use a balanced literacy model, with stations or rotations that included free writing (Luscombe, 2022).

Observations demonstrate that in many classrooms, limited time is allocated for explicit writing instruction on essential skills, such as (1) proper word usage and punctuation, (2) writing complete sentences, (3) writing a complete paragraph, (4) using descriptive language, (5) developing a three- to five-paragraph essay, (6) creating a summary or an opinion essay, and (7) responding to literature in meaningful ways. In addition, Graham (2019) determines from a review of 28 studies "that writing instruction in most classrooms is not sufficient. One indicator of this inadequacy was that a majority of teachers did not devote enough time to teaching writing" (p. 278).

An additional concern is that the writing students engage in is often not directly related to curricular standards or content-area topics and instruction. Sadly, students have limited opportunities to write in response to literature, which is a critical way to help students apply their text comprehension. The "writing activities most commonly assigned to students involved very little extended writing, as students were seldom asked to write text that was a paragraph or longer" (Graham, 2019, p. 279).

Writing is often not assessed, and no constructive or critical feedback is provided, which is another important component of effective writing instruction. Students must share their writings and receive both teacher and peer feedback to become proficient writers.

Research Related to Writing and Literacy

Over time, the characteristics of quality writing instruction have been clarified. The findings from a variety of studies from the late 1980s through 2020 are reviewed in this section, which help to identify the key features of effective instruction in the area of writing. Due to time constraints and striving to teach grade-level literacy standards well, writing has not been given as much emphasis as it should, and methods of integrating writing into other literacy tasks and other content areas will need to be put into place.

Robert Slavin, from the Johns Hopkins School of Education, finds that "there's remarkably very little high-quality evidence of what works in writing" (cited by Barshay, 2019). Early in 2019, Slavin published *A Quantitative Synthesis of Research on Writing Approaches in Grades 2 to 12* (Slavin, Lake, Baye, Dachet, & Haslam, 2019), and evidence from twelve studies shows that the approach in some classrooms is on explicitly teaching the stages of writing from planning to drafting to revising to publishing. Other teachers make writing a collaborative activity, using modeling and shared writing for instruction. Another approach is integrated reading with writing (Barshay, 2019).

Slavin and colleagues (2019) posit, "If students love to write, because their peers as well as their teachers are eager to see what they have to say, then they will write with energy and pleasure." One lesson that emerges from the twelve tested programs is that students benefit from learning to write in different genres, as writing an opinion essay is very different from fiction writing. This study also finds that students need explicit grammar and punctuation instruction, taught in the context of their writing, not as a separate stand-alone lesson (Barshay, 2019).

Explicit teaching of specific writing skills, such as formation of letters, capitalization of proper nouns, writing complete sentences, and use of adjectives, is very important. Students need to have opportunities to practice these skills in writing sentences, paragraphs, letters, and essays (Presto, 2023).

The use of *formulas* for paragraph writing, which has become a common practice, may help students who have few writing skills; however, other students may have their writing ability and intellectual development hampered by conforming to a narrow and simplistic model. Experts in English teaching recommend that "formulas should only be taught along with strategies to move beyond them" (McKnight & Woods, 2020)

Modeling Writing and Using Mentor Texts

Teachers should model writing strategies, provide assistance as students practice using the strategies on their own, and allow for independent practice with the strategies once they have learned them (Gillespie & Graham, 2011). Students should write to represent new information they have learned and to explain their opinions on a specific issue or analyze what they have read (Spear-Swerling, 2006).

Writers need knowledge of structures; thus, teachers should provide students with examples of model pieces of writing (Hillocks, 1987). Mentor texts are published pieces that serve as good examples of the type of writing students should strive to produce. Students should look at published authors' work to see how professionals write (Brown, 2007). To become proficient writers, "students need to read a lot, write a lot, and learn the fundamentals" (Whyte, 2016, p. 4).

To improve students' writing, teachers must integrate essential grammar, usage, punctuation, and other language arts skills during vocabulary and writing instruction. Some of the most valuable writing skills include understanding how to use parts of speech to communicate in writing, correct use of definite and indefinite articles, and proofreading skills (Whyte, 2016, p. 5). The teacher should select strategies to focus on as they guide students through processing and proofreading a writing example. While analyzing the next writing sample, the teacher should introduce additional strategies or new tools to apply previously taught strategies (Andrade, 2004).

In addition to providing exemplary writing models, teachers should utilize modeling and *shared writing*, both of which include writing in front of students and thinking aloud during demonstration. Teachers are "the proficient writers in the room and we want students to begin emulating the teacher's thinking processes" (Brown, 2007). The following are some tried-and-true strategies for helping students develop into proficient writers.

Shared Writing

In shared writing, the students "collaborate with the teacher to jointly construct a written text. The teacher acts as scribe, prompting, questioning and supporting the students as the text is shaped" (Victoria Department of Education, 2018). Shared writing may be for the purpose of writing an essay, composing a letter, or writing a retelling of the text they have read. It is beneficial to collaboratively brainstorm possible topics during shared writing, discuss pros and cons of each, and select a topic. The teacher then models how to write each section of the writing task. Students share ideas, and the teacher scribes them while thinking aloud and asking questions, such as "Do you think that we need some transition words here? Do you think the reader might be confused about how these ideas are connected? Do you see any edits that need to be made?" A document camera, SMART board, or whiteboard should be utilized so that the writing is visible to all students (Kruse, n.d.). Shared writing allows students to be part of the writing process without the frustration they may experience on their own. Also, students get to hear how the teacher thinks as they write, and they are part of the writing process as it is being modeled (Kruse, n.d.).

Writing Rubrics and Assessment of Writing

Using writing rubrics can be a powerful strategy to guide students in their writing. When students have criteria to use to judge their writing, they begin to internalize those criteria and use them when they write new pieces. Teachers should involve students in critiques, where short pieces of writing are reviewed with different strengths and weaknesses and then evaluated with students using a rubric (Brown, 2007). It is also helpful for students to assess their own writing and the writing of their peers using clear criteria from a rubric or checklist.

The Writing Process

Teaching students to use a sound writing process is also important. It is helpful for students to understand and to utilize a writing process that includes (1) brainstorming or prewriting, (2) writing a rough draft, (3) editing (self, peer, teacher), (4) rewriting and re-editing, and (5) publishing. A writing process chart, or checklist, can offer a graphic that reinforces the steps and illustrates the connections between the various steps in the writing process (Andrade, 2004). Use of a writing process chart can be an ongoing resource to utilize throughout the writing curriculum.

Content-Area Writing and Picture Word Induction Model

It is valuable to engage students in writing in many different content areas including science, social studies, mathematics, and health. Direct instruction, modeling, and shared writing are needed for students to apply writing skills learned in ELA to different subject areas. Students can be involved in writing in a number of ways in the content areas including the following generic suggestions.

- Explaining a concept or idea
- Describing their opinions or viewpoints in regard to an event
- Analyzing their own and others' positions about a topic or event
- Explaining their thinking or problem-solving process
- Describing a hypothesis and why it was proven or not proven
- Telling about their reactions to an experiment or event

The picture word induction model, or PWIM (Calhoun, 1999), can be a useful strategy for integrating writing into various content areas (Shaman, 2014). With PWIM, an enlarged photo with plenty of white space around it that directly relates to the content you are teaching is displayed where all students can see it. Students and the teacher together label objects in the picture, writing the words around the picture with arrows to the objects. Next, they use the words in sentences, and finally they summarize their thoughts about the photo in a paragraph (Gu & Lornklang, 2021). Most of this process is done by the students and teacher together as shared writing. Students may write their own sentences and paragraphs about the picture after these steps are completed together, to encourage application and for use as a formative assessment.

Writing for Various Purposes and in Various Genres

Students should be involved in writing for different, authentic purposes and using different formats including narratives, expository pieces, essays, letters, and poems. The purposes for writing may include a biographical piece that might be used for a job application; an essay for the newspaper or an essay competition; letters to school administrators, legislators, and authors; narratives expressing their personal viewpoints and opinions; and poetry for self-expression. Some of students' writings can be informal, where students do not engage in all of the steps of the writing process (perhaps drafting and editing only). Other writings should be more polished, and the formal writing process should be utilized.

Recommended Practices for Writing in Response to Text

One of the most effective ways to enhance both comprehension and writing skills is to involve students in writing in response to the text they are reading. Students should write in response to literature regularly, as this is a powerful way to increase vocabulary, comprehension, and writing proficiency. This may include describing aspects of the text or stating an opinion about the plot, characters' traits, a general theme, or the moral of a text. Students should make connections and provide rationale, evidence, and examples from the text (Whyte, 2016). Educators must also explicitly teach students procedures for summarizing what they read. Summarization allows students to practice concise, clear writing to convey an accurate message of a text's main ideas (Gillespie & Graham, 2011). The following are suggestions for integrating writing within reading instruction.

- Describe a character, telling about their traits, feelings, and actions.

- Write your opinion about what the character said or did and why you feel that way.

- Create a "sequel" to the book or story.

- Write a letter to a character, or to the author, telling them your thoughts and asking questions you are still wondering about.

- Summarize the book or story in 1–3 paragraphs.

- Write a 3-paragraph essay with the first paragraph telling about the beginning of the book or story, the second paragraph describing the middle of the book or story, and the third paragraph telling about the ending.

- Complete graphic organizers that ask students to write about predictions, connections, what they visualized, what they inferred and why, and so on.

- Ask students to summarize what they learned from a nonfiction or informational text.

- Summarize the sequence of the story or the plotline (what happened first, second, third, and so on) or what was the problem, climax, and solution.

- Respond in writing to exit tickets.

- Respond to writing prompts such as the following.

  - Who was telling this story or sharing this information, and what was their purpose?

  - Which character could you connect with, and why?

  - What was the motivation for the character's actions?

  - Would you make the same choices as the characters?

  - What would you change about the book or story if you could?

See figure 9.1 for a weekly planning template for writing. See separate sections for the research and strategies discussed earlier.

Day 1	Days 2 and 3	Day 4	Day 5
Whole group: Teach language arts skills during vocabulary explicit instruction. **Small group interventions:** Provide guided support for writing on vocabulary or other graphic organizers. **Independent work and rotations:** Complete writing tasks related to vocabulary instruction.	**Whole group:** Explicit instruction and modeling of writing task. Shared writing for demonstration. **Small group interventions:** Begin writing assignment/task with support. **Independent work and rotations:** Work on writing assignment or task as taught and modeled during whole group explicit instruction.	**Whole group:** Review writing instruction from prior day. Model or engage students in shared writing to focus on skills. **Small group interventions:** Continue working on writing assignment/task with support. **Independent work and rotations:** Continue to work on writing assignment and rewrite and edit.	**Whole group:** Provide time and assistance for students in completing writing assignment. **Small groups:** Share out writing tasks with small groups and some with whole group or with another audience.

Figure 9.1: Weekly planning template for writing.

Recommendations for Writing Within Literacy Instruction

- Regularly teach and model writing strategies, integrating pertinent language arts skills and standards.

- Utilize shared writing to model and teach writing skills and strategies.

- Have students engage in authentic, purposeful writing that enhances learning.

- Engage students in responding to literature on a regular basis and in writing summaries and other products integrating content-area knowledge.

- Have students fully develop *some* of their writings using the writing process and have them share their writing with an audience.

If writing is included during literacy stations or rotations, provide guidance, expectations, and tools for accountability. Utilize writing rubrics to provide clear expectations and provide constructive feedback for students.

Conclusion

Writing and language arts are essential aspects of teaching students to be strategic, proficient communicators. Time and opportunities to write should be a regular part of literacy instruction. Writing tasks should be relevant and purposeful. Modeling how good writing is done and engaging students in shared writing should be an integral part of writing instruction. Students should be held accountable for and have opportunities to actually use their written products. It is valuable to involve students in writing tasks that connect to the texts that they are reading, as this strengthens writing skills and other skills such as comprehension. Chapter 10 (page 167) will address how to structure reading instruction so that (1) all students are included in whole-group, core instruction; (2) students in need of additional supports and interventions receive them; and (3) students who are working independently, or with a partner, are involved in meaningful tasks that strengthen the skills learned in whole-group instruction.

A generic example of writing instruction and part 8 of the instructional planning template, which includes the writing component of literacy instruction, are provided on the following pages.

Part 8: Writing Instructional Planning Template

Part 8: Writing
Type of writing task:
Language arts skills focus:
Teacher actions:
Student writing activities:

Reflection Questions for Chapter 9: Literacy Development Through Writing

How often do you explicitly model writing for your students, focusing on specific writing skills, at least weekly?

How frequently are your students given opportunities to write in response to literature and for other authentic purposes?

Are students held accountable for their writing, and do they share their writing with others?

Chapter 10

Whole-Group, Small-Group, and Independent Work

There is no such thing as a child who hates to read; there
are only children who have not found the right book.

—**FRANK SERAFINI**

Teachers realize the importance of providing quality instruction in all of the major components of literacy, as recommended by the National Reading Panel (2000) and through extensive research related to the science of reading. However, many teachers struggle to find a reading format that provides the time and opportunity to include all five of the components (phonemic awareness, phonics, vocabulary, fluency, and comprehension), as well as language arts skills and writing, within their literacy instructional time. It is not uncommon for schools to require 90–120 minutes of literacy instruction daily, yet, due to factors such as directives that whole-group instruction be just 30 minutes, the perception that all students should receive small-group instruction, and trying to provide interventions for students who need additional support, this time often is not enough.

This chapter provides research-based suggestions for how to format reading instruction so that all students are included in whole-group instruction and students who require additional practice and support receive interventions. Also, recommendations for what students should be engaged in when they are not involved in large- or small-group instruction, that support the learning targets and application of learning, are discussed.

Common Practices in Regard to Reading Block Management and Formats

The trend for reading instruction in many of today's schools, particularly in the elementary grades, is to have either no whole-group instruction using a grade-appropriate text, or minimal time being allocated (30 percent or less of the literacy block) for whole-group instruction. Teachers report being told to "spend about 30 minutes delivering whole-group instruction and then spend the next 60 minutes meeting with small groups of students while the other students work in literacy stations to practice skills previously taught either independently or in partners/groups" (Shanahanonliteracy.com, 2015).

This philosophy of limiting whole-group instructional time has evolved for a number of reasons, including (1) the perceived lack of value of reading programs, such as basals or anthologies; (2) viewpoints that whole-group instruction is less meaningful and engaging for students; (3) beliefs that teaching reading in small groups using texts that match the students' reading levels is best; and (4) the perception, or perhaps the reality, that the instructional text is too difficult for the students; therefore, other easier texts are utilized for reading instruction.

Due to allocating minimal time for whole-group instruction and between 45 and 90 minutes for small-group instruction and stations or rotations, many times, students are asked to read independently (*read to self*) or read to a partner (*partner or buddy reading*) for up to 60 minutes while they are not in their small groups. More recently, some students are being asked to work in an online program for up to 60 minutes. In addition, during small-group or rotation times, students are most often not provided with specific expectations and are not held accountable for their learning.

During each group's 10–20 minutes of small group, or guided reading time, the teacher typically reads text to the students, listens to students read text, or provides guided practice on fluency or decoding. There is often little instruction in vocabulary, few opportunities for application of whole-group instruction, minimal instruction in comprehension strategies, and little or no rich discussion about literature. Although limited instruction typically occurs during small groups, at least two-thirds of elementary teachers report that they teach in small groups several times a week (Lenski et al., 2016; NCES, 2019). This format for reading instruction is concerning in a number of ways.

1. All students are not provided with instruction in grade-appropriate text.
2. Reading instruction is fragmented—meaning the skills and concepts addressed in whole-group instruction are not supported or applied during small-group times or rotations.

3. When students are expected to work independently for up to 60 minutes, it is not uncommon for them to be off-task and distracted, especially if there are no tools for accountability.

4. Stations or rotations are often not related to the curriculum standards.

5. Due to the limited time for small-group instruction, students are engaged in very little guided reading, discussion, and application of strategies.

6. Students typically receive small-group instruction three or four times per week, with higher-achieving students averaging only one or two times per week, which may constitute an equity issue.

Louise Spear-Swerling and Jamie Zibulsky (2013) find that many teachers plan little or no time for aspects of literacy such as vocabulary, phonemic awareness, and spelling; also, relatively little time was devoted to basic writing skills and virtually none to writing processes such as planning or revision. Many teachers "chose to allocate time in ways inconsistent with scientific recommendations, for writing as well as for reading" (Spear-Swerling & Zibulsky, 2013, p. 1354).

Research Related to Reading Instructional Formats

When students receive only short periods of teacher-guided instruction, they are not held accountable for completion of meaningful tasks or supervised during rotations, and they are engaged in work that does not directly support the curriculum standards. This can be detrimental to the development of reading proficiency.

Scientifically based research about reading development and reading instruction supports direct instruction in the five components identified by the National Reading Panel (2000): phonemic awareness, phonics, comprehension, vocabulary, and fluency. Unfortunately, due to the limited time for whole-group reading instruction and short, small-group time frames, students do not receive instruction in all five of these critical areas.

Somewhere along the way, schools determined that all elementary, and even middle school, students need to receive reading instruction in small groups. Providing solid whole-group instruction for 45–60 minutes, which should be a priority, leaves less time for small-group instruction. All students do not need to be involved in small-group reading instruction. When the number of small groups is decreased to one or two for the purpose of providing interventions based on students' needs, this allows more time for both whole-group instruction and longer small-group instruction. Shanahan (2018) provides the following narrative regarding whole-group and small-group instruction:

Commonly, teachers provide approximately 30 minutes of whole group instruction focused on: 1) developing fluency, 2) mini-lessons, often not related to a specific text, and 3) reading to students. Then, students work in small, leveled groups with the teacher for 10-15 minutes, while other students work independently or in small groups on other literacy tasks. These tasks are most often not related to the concepts, skills, and strategies that were taught during whole group instruction and do not assist the students in applying their learning. I'd never organize classrooms in order to ensure that they specifically receive small group teaching. And, I'd always try to minimize small group teaching whenever possible for the sake of efficiency. Never do with a small group, what could be done as well with the whole class.

Whole-Group Instruction

The key component of literacy instruction is that all students receive core, grade-level instruction within a scientifically researched core program. Norma Hancock (2022) reiterates that all students must have equitable access to core instruction that addresses grade-level expectations for learning. Usually, the core instructional program is a comprehensive reading curriculum that is aligned with Common Core State Standards, with the intent of delivering a high-quality instructional program in reading. Surveys and observational studies indicate that in many schools core, whole-group reading instruction is often allotted 15–30 minutes of the 90- to 120-minute literacy block.

Around 75–80 percent of students should be expected to achieve competency through core instructional delivery (Shapiro, n.d.). This supports the practice of reducing both numbers of small groups and the time used for small-group instruction, leaving more time for universal, grade-level instruction for all students.

All students should receive instruction in the research-based core curriculum and be assessed on an initial screening at the beginning of the year and again in the winter and spring to ensure that they continue to perform at benchmark levels. Students who are meeting benchmarks, or reaching the established proficiency levels, may receive extra instruction in flexible, temporary small groups to focus on particular skills if needed (Read Naturally, Inc., 1999). Approximately 70 percent of students in most classrooms do not require daily or even regularly scheduled small-group reading instruction.

Small-Group Instruction

Approximately 25 percent of students in a typical classroom may need additional teaching and support to address skills gaps and to work toward meeting performance expectations. These students should receive regular—daily, if possible—supplemental interventions to support their learning and raise their achievement in the core curriculum. For these students, small groups should be formed, based on assessment data, to focus on the specific components of reading in which these students are deficient.

This instruction should focus on more time, reteaching, and additional practice in the core curriculum through the reading program's intervention support materials and other research-based, supplementary materials. Students served at this level are assessed regularly using progress-monitoring assessments to determine whether or not the intervention is effective (Shapiro, n.d.).

Small-group instruction should follow whole-group instruction to reinforce or reteach specific skills and concepts in a setting with a lower student-teacher ratio. Small groups typically range in size from four to six students. Small-group instruction is a "good strategy whenever a group of students has a specific need that the rest of the class does not or where there is great variance in the level or amount of instruction needed" (Slavin, Lake, Davis, & Madden, 2011, p. 5).

The "challenge of small group instruction is the management of other students who must be engaged in meaningful assignments during independent work time while the teacher is working with a small group" (Van Zant & Volpe, 2018). When some students work in a small group with the teacher, students who are not in the group must have productive work to do. They must know the routines for working alone or in small groups on their own (Slavin et al., 2011). This time should be used to solidify students' understanding of key literacy skills and strategies. Organizing "engaging and differentiated assignments and activities designed to reinforce skills taught during whole group instruction is the key to managing successful independent work" (Van Zant & Volpe, 2018).

Computer-Assisted Instruction in Reading

A significant trend in literacy instruction is to assign students to work in software programs when they are not in small groups with the teacher or during some part of the literacy block. It is not uncommon for students to work on computer-assisted instruction (CAI) such as IXL, Read 180, or Lexia (www.ixl.com, www.hmhco.com/programs/read-180, and www.lexialearning.com, respectively). These are programs that have been created to help students achieve reading standards through a phonics-based approach. Studies indicate that CAI seemed to positively affect younger students who need support in decoding skills and had a lesser impact on older students and the area of reading comprehension (Toonder & Sawyer, 2021). Table 10.1 (page 172) provides an overview of key studies over time and the findings related to CAI and its impact on students' literacy learning.

Table 10.1: Computer-Assisted Reading Instruction Research

Researchers	Findings
Macaruso & Walker (2008)	This study compares learning of students who receive CAI support and students taught by the same teacher but without CAI. The two groups perform similarly on measures of preliteracy skills. There are, however, significant positive differences between groups on posttest measures of phonological awareness skills, particularly for students with the lowest pretest scores.
Stetter & Hughes (2010)	Research indicates a more considerable positive impact on students with cognitive delays and English learners (ELs) than on the general student population.
Ness, Couperus, & Willey (2013)	These researchers study the effects of one widely used CAI program and determine that students who use the CAI program do not outperform students in the control group, consisting of students who are not involved in using the CAI program.
Slavin & Cheung (2016)	Computer-based tools offer students with learning disabilities support; however, results are mixed, with positive effects not being consistently shown.
Norton (2018)	This researcher studies the impact of three CAI programs on the reading achievement of fourth-grade ELs. The results do not show any significant gains for students enrolled in this intervention.
Kazakoff, Macaruso, & Hook (2018)	These researchers find that a blended learning approach that integrates teacher-led instruction with online, digital activities contributes to significant gains in reading in a large sample of ELs
Macaruso, Marchall, & Hurwitz (2019)	These authors research CAI's effect on students from kindergarten through third grade. Results suggest that the CAI program helps to improve students' literacy skills from kindergarten through second grade. Although literacy scores plateau in third grade, students in the sample are reading slightly above national averages.

In addition to the limitations of CAI indicated by these studies, reading online text differs from the way one reads a real story or a book. Reading a book requires sustained focus and absorption that a short passage followed by multiple-choice questions cannot match. If students are reading just to move on to the next level or unit, they are reading as a means to an end. If we teach that the purpose of reading is to accomplish a task, we are not building lifelong readers (We Are Teachers, 2017). Online reading programs might help students improve their multiple-choice skills; however, they still need someone working with them and asking the right questions (We Are Teachers, 2017).

Sound practice might be to engage students in CAI as part of a comprehensive reading program; however, these programs must be used with fidelity, monitored and supported by the teacher and limited to no more than 30 minutes, no more than three or four days a week. CAI should not be relied upon to teach students all of the standards or serve as a replacement for research-based reading instruction. Students must continue to receive teacher-directed, explicit instruction, engage in rich discussion of text, and learn to enjoy reading.

Recommendations Related to Reading Instructional Formats Based on Research

Please note that not all students need to have small-group instruction on a daily basis. Students who are in need of interventions should have additional instruction and practice in a small-group on a regular basis, for the purpose of supporting their progress in the instructional text and to work on their specific needs and learning gaps. The following are recommendations for structuring reading instruction to provide core instruction for all students and small-group interventions for students who need additional support in specific areas of literacy. This format is effective with all grade levels of students; however, the time suggestions may need to be adjusted based on grade level and students' needs.

- Whole-group instruction should be utilized for 45–60 minutes of the literacy block.

- During whole-group time, teachers teach and model phonemic awareness, phonics, vocabulary, comprehension, fluency, and writing skills and strategies using a grade-level common text for all students.

- Small-group interventions should take place during 30–60 minutes of the literacy block.

- During small groups with the teacher, skills and strategies from whole-group instruction should be pretaught and retaught and practiced, using the grade-level text or another text.

- Additional time should be spent with students who have been identified as at risk, based on literacy assessments. Resources and strategies based on their specific skill gaps should be addressed during this additional time.

- While some students are in small group for interventions, the other students should be engaged in meaningful work, such as tasks that are described as follows.

Here is an illustration of the time structure for literacy instruction, based on the recommendations provided earlier.

- **Whole-Group Instruction: 45–60 minutes for all students using grade-level text**
  - Vocabulary, Phonemic Awareness, Phonics, Language Arts Explicit Instruction
  - Comprehension Explicit Instruction
  - Reading and Discussion of Grade-Level Text
  - Writing Explicit Instruction
- **Small-Group Instruction: 30–45 minutes (for students in need of additional support)**
  - Small-group review, reteaching, extra guided practice in vocabulary, phonemic awareness, phonics, language arts skills, and comprehension strategy (from large group)
  - Reading of instructional grade-level or related text, with support as needed
  - Reteaching, review, and guided practice in writing
  - Support and guidance for other reading assignments or tasks
- **Independent or Partner Work: 30–45 minutes (for those not in small group)**
  - Reading of assigned grade-level text (practicing fluency)
  - Phonics or vocabulary work (graphic organizer, for example)
  - Comprehension tasks for application of strategies
  - Writing tasks

For independent work time to be the most effective and to enhance students' learning of grade-level standards, assignments and activities should be selected that directly reinforce the skills and concepts taught during whole-group literacy instruction. Suggested independent or partner work for students who are not in a small group include the following.

- **Word study:** Activities based on the phonics and vocabulary work from whole-group instruction
- **Comprehension:** Graphic organizers and other activities to apply whole-group instruction to instructional or student-selected text

- **Independent reading:** Reading the assigned portions of the instructional text (or student-selected text), with application of skills and strategies from whole group and with accountability for reading

- **Writing:** Writing tasks that are related to whole-group instruction, standards-based, and in response to literature (with clear expectations and accountability)

- **Fluency:** Reading of instructional text, practice on expert passages, reading and rereading of poems, scripts, and so on

- **Preparation for student-led discussions:** Generating higher-order questions, preparing for their roles in the discussion

Figure 10.1 is a generic example of what independent work time and rotations might look like. The tasks are directly aligned to whole-group instruction.

Day 1	Day 2	Day 3	Day 4	Day 5
Independent work and rotations:	**Independent work and rotations:**	**Independent work and rotations:**	**Independent work and rotations:**	**Independent work and rotations:**
Read assignment from instructional text independently and work on vocabulary graphic organizer. Read to self or partner with accountability task. Practice sight words.	Read assignment independently or with a partner and work on vocabulary graphic organizer. Read to self or partner. Start comprehension strategy task. Work on expert page.	Read assignment and independent practice with comprehension strategy. Begin writing task. Work on vocabulary activity with partners.	Read assignment in instructional text. Continue to work on comprehension task. Work on writing assignments. Read to self or partner with accountability task. Prepare for role in discussion or literature circle. Practice sight and vocabulary words.	Share out vocabulary task, comprehension activity. Complete writing task and share with an audience. Complete assessments. Engage in discussion protocol or literature circle.

Figure 10.1: Weekly independent or partner work.

Conclusion

Determining a format for literacy instruction that includes all students receiving high-quality instruction in all of the major components of reading can be challenging. All students should be involved in core, universal instruction for a good portion of the reading block so they receive explicit instruction and modeling of phonics, fluency, vocabulary skills, and comprehension. Small-group instruction does not need to include all students. If only the students who need interventions are pretaught or retaught skills or provided with extra support and practice, this can reduce the small-group instructional time, allowing for more whole-group, grade-level instruction to happen. It is important to engage students who are working independently or with a partner with meaningful tasks in which they practice and apply the skills taught in whole group, with both instructional texts and self-selected texts. CAI programs should be used in moderation, and students' progress must be monitored frequently.

Reflection Questions for Chapter 10: Whole-Group, Small-Group, and Independent Work

How often do all students receive quality, whole-group instruction for 40–60 minutes daily using a grade-level-appropriate text?

Does small-group instruction support and clearly connect to whole-group instructional content, skills, and strategies by using either the instructional text or another text?

Are students who are not working in a small group with the teacher engaged in meaningful tasks that help them to apply the content, skills, and strategies from whole-group instruction (using either the instructional text or other texts)?

Final Thoughts and Moving Forward

Each chapter of this book presented some concerns about current literacy instructional practices in many of today's schools, as well as a sound review of research related to each component of reading instruction. This research should be used to guide instructional decision making and planning. In addition, the following realities indicate the pressures that teachers currently face, many of which could be remedied through the implementation of *Solving the Literacy Puzzle*.

- Currently teachers are expected to instruct students on a wide range of levels (from several years below grade level to several years above grade level).

- When a literacy framework is in place where much of the academic block is used for small-group instruction, teachers are expected to teach vocabulary, comprehension fluency, phonics, and writing within 15- to 30-minute small groups, based on the specific needs of the students. This is virtually impossible. Teachers are human, and time is limited.

- All students are being assessed frequently, which is time-consuming, as is the analysis of the data. Teachers are expected to design individualized instruction for a significant number of students.

Our goal should be to have all students performing *on grade level at the end of kindergarten and at the end of first grade*. Teachers of second grade and beyond will then have a more manageable range of abilities for which to plan instruction, and much of the reading instruction can occur during whole-group instruction.

Nearly all students, regardless of their family, ethnic, socioeconomic, and cultural backgrounds, have the ability to perform on grade level in kindergarten and first grade, unless they have significant cognitive disabilities. Literacy researchers Richard Allington, Peter Johnston, and Jeni Pollack-Day (2022) determine that "virtually *every student could be reading on grade level* by the end of 1st grade" (cited by Schmoker, 2019).

If we utilize the strategies and recommendations from *Solving the Literacy Puzzle* and are diligent in working toward the goal of having all students in grades K–1 perform on or above grade level, students from grades 2 and beyond will be able to be successful, and learning gaps will be much smaller. Teachers will not need to have differentiated small-group instruction for a large number of students. Through implementation of the *Solving the Literacy Puzzle* model, high-quality grade-level instruction will be provided for all students (10–25 percent may still need small-group interventions).

Shanahan's (2020b) advice includes, "Brush up your skills in working with larger groups," and use the windfall of precious time to multiply the amount of instruction we provide in the most indispensable elements of K–3 literacy. Then as night follows day, third-grade literacy rates will rise" (as cited by Schmoker, 2019, p. 462).

At the beginning of this book, the topic of cognitive dissonance was presented, and readers were made aware that this dissonance might occur at times throughout the reading of the chapters. You may have been led to question your beliefs about reading instruction and your teaching practices. Readers were also encouraged to be open to new ideas, based on research.

The cognitive dissonance that you may have encountered might indicate the need for a shift in paradigms related to certain aspects of literacy instruction. Hopefully, the review of research and recommendations this book has provided will lead to some changes in thinking about reading instruction that will lead to positive changes in student learning.

Implementing Solving the Literacy Puzzle

Early in the book, readers were encouraged to candidly complete the reading instruction self-assessment, and throughout chapters 3–10 (pages 43, 65, 83, 111, 129, 143, 157, and 167 respectively), readers were asked to reflect on several questions related to the chapter. After reading this book, it is recommended that readers revisit the "Literacy Practices Self-Assessment" found on page 10 on their own or, better yet, with a group of teachers, an administrative team, a school leadership team, or literacy specialists in your district.

Readers are encouraged to engage in candid sharing of their responses to the Literacy Practices Self-Assessment and the reflective thoughts they have had about the questions in each chapter and use this discussion to determine actions that they may want to take. This process could occur with a single teacher, within a grade-level team, or with the teachers from the entire building or school district. Any level of change has the potential to have a positive impact on teaching and students' learning; however, when a cadre of teachers or an entire school collaborates, sets goals, and works together to implement change, this can have an even higher positive effect on literacy instruction and student achievement. As you review your self-assessments and reflections, you may want to indicate which of the components of your current practices are aligned with the research and the recommendations provided in this book.

Next, it is beneficial to dig deeper into which components you would like to focus on for improvement. For example, if you believe your grade-level team, or your school as a whole, is doing well in the areas of vocabulary instruction and fluency, you may want to identify a few ways that you might tweak your instruction to make it even more evidence based.

If your team or school's practices in one or two components are deemed as not well aligned with *Solving the Literacy Puzzle*'s research review and recommendations, you may want to choose those components as your focus for collaboration and change. If most of the components of literacy instruction in your classroom or school are not aligned with the research, you may want to work through each chapter or component of *Solving the Literacy Puzzle*.

The important thing is that you review and reflect upon your current practices, look at their alignment with the research and recommendations discussed in this book, and then set manageable goals that integrate sound, research-based practices. The change process can start small and happen over time. It is vital, however, that goals are set, actions are planned, and there is time allocated for collaboration and monitoring the progress related to your goals. Setting reasonable timelines for actions to occur is also important in the process of moving forward.

This book was intended to serve as a guide for K–12 teachers in how to plan and implement effective, comprehensive, research-based instruction; therefore, it is a promising idea to use this book as a tool for change. The recommendations for each component, the planning templates, and the examples should prove to be beneficial.

Some schools may want to use this book as a format for ongoing professional development for PLCs or for the teaching staff as a whole. Appendix A (page 183) is a suggested format for using the book as a guide for professional learning. This format would be appropriate for all grade levels of teachers. Templates for use in professional development sessions may be found in appendix B (page 195). It is recommended that you use the chapters in order from 1 through 10, focusing on one chapter, or literacy component, at a time. The time frame may be weekly during professional development or PLC times, or once or twice a month. Appendix C (page 197) provides additional guidance and templates in using *Solving the Literacy Puzzle* for professional learning.

Appendix A

Literacy Practices

5 Day Instructional Plan Example

This is an example of a completed comprehensive weekly instructional plan for grade 3 for the story *The Scavenger Hunt* by Ajit Narra (2019). A related story, called *After the Flood* (K5 Learning, n.d.), is also included in the plans as an additional instructional text. This instructional plan integrates the research and recommendations from *Solving the Literacy Puzzle*. There are instructional plans for core instruction, whole-group instruction, small-group instruction, and independent work. All of the components of the science of reading are addressed. Following the example template is specific information about each of the components of instruction. In addition, a scannable QR code leading to the full text of each story is available at the end of this appendix (page 193).

Example of Completed Five-Day Instructional Plan Using *Solving the Literacy Puzzle*

Day 1	Day 2	Day 3	Day 4	Day 5
Whole-Group Instruction (45–60 minutes)	**Whole-Group Instruction (45–60 minutes)**	**Whole-Group Instruction (45–60 minutes)**	**Whole-Group Instruction (45–60 minutes)**	**Whole-Group Instruction (45–60 minutes)**
Comprehension strategy: Explicit instruction and modeling of questioning strategy (10 minutes) **Vocabulary and phonics:** Introduce the words *scavenger, flooded, thirsty, village,* and *items* using sentences from the book, modeling use of context clues and structural analysis. Have students write the words and short definitions on their graphic organizers. (15 minutes) **Establish prior knowledge and anticipatory set:** Read aloud a passage from a book or watch a video clip about floods. (5–10 minutes) **Introduction to and reading of whole group text:** Text walk and discuss setting of *The Scavenger Hunt* (Narra, 2019). **Go over the characters' names.** Read pages 1–2 aloud to students, modeling fluency and questioning. (15 minutes)	**Comprehension strategy:** Review the importance of questioning (both to better own understanding and to monitor thinking). (5 minutes) **Vocabulary and language arts:** Introduce new words *banks, puzzled, relieved,* and *survivors* in context, using the sentences from the text modeling context clues and decoding. Have students add these words and short definitions to vocabulary graphic organizers. (20 minutes) **Reading of whole group text:** Read orally (taking turns, playing parts, etc.) and discuss pages 1–8 of *The Scavenger Hunt* (Narra, 2019) using the preplanned questions. Have students share the questions they wrote for pages 1–8 from day 1. Read page 9 orally to the students and assign pages 9–17 to read independently and to write questions as they read. (15–20 minutes)	**Writing:** Explicit instruction and modeling of writing a five-sentence informational paragraph (topic: winter storms or tornados). Develop introductory or topic sentence, three sentences with information, and a concluding sentence. Review capitalization and punctuation. Add some dialogue while modeling to review commas and quotation marks. (20 minutes) **Vocabulary:** Review all 9 vocabulary words, and their meanings, from days 1 and 2 using the context sentences or word cards. Engage students in Word Sorts using the word cards in pocket chart. (15 minutes) **Reading of whole group text:** Read orally and discuss *The Scavenger Hunt* (Narra, 2019, pp. 9–17) using preplanned questions. Continue to have students share out the questions that they wrote while they were reading. (10–15 minutes)	**Comprehension strategy and guided or independent practice:** Review questioning and why it is important. Ask students what questions they have about the passage *After the Flood* (K5 Learning, n.d.). (10 minutes) **Writing:** Review writing a five-sentence informational paragraph (about floods) and the components. Read aloud *After the Flood* (K5 Learning, n.d.) and model writing a topic sentence and one informational sentence. Have some students share out their introductory or topic sentences. (15 minutes) **Vocabulary:** Play the Flyswatter vocabulary game using the 9 new words for *The Scavenger Hunt* (Narra, 2019) and some words from prior books or stories. (10 minutes) **Reading of whole group text:** Allow students five minutes to practice their part. Reread selected pages of *The Scavenger Hunt* (Narra, 2019) with students modeling their "expert reader" parts. (15–20 minutes)	**Writing:** Guided or independent practice and "sharing out" of students' writing. (15 minutes) **Comprehension:** Review activity or students share their comprehension graphic organizers. (10 minutes) **Formative weekly assessment:** Vocabulary, comprehension, writing. (15 minutes) **Reading of whole group text:** Read orally and discuss portions from previous day using preplanned questions, discussion groups, or literature circles. (20 minutes)

Day 1	Day 2	Day 3	Day 4	Day 5
Small-group interventions (30–45 minutes)	**Small-group interventions (30–45 minutes)**	**Small-group interventions (30–45 minutes)**	**Small-group interventions (30–45 min)**	**Small-group interventions (30–45 minutes)**
Review vocabulary for *The Scavenger Hunt* (Narra, 2019) and practice vocabularuy words. Assist students with visuals and synonyms on their vocabulary graphic organizers and read assigned pages 1–8 with small group (taking turns). Assist students in writing questions about the book as they read.	Review four new vocabulary words for *The Scavenger Hunt* (Narra, 2019) and practice vocabulary words. Assist students with antonyms on their vocabulary graphic organizers and read assigned pages 1–8 with small group (taking turns). Encourage students to verbally ask questions about the book while they read. Read together the passage *After the Flood* (K5 Learning, n.d.).	Review all nine vocabulary words and their meanings and assist in finishing vocabulary graphic organizer. Read pages 9–17 (taking turns). Assist students in writing their topic sentence and one informational sentence about floods for their five-sentence paragraph.	Reread parts of *After the Flood* (K5 Learning, n.d.) together, noting key ideas. Assist students in continuing to write their five-sentence informational paragraphs about floods.	Review writing skills and read assigned pages with small group. Others read assignment and complete other work as needed.
Independent Work or Rotation Time (30–45 minutes)	**Independent Work or Rotation Time (30–45 minutes)**	**Independent Work or Rotation Time (30–45 minutes)**	**Independent Work or Rotation Time (30–45 minutes)**	**Independent Work or Rotation Time (30–45 minutes)**
Read pages 1–8 of *The Scavenger Hunt* (Narra, 2019) independently and note a question or two on graphic organizer. Add visual images and synonyms to vocabulary graphic organizer. Visit websites on floods and jot some notes.	Read pages 9–17 of *The Scavenger Hunt* (Narra, 2019) independently and note a question or two on graphic organizer. Add antonyms and "what this word makes me think of" to vocabulary graphic organizer. Visit websites on floods and jot some notes. Independent reading of student-selected books.	Complete vocabulary graphic organizer. Reread *The Scavenger Hunt* (Narra, 2019) with a partner. Read the passage *After the Flood* (K5 Learning, n.d.). Jot some notes. Begin to write their five-sentence information paragraph about floods. Independent reading of student-selected books.	Continue writing their informational paragraphs about floods, using their notes. Practice vocabulary and sight words on word cards. Independent reading of student-selected books. Write two questions on graphic organizer.	Finish and share out their informational paragraphs (in small groups, some in large group). Share their vocabulary graphic organizers in small groups. Independent reading of student-selected books. Prepare for Book Talk next week.

Part 1: Selection of Text and Grouping Formats

- **Instructional text for universal, core whole-group instruction:**
    - *The Scavenger Hunt* by Ajit Narra (2019) and *After the Flood* (K5 Learning, n.d.)
- **Instructional groupings:**
    - Whole group followed by small group, independent, and partner work

Part 2: Vocabulary and Language Arts Instruction

- **Vocabulary words for instruction (Tier II) and words important to comprehend text):**

scavenger (hunt)	village	relieved
flooded	puzzled	survivors
thirsty	banks	items

- **Sentences to use to teach words in context:**

  1. "A game!" says Lajjo, brightening up.

  2. "Yes! It's a scavenger hunt. You have to find all the items on this list."

  3. The banks of the river break. In just a few minutes, the village is flooded with muddy water from the river.

  4. "Lajjo, I'm thirsty. Do you have some water?" asks her friend, Prateek.

  5. "Why did you do that?" Lajjo asks, puzzled.

  6. The army comes in boats laden with supplies for the flood survivors. Lajjo's family is relieved.

Part 3: Vocabulary and Language Arts Instruction (continued):

- **Word-learning focus during instruction and modeling (decoding, context clues, and so on):**
  - scavenger (hunt)—context and decoding
  - flood(ed)—decoding
  - banks—context clues (multimeaning word)
  - thirsty—context clues
  - items—decoding
  - relieved—context clues
  - village—context and decoding
  - survivors—context clues
  - puzzled—context and decoding (multi-meaning word)
  - scavenger—context clues
- **Language arts skills focus:**

- Use commas and quotation marks to mark direct speech and quotations from a text.
- Use multimeaning words: *banks*, *puzzles*.

- **Whole-group activities:**
  - Engage in explicit instruction using the sentences to model the use of context clues and decoding skills.
  - Review use of punctuation for dialogue (commas, capitals, quotation marks).
  - Review phonics skills as applicable.
  - Students write vocabulary words on graphic organizer, the part of speech, and a short student-friendly definition of the word as each word is taught.
  - Students play the Flyswatter game and take a vocabulary quiz.

- **Small group activities:**
  - Assist in completion of vocabulary graphic organizer.
  - Review vocabulary words and sight words.
  - Take a vocabulary quiz.

- **Independent work:**
  - Work on the vocabulary graphic organizer.
  - Read *After the Flood* (K5 Learning, n.d.) and note commas and quotation marks for dialogue.
  - Practice vocabulary word cards or on Quizmo.

Part 4: Comprehension Strategies

- **Research-based comprehension strategies:**
  - Questioning as we read (generating questions about the text and about our own understanding—developing metacognition)
  - Use of context clues to determine meaning of a word

- **Text for explicit instruction:**
  - *The Scavenger Hunt* (Narra, 2019) (whole-group, grade-level text)
  - *After the Flood* (K5 Learning, n.d) passage

- **Text for modeling strategy read-aloud or think-aloud:**

- Explicit instruction script for the questioning strategy
- Sharing and discussion of student-generated questions during whole-group reading of *The Scavenger Hunt* (Narra, 2019)
- Model generating questions during reading of *After the Flood* (K5 Learning, n.d), and share students' questions

- **Small-group activity for application of strategy:**
  - Review of explicit instruction in *questioning* from whole group.
  - Guided practice in asking questions prior to reading and while reading pages 1–8 and pages 9–17. Verbal questions from students while reading *After the Flood* (K5 Learning, n.d.).
  - Context clues activity.

- **Independent practice activities for application of strategy:**
  - As students read pages 1–8 of *The Scavenger Hunt* (Narra, 2019), write questions that they have about the text or floods on the questioning graphic organizer.
  - Continue to work on the questioning graphic organizer for pages 9–17 and with additional text, *After the Flood* (K5 Learning, n.d.), and student-selected text.
  - Context clues activity.

Part 5: Questioning and Discussion of Text During Whole Group

- **Preplanned questions (related to comprehension strategy and learning targets)** *for use when reading the text with the teacher*:
  - **For pages 1–8:**
    + Page 1 (after text walk)—Do you think the setting of this story is in the United States? Why or why not?
    + Page 3—Why do you think Lajja is scared? What do you think she is afraid will happen?
    + Page 4—Why might the family be safer on higher ground? What do people living in homes near rivers do to avoid flooding?
    + Page 6—What did Mai mean when she said, "All you care about is a doll?" Why do you think she is angry?
    + Page 8—Why is Lajja so excited about a game?

+ Page 8—Do you have any ideas about why Daddu is asking Lajja to find those specific items?

While reading, ask students to share the questions that they generated while they were reading pages 1–8 independently.

- **For pages 9–17:**
    + Page 9—Why do you think Mai gave Lajju a piece of her sari? How do you think this made Lajju feel (remember that Mai was angry with her earlier)?
    + Page 11—How would you describe how Lajju probably felt about not being able to give Preteek some water?
    + Page 12—How does the carpenter feel about Lajju playing a game? Why does he feel this way?
    + Page 14—What were you asking yourself or wondering about when Daddu was working with the bucket and other items? (Questioning strategy)
    + Page 16—Why was what Daddu did so important? What are your thoughts about how Daddu knew how to do this?
    + Page 17—What was the surprise for Lajju when the army came? Would Lajju think getting her doll back was the best thing that could happen?

Part 6: Fluency

- **Sight words and words from text for students to practice:**

scavenger	village	relieved
flood	puzzled	survivors
thirsty	banks	items

Additional vocabulary words from past several stories/books and grade-level sight words on word cards.

- **Common text to use for fluency development:**
    - *The Scavenger Hunt* (Narra, 2019)
- **Teacher actions:**
    - Model fluency during shared reading of the book in whole group.
- **Student activities for fluency practice:**

- Choose a page of the book to be the expert reader.
- Practice and "perform" during whole-group reading.
- Practice sight word flashcards and words from the book.

Part 7: Independent Reading of Instructional Text and Other Texts

- **Common, grade-level text to use for instruction:**
  - Day 1—Pages 1–8
  - Day 2—Pages 9–17
  - Day 3—Pages 1-17
  - Days 4–5—Reading passage *After the Flood* (K5 Learning, n.d.)
- **Vocabulary and "tricky" words to preteach:**
  - Nine identified vocabulary words for explicit instruction and character names: Lajju, Mai, Preteek, Babu, Daddu, Gudiya
- **Steps to build prior knowledge:**
  - Read a short book to the class about a flood (preferably nonfiction).
  - Show video clips of floods.
  - Discuss the setting of the story after a text walk (India).
- **What part of the text will the teacher model by reading aloud?**
  - Day 1—Pages 1 and 2
  - Day 2—Page 9
- **What pages or chapters will students be asked to read independently from the grade-level instructional text?**
  - Day 1—Pages 1–8
  - Day 2—Pages 9–17
  - Day 3—Reread Pages 1–17
  - Day 4—Article *After the Flood* (K5 Learning, n.d.)
- **How will students apply vocabulary, comprehension, and other skills from whole-group instruction?**
  - Vocabulary graphic organizer (and multimeaning words)
  - Comprehension activity on questioning
  - Use of context clues activity

- **How much time will be allocated for independent reading of a *student-selected* text?**
  - 15 minutes on days 2, 4, and 5
- **How students will be held accountable for their independent reading:**
  - Comprehension activity on questioning (same as one used with whole-group, grade-level text and *After the Flood* [K5 Learning, n.d.])

Part 8: Writing and Language Arts Skills

- **Type of writing task:**
  - Informational (five-sentence) paragraph—synthesizing what the student learned about flooding from the book and the other texts they read
  - Introductory sentence, three informational sentences, a concluding sentence
- **Language arts skills focus:**
  - Developing a complete informational, summarizing paragraph with correct punctuation and capitalization
- **Teacher actions:**
  - Explicit instruction and modeling of writing a complete informational paragraph
- **Student independent or small-group work:**
  - Writing a five-sentence informational paragraph about floods with correct punctuation and capitalization

Independent and Partner Work Time Details for *The Scavenger Hunt* and *After the Flood*

- **Day 1:**
  - Read *The Scavenger Hunt* (Narra, 2019, pp. 1–8). Generate questions as they read using the graphic organizer.
  - Add visual images and synonyms to vocabulary graphic organizer.
  - Visit the following sites to read about floods:
    + study.com/academy/lesson/flood-lesson-for-kids-definition -facts.html

+ www.slideshare.net/ohteikbin/the-flood-a-story-for
   -children-presentation

- Write down some notes about what they learned from these sources.

- **Day 2:**

  - Read *The Scavenger Hunt* (Narra, 2019, pp. 9–17). Generate questions as they read using the graphic organizer.

  - Add antonyms and "what this word makes me think of" to vocabulary graphic organizer.

  - Continue to visit the websites provided to read about floods.

  - Write down some notes about what they learned from these sources.

  - Independent reading of student-selected books.

- **Day 3:**

  - Reread *The Scavenger Hunt* practicing their "expert reader" page.

  - Finish vocabulary graphic organizer.

  - Read *After the Flood*, highlighting or circling punctuation for the dialogue and jotting questions on the graphic organizer.

  - Begin writing their informational paragraphs using their notes.

- **Day 4:**

  - Continue writing their informational paragraphs about floods, using their notes.

  - Practice vocabulary and sight words on word cards or Quizmo.

  - Engage in independent reading of student-selected books. Write two questions on graphic organizer.

- **Day 5:**

  - Finish and share out their informational paragraphs (in small groups, some in large group).

  - Share their vocabulary graphic organizers in small groups.

  - Engage in independent reading of student-selected books.

  - Prepare for Book Talk next week.

**Scan the following
code to read Ajit Nara's (2019)
*The Scavenger Hunt.***

**Scan the following code to read K–5 Learning's
*After the Flood.***

Appendix B

Generic Five-Day Instructional Planning Template

This is a blank template, with headings for whole-group, small-group, and independent work and all of the literacy components, to use for planning literacy instruction using the strategies and recommendations from *Solving the Literacy Puzzle*. The template includes suggested time frames for each portion of the literacy block. The following is the comprehensive literacy block template for each portion of literacy instruction.

45–60 Minutes Literacy Whole-Group Instructional Planning Template

Day 1	Day 2	Day 3	Day 4	Day 5
Whole-group Instruction (45–60 minutes)	Whole-group Instruction (45–60 minutes)	Whole-group Instruction (45–60 minutes)	Whole-group Instruction (45–60 minutes)	Whole-group Instruction (45–60 minutes)
Small-group interventions (30–45 minutes)	Small-group interventions (30–45 minutes)	Small-group interventions (30–45 minutes)	Small-group interventions (30–45 min)	Small-group interventions (30–45 minutes)
Independent work or rotation time (30–45 minutes)	Independent work or rotation time (30–45 minutes)	Independent work or rotation time (30–45 minutes)	Independent work or rotation time (30–45 minutes)	Independent work or rotation time (30–45 minutes)

Appendix C

Guides for Professional Development for *Solving the Literacy Puzzle*

If *Solving the Literacy Puzzle* will be used by individual teachers, teacher teams, literacy teams, or school staff, the following will provide guidance for professional learning sessions.

Professional Development Session 1

- Individual responses to the Literacy Practices Self-Assessment (candidly share and discuss):
    - Commonalities among group members' responses (areas of strength and alignment and areas to focus on for better alignment between the research and current practices)
    - Discussion about the literacy components and related chapters that the group wants to focus professional development around, based on the self-assessment responses
    - Group goals (2–3 long-range goals)
    - Next steps (component of focus for next meeting)
    - Specific actions and goals for next meeting

Professional Development Session 2

- Discussion of the self-assessment and the reflection questions at the beginning of the chapter related to the specific literacy component or chapter of the book that the group determined as the focus area during session 1.

- Read the designated chapter independently before the meeting, or collaboratively and do the following. Share out with the group.
  - Note the current reality in your classroom or school.
  - Think about what research-based practices you believe should be implemented.
  - Think about what changes and additions may need to be made to better align with the *Solving the Literacy Puzzle* research and recommendations.
- Determine, as a team, the goals that you want to set and discuss the specific changes or additions you want to make in your literacy instruction, based on that chapter, or component.
- Record next steps.
- Record specific actions and goals for next meeting.

Professional Development Session 3 and Beyond

- Review the group goals set during session 1.
- Share out during each subsequent session what actions you have taken, what strategies or resources you used, and how things are going.
- Read the designated chapter independently before the meeting, or collaboratively, or review if no new chapter or component.
- Review the sample lesson plans in the book and discuss how and when you might implement these practices
- Engage in collaborative instructional planning to address the goals.
- Record next steps.
- Record specific actions and goals for next meeting.

Notes to consider:

- Continue this process until your group feels comfortable with your understanding and implementation of research-based practices for that chapter or component.
- Continue onto the next component and engage in a similar process.
- At the end of each component or every two or three sessions, review the self-assessment and discuss the changes that have been implemented and the progress being made toward your goals.

References and Resources

A World of Language Learners. (2021). *Using poetry to teach reading fluency.* Accessed at www.aworldoflanguagelearners.com/poetry-reading-fluency on February 8, 2024.

Alcock, K. J., Ngorosho, D., Deus, C., & Jukes, M. C. H. (2010). We don't have language at our house: Disentangling the relationship between phonological awareness, schooling, and literacy. *British Journal of Educational Psychology, 80*(1), 55–76.

Alghazo, E. M., & Al-Hilawani, Y. A. (2010). Knowledge, skills, and practices concerning phonological awareness among early childhood education teachers. *Journal of Research in Childhood Education, 24*(2), 172–185.

Allington, R., Johnston, P., & Day, J. P. (2002). Exemplary fourth-grade teachers. *Language Arts, 79*(6), 462–466.

Andrade, H. (2004). The writing rubric. *Educational Leadership, 62*(2), 48–52. Accessed at www.ascd.org/publications/educational-leadership/oct04/vol62/num02/The-Writing-Rubric.aspx on February 7, 2024.

Armbruster, B. B., Lehr, F., Osborn, J., & Adler, C. R. (2003). *Put reading first: The research building blocks of reading instruction: Kindergarten through grade 3* (2nd ed.). Washington, DC: National Institute for Literacy.

Austin, A. (2022). *Seven strategies to improve reading comprehension.* Connections Academy, Baltimore, MD: Pearson. Accessed at www.connectionsacademy.com/support/resources/article/an-introduction-to-using-effective-reading-comprehension-strategies on May 14, 2024.

Awesome, C. (2017). *3 reasons no online reading program can measure up to a good book.* Accessed at www.weareteachers.com/online-reading-programs-vs-books on February 8, 2024.

Ayala, S. M., & O'Connor, R. (2013). The effects of video self-modeling on the decoding skills of children at risk for reading disabilities. *Learning Disabilities Research and Practice, 28*(3), 142–154.

Bafile, C. (n.d.). *Reader's theater: Giving students a reason to read aloud.* Accessed at www.reading rockets.org/topics/fluency/articles/readers-theater-giving-students-reason-read-aloud on January 16, 2024.

Barak, M., & Rafaeli, S. (2004). On-line question-posing and peer-assessment as means for web-based knowledge sharing in learning. *International Journal of Human-Computer Studies, 61*(1), 84–103. Accessed at https://doi .org/10.1016/j.ijhcs.2003.12.005 on February 24, 2024.

Barr, R. (1989). The social organization of literacy instruction. In S. McCormick & J. Zuttell (Eds.), *Cognitive and social perspectives for literacy research and instruction* (Thirty-eighth Yearbook of the National Reading Conference, pp. 19–34). Chicago: National Reading Conference.

Barshay, J. (2019, November 4). *Scientific evidence on how to teach writing is slim.* Accessed at https://hechingerreport.org/scientific-evidence-on-how-to-teach -writing-is-slim/ on February 24, 2024.

Barshay, J. (2022). *Proof points: Six puzzling questions from the disastrous NAEP results.* Accessed at hechingerreport.org/proof-points-six-puzzling-questions -from-the-disastrous-naep-results on January 26, 2024.

Barshay, J., Flynn, H., Sheasley, C., Richman, T., Bazzaz, D., & Griesbach, R. (2021, November 10). *America's reading problem: Scores were dropping even before the pandemic.* Accessed at https://hechingerreport.org/americas -reading-problem-scores-were-dropping-even-before-the-pandemic/ on February 24, 2024.

Bauer, T., & Tang, H. (2022). Explicit vocabulary instruction for fifth graders' vocabulary knowledge and reading comprehension: An action research study. *Journal of Educational Technology Development and Exchange, 15*(1), 124–141. Accessed at https://doi.org/10.18785/jetde.1501.08 on February 24, 2024.

Baumann, J. F., & Heubach, K. M. (1996). Do basal readers deskill teachers? A national survey of educators' use and opinions of basals. *The Elementary School Journal, 96*(5), 511–526.

Baumann, J. F., Edwards, E. C., Boland, E. M., Olejnik, S., & Kame'enui, E. J. (2003). Vocabulary tricks: Effects of instruction in morphology and context on fifth-grade students' ability to derive and infer word meanings. *American Educational Research Journal, 40*(2), 447–494. Accessed at https://doi .org/10.3102/00028312040002447 on February 24, 2024.

Baumann, J. F., Hoffman, J. V., Duffy-Hester, A. M., & Ro, J. M. (2000). *The first R* yesterday and today: U.S. elementary reading instruction practices reported by teachers and administrators. *Reading Research Quarterly, 35*(3), 338–377. Accessed at https://doi:10.1598/RRQ.35.3.2 on February 24, 2024.

Bayat, N., & Cetinkaya, G. (2020). The relationship between inference skills and reading comprehension. *Egitim ve Bilim, 45*(203). Accessed at https:// doi:10.15390/EB.2020.8782 on February 24, 2024.

Beck, I. L., McKeown, M. G., & Kucan, L. (2002). *Bringing words to life: Robust vocabulary instruction.* New York: Guilford Press.

Bell, D. D. (2010). *Exploring phonemic awareness in preschool English language learners.* [Doctoral dissertation, Florida State University]. FSU Libraries. Accessed at https://diginole.lib.fsu.edu/islandora/object/fsu%3A175849 on January 26, 2024.

Bernard, M. (2022). *The importance of grammar in reading comprehension.* Accessed at https://ortongillinghamonlinetutor.com/the-importance-of-grammar-in-reading-comprehension on February 7, 2024.

Blachowicz, C. L. Z., & Fisher, P. (2006). *Teaching vocabulary in all classrooms.* Upper Saddle River, NJ: Pearson.

Bouhali, F., Bezagu, Z., Dehaene, S., & Cohen, L. (2019). A mesial-to-lateral dissociation for orthographic processing in the visual cortex. *Proceedings of the National Academy of Sciences of the United States of America, 116*(43), 21936–21946.

Boushey, G., & Behne, A. (2019). *The CAFE book: Engaging all students in daily literacy assessment and instruction* (2nd ed.). Portsmouth, NH: Stenhouse.

Boushey, G., & Moser, J. (2006). *The Daily Five: Fostering literacy independence in the elementary grades.* Portland, ME: Stenhouse.

Brady, S. (2020). A 2020 perspective on research findings on alphabetics (phoneme awareness and phonics): Implications for instruction (expanded version). *The Reading League Journal, 1*(3), 20–28.

Brandon, D. (2021, March 26). *The importance of reading comprehension.* Accessed at www.aces.edu/blog/topics/home-family-urban/the-importance-of-reading-comprehension/ on January 26, 2024.

Braun, H. (2015, August 8). *8 smart strategies for teaching writing.* Accessed at www.theclassroomkey.com/2015/08/8-smart-strategies-for-teaching-writing.html on January 26, 2024.

Braunshausen, S. (n.d.). *What is the basal reading approach?* Accessed at http://education.seattlepi.com/basal-reading-approach-1838.html on January 26, 2024.

Brevik, L. M. (2019). Explicit reading strategy instruction or daily use of strategies? Studying the teaching of reading comprehension through naturalistic classroom observation in English L2. *Reading and Writing: An Interdisciplinary Journal, 32,* 2281–2310.

Brown, H. (2007). *8 Smart strategies for teaching writing.* Accessed at www.theclassroomkey.com/2015/08/8-smart-strategies-for-teaching-writing.html on May 14, 2024.

Brown, L., Mohr, K., Wilcox, B., & Barrett, T. (2017). The effects of dyad reading and text difficulty on third-graders' reading achievement. *The Journal of Educational Research.* DOI: 10.1080/00220671.2017.1310711.

Brown, S., Fabiano, G. & Pechacek, K. (2022). *Understanding tier 1 instructional strategies that support an engaged classroom.* Accessed at www.renaissance .com/2022/06/02/blog-understanding-tier-1-instructional-strategies-tha t-support-an-engaged-classroom on April 15, 2024.

Bush, L. (2008, July 28). *Reading First.* [Conference Presentation]. Fifth Annual Reading First. Nashville, Tennessee, United States.

Busheri, D. (2022, May 9). How to Encourage Kids to Read? 10 Easy Ways for Motivation. Zoog. Accessed at www.getzoog.com/how-encourage-kids -read/#:~:text=Choose%20Age% on April 23, 2024.

Buttaro, A., Jr., & Catsambis, S. (2019). Ability grouping in the early grades: Long-term consequences for educational equity in the United States. *Teachers College Record, 121*(2), 1–50.

Cabell, S. Q., Justice, L. M., McGinty, A. S., De Coster, J., & Forston, L. D. (2015). Teacher–child conversations in preschool classrooms: Contributions to children's vocabulary development. *Early Childhood Research Quarterly, 30*(A), 80–92.

Calhoun, E. F. (1999). *Teaching beginning reading and writing with picture-word inductive model.* Arlington, VA: ASCD. Accessed at https://files.eric.ed.gov / fulltext/EJ1307957.pdf on April 23, 2024.

Callaghan, G., & Madelaine, A. (2012). Levelling the playing field for kindergarten entry: Research implications for preschool early literacy instruction. *Australian Journal of Early Childhood, 37*(1), 13–23. Accessed at https://doi.org/10.1177/183693911203700103 on February 24, 2024.

Carnine, D. W., Silbert, J., Kame'enui, E. J., & Tarver, S. G. (2004). *Direct instruction reading* (4th ed.). Upper Saddle River, NJ: Pearson Prentice Hall.

Carol Pufahl Literacy Foundation. (n.d.). *Why early childhood literacy is so important.* Accessed at www.cpliteracyfoundation.org/about-us/why-early -childhood-literacy-is-so-important/ on January 26, 2024.

Carroll, K., & Olson, P. (2023, November 21). *Ability grouping in school.* Accessed at http://study.com/learn/lesson/ability-grouping-pros-cons-school.html on January 26, 2024.

Carson, K. L., Gillon, G. T., & Boustead, T. M. (2012). Classroom phonological awareness instruction and literacy outcomes in the first year of school. *Language, Speech, and Hearing Services in Schools, 44*(2), 147–160. Accessed at https://doi.org/10.1044/0161-1461(2012/11-0061) on February 24, 2024.

Cavanaugh, C. (2008). *Guide to classroom discussions.* Accessed at https:// qureshiuniversity.com/guidetoclassroomdiscussions.htm on March 11, 2024.

SIOP. (n.d.). *Learn about SIOP.* Accessed at www.cal.org /siop/about on April 23, 2024.

Center for the Improvement of Early Reading Achievement. (2006). *Connections to effective schools and effective teaching traditions*. Washington, DC: Office of Educational Research and Improvement, United States Department of Education.

Cheesman, E. A., McGuire, J. M., Shankweiler, D., & Coyne, M. (2009). First-year teacher knowledge of phonemic awareness and its instruction. *Teacher Education and Special Education*, *32*(3), 270–289. Accessed at https://doi.org/10.1177/0888406409339685 on February 24, 2024.

Cheng, Ching-Hsue & Su, Chung-Ho. (2012). A game-based learning system for improving student's learning effectiveness in system analysis course. *Procedia - Social and Behavioral Sciences*. *31*, 669-675. DOI:10.1016/j.sbspro.2011.12.122.

Child, A. E., Cirino, P. T., Fletcher, J. M., Willcutt, E. G., & Fuchs, L. S. (2019). A cognitive dimensional approach to understanding shared and unique contributions to reading, math, and attention skills. *Journal of Learning Disabilities*, *52*(1), 15–30.

Cognitive dissonance. (n.d.). In *Merriam-Webster's online dictionary*. Accessed at www.merriamwebster.com/dictionary/cognitive%20dissonance on February 7, 2024.

Coleman, J. S., et al. (1966). *The Coleman report: Equality of educational opportunity*. Washington, DC: U.S. Government Printing Office.

Colorado Department of Education (2022). *Tier 1 (core) universal instruction: Reading*. Accessed at www.cde.state.co.us/standardsandinstruction/tier-1-core-universal-instruction-reading on April 23, 2024.

Connor, C. M., Piasta, S. B., Fishman, B., Glasney, S., Schatschneider, C., Crowe, E., et al. (2009). Individualizing student instruction precisely: Effects of child × instruction interactions on first graders' literacy development. *Child Development*, *80*(1), 77–100. Accessed at https://doi:10.1111/j.1467-8624.2008.01247.x on February 24, 2024.

Cornwell, L. (2015). Scholastic.com for Librarians | What Is Readers Theater. Accessed at www.scholastic.com/librarians/programs/whatisrt.htm on June 8, 2015.

Council for Advancement of Adult Literacy. (2008). Report of the national commission on adult literacy. New York: Author. Accessed at https://eric.ed.gov/?id=ED511933 on March 11. 2024.

Council of Chief State School Officers. (2015). *Fact sheet: Testing action plan*. Accessed at www2.ed.gov/documents/press-releases/testing-action-plan-profiles.pdf on March 11, 2024.

Cox, T. (2023, November 21). *300 most common English words (and how to learn them fast)*. Accessed at https://preply.com/en/blog/300-most-common-english-words/ on January 26, 2024.

Cummings, K. D., Kaminski, R. A., Good, R. H., III, & O'Neil, M. (2011). Assessing phonemic awareness in preschool and kindergarten: Development and initial validation of first sound fluency. *Assessment for Effective Intervention*, *36*(2), 94–106.

D'Souza, K. (2022, November 14). *"Just-right" books: Does leveled reading hurt the weakest readers*. Accessed at https://edsource.org/2022/just-right-books-does -leveled-reading-hurt-the-weakest-readers/680958 on January 26, 2024.

de Koning, B. B., Bos, L. T., Wassenburg, S. I., & van der Schoot, M. (2017). Effects of a reading strategy training aimed at improving mental simulation in primary school children. *Educational Psychology Review*, *29*(4), 869–889. Accessed at https://doi.org/10.1007/s10648-016-9380-4 on February 24, 2024.

Dehaene, S. (2010). *Reading in the brain: The new science of how we read*. New York: Penguin Publishing Group.

Del Campo, R., Buchanan, W. R., Abbott, R. D., & Berninger, V. W. (2015). Levels of phonology related to reading and writing in middle childhood. *Reading and Writing*, *28*(2), 183–198. Accessed at https://doi:10.1007/s11145 -014-9520-5 on November 24, 2024.

Derakhshan, A., & Khatir, E. D. (2015). The effects of using games on English vocabulary learning. *Journal of Applied Linguistics and Language Research*, *2*(3), 39–47.

DeSilver, D. (2017, February 15). *U.S. students' academic achievement still lags that of their peers in many other countries*. Accessed at www.pewresearch.org /fact-tank/2017/02/15/u-s-students-internationally-math-science on January 26, 2024.

DiSciscio, M. T. (2022). Responding: A discussion protocol for creative classrooms. *Music Educators Journal*, *108*(4), 45–50. Accessed at https://doi .org/10.1177/00274321221107138 on November 24, 2024.

Dolch, E. W. (1936). A basic sight vocabulary. *The Elementary School Journal*, *36*, 456-460. doi:10.1086/457353

Dong, Y., Tang, Y., Chow, B. W., Wang, W., & Dong, W. (2020). Contribution of vocabulary knowledge to reading comprehension among Chinese students: A meta-analysis. *Frontiers in Psychology*, *11*, 525369. Accessed at https://doi .org/10.3389/fpsyg.2020.525369 on November 24, 2024.

Dougherty Stahl, K. A. (2004). Proof, practice, and promise: Comprehension strategy instruction in the primary grades. *Reading Teacher*, *57*(7), 598–609.

Duffy, G. G. (2003). *Explaining reading: A resource for teaching concepts, skills, and strategies*. New York: Guilford Publications.

Duke, N. K. (2010). Choosing the right text. Doing what works. Accessed at https://dwwlibrary.wested.org/resources/1021 on March 11, 2024.

Duke, N. K., Pearson, P. D., Strachan, S. L., & Billman, A. K. (2011). *Essential elements of fostering and teaching reading comprehension*. Reading Hall of Fame. Accessed at www.readinghalloffame.org/sites/default/files/03-duke -pearson-strachan-billman.2011_rev_copy.pdf on January 26, 2024.

Duke, N. K., Ward, A. E., & Pearson, P. D. (2021). *The science of reading* comprehension instruction. *The Reading Teacher*, *74*(6), 663–672. Accessed at https://doi.org/10.1002/trtr.1993 on November 24, 2024.

Duke, N., & Varlas, L. (2019, July 1). *Turn small reading groups into big wins*. Accessed at www.ascd.org/publications/newsletters/education -update/jul19/vol61/num07/Turn-Small-Reading-Groups-into-Big-Wins.aspx on January 26, 2024.

Durkin, D. (1978). What classroom observations reveal about reading comprehension instruction. *Reading Research Quarterly*, *14*(4), 481–533.

Eisenberg, M. (2013, September 23). *The importance of studying language arts*. Accessed at https://naturalhealingnews.com/the-importance-of-studying -language-arts/#.YBSGh-hKiUl on January 26, 2024.

Elleman, A. M., & Oslund, E. L. (2019). Reading comprehension research: Implications for practice and policy. *Policy Insights From the Behavioral and Brain Sciences*, *6*(1), 3–11.

Elosúa, M. R., García-Madruga, J. A., Vila, J. O., Gómez-Veiga, I., & Gil, L. (2013). Improving reading comprehension: From metacognitive intervention on strategies to the intervention on working memory executive processes. *Universitas Psychologica*, *12*(5), 1425–1438. Accessed at https://doi.org /10.11144/Javeriana.UPSY12-5.ircm on November 24, 2024.

Emmitt, M., Hornsby, D., & Wilson, L. (2013). *The place of phonics in learning to read and write*. Norwood, South Australia: Australian Literacy Education Association.

Ewing, R., & Maher, M. (2016). *Phonics: Its place in the literacy story*. Accessed at https://readingaustralia.com.au/2016/11/phonics-its-place-in-the -literacy-story/ on March 11, 2024.

Festinger, L. (1957). *A theory of cognitive dissonance*. Stanford, CA: Stanford University Press.

Fisher, D., & Frey, N. (2014). Content area vocabulary learning. *The Reading Teacher*, *67*(8), 594–599. Accessed at https://ila.onlinelibrary.wiley.com/doi/abs/10.1002/trtr.1258 on April 23, 2024.

Fisher, D. (2004). Setting the "opportunity to read" standard: Resuscitating the SSR program in an urban high school. *Journal of Adolescent and Adult Literacy*, *48*(2), 138–150. Accessed at https://doi.org/10.1598/JAAL.48.2.5 on November 24, 2024.

Fisher, D., & Frey, N. (2020). The skill, will, and thrill of reading comprehension. *Educational Leadership*, *77*(5). Accessed at www.ascd.org/el/articles/the-skill-will-and-thrill-of-reading-comprehension on March 11, 2024.

Fletcher, J. M., Lyon, G. R., Fuchs, L. S., & Barnes, M. A. (2019). *Learning disabilities: From identification to intervention* (2nd ed.). New York: Guilford Press.

Foorman, B., Coyne, M., Denton, C. A., Dimino, J., Hayes, L., Justice, L., et al. (2016). *Foundational skills to support reading for understanding in kindergarten through 3rd grade*. Washington, DC: National Center for Education Evaluation and Regional Assistance (NCEE). Accessed at https://ies.ed.gov/ncee/WWC/Docs/PracticeGuide/wwc_foundationalreading_040717.pdf on January 26, 2024.

Frey, B. B., Lee, S. W., Tollefson, N., Pass, L., & Massengill Shaw, D. (2005). Balanced literacy in an urban school district. *The Journal of Educational Research*, *98*(5), 272–280.

Fry, E. (1999). *1000 instant words: The most common words for teaching reading, writing and spelling*. Garden Grove, CA: Teacher Created Resources.

Fry, E. B., & Kress, J. E. (2006). *The reading teacher's book of lists: Grades K–12* (5th ed.). Hoboken, NJ: Jossey-Bass.

Ganske, K. (2000). *Word journeys: Assessment-guided phonics, spelling, and vocabulary instruction*. New York: Guilford Press.

Garcia, V. (2017, July 25). *The problem with illiteracy and how it affects all of us*. Accessed at http://readingpartners.org/blog/problem-illiteracy-affects-us on January 26, 2024.

Georgiou, G. K., Parrila, R., Cui, Y., & Papadopoulos, T. C. (2013). Why is rapid automatized naming related to reading? *Journal of Experimental Child Psychology*, *115*(1), 218–225. Accessed at https://doi.org/10.1016/j.jecp.2012.10.015 on February 24, 2024.

Gillespie, A., & Graham, S. (2011). *Evidence-based practices for teaching writing better: Evidence-based education*. Accessed at www.betterevidence.org/us-edition/issue-6/evidence-based-practices-for-teaching-writing on February 8, 2024.

Goldberg, M. (2019, October 21). *Making changes that last: The end of the pendulum?* Accessed at www.readingrockets.org/blogs/right-to-read/making-changes-last-end-pendulum on February 26, 2024.

Goldman, S. R., Snow, C., & Vaughn, S. (2016). Common themes in teaching reading for understanding: Lessons from three projects. *Journal of Adolescent and Adult Literacy*, *60*(3), 255–264.

Gonzalez, M. (2014). The effect of embedded text-to-speech and vocabulary e-book scaffolds on the comprehension of students with reading disabilities. *International Journal of Special Education*, *29*(3), 111–125.

Graham, S. (2019). Changing How Writing Is Taught. *Review of Research in Education, 43*(1), 277-303. Accessed at https://doi.org/10.3102/0091732X18821125 on April 23, 2024.

Graham, S., Bollinger, A., Olson, C. B., D'Aoust, C., MacArthur, C., McCutchen, D., et al. (2012, June). *Teaching elementary school students to be effective writers: A practice guide* (NCEE 2012–4058). Washington, DC: National Center for Education Evaluation and Regional Assistance, Institute of Education Sciences, U.S. Department of Education. Accessed at https://ies.ed.gov/ncee/wwc/Docs/practiceguide/writing_pg_062612.pdf on January 26, 2024.

Gul, C., & Lornklang, T. (2021). The use of Picture-Word Inductive Model and Readers' Theater to improve Chinese EFL learners' vocabulary learning achievement. *Advances in Language and Literary Studies, 12*, 120. DOI: 10.7575/aiac.alls.v.12n.3.p.120.

Gunderson, L., D'Silva, R. A., & Oto, D. M. (2019). *ESL (ELL) literacy instruction: A guidebook to theory and practice* (4th ed.). New York: Routledge.

Gunn, J. (2018). The serious, lifelong impacts of illiteracy. *The Resilient Educator.* Accessed at https://resilienteducator.com/classroom-resources/illiteracy-impacts/ on April 23, 2024.

Gustafson, J. (2019). *Robust vocabulary instruction.* Accessed at https://achievethecore.org/peersandpedagogy/robust-vocabulary-instruction on April 23, 2024.

Guthrie, J. T. (2008). Reading motivation and engagement in middle and high school: Appraisal and intervention. In J. T. Guthrie (Ed.), *Engaging adolescents in reading* (pp. 1–16). Thousand Oaks, CA: Corwin.

Hallinan, M. T., & Sorensen, A. B. (1983). The formation and stability of instructional groups. *American Sociological Review, 48*(6), 838–851.

Han, F., & Ellis, R. A. (2021). Predicting students' academic performance by their online learning patterns in a blended course: To what extent is a theory driven approach and a data driven approach consistent? *Educational Technology and Society, 24*(1), 191–204. Accessed at www.jstor.org/stable/26977867 on February 8, 2024.

Hancock, N. (2022, December 29). *Tiered instruction within the MTSS model.* Accessed at www.doe.mass.edu/massliteracy/leading-mtss/tiered-instruction.html on January 26, 2024.

Harmon-Jones, E., & Mills, J. S. (1999). *Cognitive dissonance: Progress on a pivotal theory in social psychology.* Washington, DC: American Psychological Association.

Harvey, S., & Goudvis, A. (2000). *Strategies that work.* Portland, ME: Stenhouse.

Hattie, J., & Yates, G. C. R. (2013). *Visible learning and the science of how we learn.* London: Routledge.

Heal, J. (2023, January 5). *Balancing teacher-led instruction and student-centered learning.* Accessed at www.edutopia.org/article/teacher-led-instruction -student-centered-learning/ on January 26, 2024.

Hebzynski, S. J. (2017). *Balanced literacy strategies* [Dissertation, St. Cloud State University]. Culminating Projects in Teacher Development. Accessed at https://repository.stcloudstate.edu/ed_etds/21 on January 26, 2024.

Heggerty.org. (2023). *The Heggerty phonemic awareness curriculum.* Accessed at https://heggerty.org/curriculum/ on January 26, 2024.

Heinemann Publishing. (2016, June 8). *These 18 practices are proven effective for teaching reading.* Accessed at https://medium.com/@heinemann/these-18 -practices-are-proven-effective-for-teaching-reading-5ea6c9424fa0 on January 26, 2024.

Hermann, E. (n.d.). *Teach and kids learn.* Accessed at www.teachnkidslearn.com /members/erick-herrmann/ on April 23, 2024.

Hiebert, E. H. (2020) The core vocabulary: The foundation of proficient comprehension. *The Reading Teacher, 73*(6), 757–768.

Hiebert, E. H., & Reutzel, D. R. (2010). *Revisiting silent reading: New directions for teachers and researchers.* Newark, DE: International Reading Association.

Hill, H. C. (2017). The Coleman Report, 50 years on: What do we know about the role of schools in academic inequality? *The ANNALS of the American Academy of Political and Social Science, 674*(1), 9–26. Accessed at https://doi .org/10.1177/0002716217727510 on February 24, 2024.

Hillocks, G., Jr. (1987). Synthesis of research on teaching writing. *Educational Leadership, 44*(8), 71–76, 78, 80–82.

Hoines, B. (2001). *Exceptional reading practices used by fourth grade teachers in high poverty schools.* Orlando, FL: University of Central Florida.

Homeschool Compass. (2021). *How to teach language arts in your homeschool.* Accessed at https://homeschoolcompass.com/teaching-language-arts on January 26, 2024.

Huang, F. L., Moon, T. R., & Boren, R. (2014). Are the reading rich getting richer? Testing for the presence of the Matthew effect. *Reading and Writing Quarterly, 30*(2), 95–115. Accessed at https://doi.org/10.1080/10573569 .2013.789784 on February 24, 2024.

Hunt, F. (2020, July 24). *Getting your students to engage with course reading.* Accessed at www.facultyfocus.com/articles/course-design-ideas/getting -your-students-to-engage-with-course-readings/ on January 26, 2024.

Huyvaert, S. H. (1998). *Time is of the essence: Learning in schools.* Needham Heights, MA: Allyn & Bacon.

Illinois Center for Innovative Teaching and Learning. (n.d.). *Using advanced questioning techniques.* Accessed at www.niu.edu/citl/resources /literature/effective-teaching-practices-bibliography.shtml#ll5 on January 26, 2024.

Iowa Department of Education (2018). *Every child succeeds act in Iowa.* Accessed at https://oese.ed.gov/files/2020/03/Iowa-Final-Consolidated-State -Plan-PDF.pdf on April 23, 2024.

Iowa Department of Education. (2011, December). *Guidance document: Response to intervention.* Accessed at https://files.eric.ed.gov/fulltext/ED544325.pdf on January 26, 2024.

Jacoby, J. W., & Lesaux, N. K. (2017). Language and literacy instruction in preschool classes that serve Latino dual-language learners. *Early Childhood Research Quarterly, 40*(30), 77–86. Accessed at https://doi.org/10.1016/j .ecresq.2016.10.001 on February 24, 2024.

January, S. A., Lovelace, M. E., Foster, T. E., & Ardoin, S. P. (2017). A comparison of two flashcard interventions for teaching sight words to early readers. *Journal of Behavioral Education, 26*(2), 151–168. Accessed at https://doi.org/10.1007 /s10864-016-9263-2 on February 24, 2024.

Jenkins, J. R., Graff, J. J., & Miglioretti, D. L. (2009). Estimating reading growth using intermittent CBM progress monitoring. *Exceptional Children, 75*(2), 151–163. Accessed at https://doi.org/10.1177/001440290907500202 on February 24, 2024.

Jenkins, J. R., Hudson, R. F., & Lee, S. H. (2007). Using CBM-reading assessments to monitor progress. *Perspectives on Language and Literacy, 33*(2). Accessed at www.rtinetwork.org/essential/assessment/progress /usingcbm on March 11, 2024.

Jennings, J. H., Lerner, J. W., & Caldwell, J. S., (2010). *Reading problems: Assessment and teaching strategies* (6th ed.). Boston: Allyn & Bacon.

Jiban, C. (2020, June 25). *Let's talk equity: Reading levels, scaffolds, and grade-level text.* Accessed at www.nwea.org/blog/2020/equity-in-reading-levels -scaffolds-and-grade-level-text/ on February 26, 2024.

Jiban, C. (2022, January 25). The science of reading explained [Blog post]. *Teach. Learn. Grow.* Accessed at www.nwea.org/blog/2022/the-science-of-reading -explained on January 26, 2024.

Jones, B. C. (2006). *The effects of a basal reading program on reading achievement in selected Tennessee schools* [Dissertation, Tennessee State University]. ETD Collection for Tennessee State University. Accessed at https:// digitalscholarship.tnstate.edu/dissertations/AAI3222584 on February 24, 2024.

Joseph, H. S. S. L., Nation, K., & Liversedge, S. P. (2013). Using eye movements to investigate word frequency effects in children's sentence reading. *School Psychology Review, 42*(2), 207–222. Accessed at https://doi.org/10.1080/02796015.2013.12087485 on February 24, 2024.

Juarez-Tillery, M. N. (2015). *The effects of the Lexia Reading Core5 Intervention Program on the reading achievement of third-grade students* [Master's thesis, California State University]. ScholarWorks. Accessed at https://scholarworks.calstate.edu/concern/theses/ww72bc248 on February 24, 2024.

Juel, C. (1988). Learning to read and write: A longitudinal study of 54 children from first through fourth grades. *Journal of Educational Psychology, 80*(4), 437–447. Accessed at https://doi.org/10.1037/0022-0663.80.4.437 on February 24, 2024.

K5 Learning. (n.d.). *After the flood: Children's story and worksheet.* Accessed at www.k5learning.com/reading-comprehension-worksheets/fifth-grade-5/childrens-stories/after-the-flood on January 26, 2024.

Kaminski, R. A., Abbott, M., Bravo Aguayo, K., Latimer, R., & Good, R. H., III (2014). The preschool early literacy indicators: Validity and benchmark goals. *Topics in Early Childhood Special Education, 34*(2), 71–82. Accessed at https://doi.org/10.1177/0271121414527003 on February 24, 2024.

Kazakoff, E. R., Macaruso, P., & Hook, P. (2018). Efficacy of a blended learning approach to elementary school reading instruction for students who are English learners. *Education Tech Research and Development, 66,* 429–449. Accessed at https://doi.org/10.1007/s11423-017-9565-7 on February 24, 2024.

Keene, E. O., & Zimmermann, S. (1997). *Mosaic of thought: Teaching comprehension in a reader's workshop.* Portsmouth, NH: Heinemann.

Kendall Hunt Publishing. (2019). *Advantages of shared reading.* Accessed at https://rpd.kendallhunt.com/content/read-aloud-shared-reading-and-shared-read-aloud-crash-course on January 26, 2024.

Kilpatrick, D. A. (2015). *Essentials of assessing, preventing, and overcoming reading difficulties.* Hoboken, NJ: Wiley.

Kjeldsen, A.-C., Kärnä, A., Niemi, P., Olofsson, Å., & Witting, K. (2014). Gains from training in phonological awareness in kindergarten predict reading comprehension in Grade 9. *Scientific Studies of Reading, 18*(6), 452–467. Accessed at https://doi.org/10.1080/10888438.2014.940080 on February 24, 2024.

Klingbeil, M. K. (2003). *Nine-week gains in vocabulary, decoding, comprehension, and attitude of third-grade students who were in guided reading and literature-based reading instruction.* Kansas City, MO: University of Missouri.

Korat, O., & Shamir, A. (2012). Direct and indirect teaching: Using e-books for supporting vocabulary, word reading, and story comprehension for young children. *Journal of Educational Computing Research*, *46*(2), 135–152. Accessed at https://doi.org/10.2190/EC.46.2.b on February 24, 2024.

Kruse, M. (n.d.). Writing aloud: A powerful way to model writing [Blog post]. *Reading & Writing Haven*. Accessed at www.readingandwritinghaven.com /writing-aloud-a-powerful-way-to-model-writing/ on January 26, 2024.

Kulikand, J. A., & Kulik, C. C. (1987). Effects of ability grouping on student achievement. *Equity and Excellence in Education*, *23*(1–2), 22–30.

Lavrijsen, J., Dockx, J., Struyf, E., & Verschueren, K. (2022). Class composition, student achievement, and the role of the learning environment. *Journal of Educational Psychology*, *114*(3), 498–512. https://doi.org/10.1037/ edu0000709

Lavrijsen, J., Dockx, J., Struyf, E., & Verschueren, K. (2022). Class composition, student achievement, and the role of the learning environment. *Journal of Educational Psychology*, *114*(3), 498–512. Accessed at https://doi.org/10.1037 /edu0000709 on November 24, 2024.

Learning at the Primary Pond. (2020). How to help all your students read grade-level text (even if they aren't yet reading at grade level! [Blog post]. *Learning at the Primary Pond.* Accessed at https://learningattheprimarypond.com/blog /how-to-help-all-your-students-read-grade-level-text-even-if-they-arent-yet -reading-at-grade-level/ on February 8, 2024.

Learning First Alliance. (2004). *Major changes to ESEA in the No Child Left Behind Act.* Accessed at www.understood.org/en/articles/the-difference -between-the-every-student-succeeds-act-and-no-child-left-behind on March 8, 2008.

Lenski, S., Larson, M., McElhone, D., Davis, D. S., Lauritzen, C., Villagómez, A., et al. (2016). What teachers want: A statewide survey of reading and English language arts teachers' instructional materials, preferences, and practices. *Literacy Research and Instruction*, *55*(3), 237–261.

Leppänen, U., Aunola, K., & Nurmi, J. (2005). Beginning readers' reading performance and reading habits. *Journal of Research in Reading*, *28*(4), 383–399. Accessed at https://onlinelibrary.wiley.com/doi/10.1111/j.1467 -9817.2005.00281.x on February 7, 2024.

Lexia. (2023). The science of reading vs. balanced literacy [Blog post]. *Lexia.* Accessed at www.lexialearning.com/blog/the-science-of-reading-vs-balanced -literacy on February 8, 2024.

Liban, M., & Liban, D. (2019). *Sounds first phonemic awareness program.* Accessed at www.readingdoneright.org/programs-by-grade on February 8, 2024.

Literacy for All. (n.d.). *Get Georgia reading.* Accessed at www.literacyforallfund .org/facts on February 8, 2024.

Livingston, N. (n.d.). *Word lists: Fry instant words in phrases*. Accessed at www.uen .org/lessonplan/view/13705 on February 8, 2024.

Loewus, L. (2015). *Reading fluency viewed as neglected skill.* Accessed at www. edweek.org/teaching-learning/reading-fluency-viewed-as-neglected- skill/2015/05 on May 14, 2024.

Lorimor-Easley, N. A., & Reed, D. K. (2019, August). An explanation of structured literacy, and a comparison to balanced literacy [Blog post]. *Iowa Reading Research Center.* Accessed at https://irrc.education.uiowa.edu/blog /2019/04/explanation-structured-literacy-and-comparison-balanced-literacy on February 8, 2024.

Lupo, S. M., Strong, J. Z., & Smith, K. C. (2019). Struggle is not a bad word: Misconceptions and recommendations about readers struggling with difficult texts. *Journal of Adolescent & Adult Literacy, 62*(5), 551–560.

Lupo, S. M., Strong, J. Z., Lewis, W., Walpole, S., & McKenna, M. C. (2017). Building background knowledge through reading: Rethinking text sets. *Journal of Adolescent and and Adult Literacy, 61*(4), 433–444.

Luscombe, B. (2022). *Inside the massive effort to change the way kids are taught to read.* Accessed at https://time.com/6205084/phonics-science-of-reading -teachers/ on February 8, 2024.

Macaruso P., Marshall V., & Hurwitz, L. B. (2019). *Longitudinal blended learning in a low SES elementary school* [Conference session]. Proceedings of Global Conference on Learning and Technology (Global Learn 2019), 253–262. Accessed at www.learntechlib.org/primary/p/210313/ on April 23, 2024.

Macaruso, P., & Walker, A. (2008). The efficacy of computer-assisted instruction for advancing literacy skills in kindergarten children. *Reading Psychology, 29*(3), 266–287. Accessed at www.tandfonline.com/doi/abs/10.1080 /02702710801982019 on February 7, 2024.

MacPhee, K. (2018, August 15). *The critical role of phonemic awareness in reading instruction.* Accessed at https://edublog.scholastic.com/post/critical-role -phonemic-awareness-reading-instruction on February 27, 2024.

Magnusson, C. G., Roe, A., & Blikstad-Balas, M. (2018). To what extent and how are reading comprehension strategies part of language arts instruction? A study of lower secondary classrooms. *Reading Research Quarterly, 54*(2), 187–212. Accessed at https://ila.onlinelibrary.wiley.com/doi/10.1002/rrq.231 on February 7, 2024.

Manurung, A. M., Pardede, H., & Purba, C. N. (2020). The effect of using sustained silent reading (SSR) method to the students' ability in Reading Report Text at the eleven grade of SMA Negeri 2 Pematangsiantar. *Journal of English Teaching as a Foreign Language, 6*(2), 39–65.

Marcotte, A. A. M., & Hintze, J. M. (2009). Incremental and predictive utility of formative assessment methods of reading comprehension. *Journal of School Psychology, 47*(5), 315–335. Accessed at www.sciencedirect.com/science/article/abs/pii/S0022440509000272?via%3Dihub on February 7, 2024.

Marzano, R. J. (2009). Six steps to better vocabulary instruction. *Educational Leadership, 67*(1), 83–84.

Marzano, R. J. (2020). *Teaching basic, advanced, and academic vocabulary: A comprehensive framework for elementary instruction.* Bloomington, IN: Marzano Resources.

Marzano, R. J., Pickering, D. J., & Pollock, J. E. (2001). *Classroom instruction that works: Research-based strategies for increasing student achievement.* Arlington, VA: ASCD.

Matthewes, S. H. (2021). Better together? Heterogeneous effects of tracking on student achievement. *The Economic Journal, 131*(635), 1269–1307. Accessed at https://academic.oup.com/ej/article/131/635/1269/5895319 on February 7, 2024.

McArthur, G., Castles, A., Kohnen, S., Larsen, L., Jones, K., Anandakumar, T., et al. (2013). Sight word and phonics training in children with dyslexia. *Journal of Learning Disabilities, 48*(4), 391–407. Accessed at https://journals.sagepub.com/doi/10.1177/0022219413504996 on February 7, 2024.

McBride, S. (2023). *Tier 1 strategies.* Accessed at www.reading-fluency.com/tier1/ on February 7, 2024.

McGuffey, W. H. (1836). *McGuffey readers.* Cincinnati, OH: Truman and Smith.

McKeown, M. G., Beck, I. L., & Worthy, M. J. (1993). Grappling with text ideas: Questioning the author. *The Reading Teacher, 46*(7), 560–566.

McKnight, L., & Woods, N. (2020). *Death by TEEL: Are formulas for writing harmful?* Accessed at https://collect.readwriterespond.com/death-by-teel-are-formulas-for-writing-harmful/ on February 7, 2024.

McQuillan, J. L. (2019). The inefficiency of vocabulary instruction. *International Electronic Journal of Elementary Education, 11*(4), 309–318. Accessed at www.iejee.com/index.php/IEJEE/article/view/730/400 on February 7, 2024.

Meador, D. (2023). *Exploring the value of whole group instruction in the classroom.* Accessed at www.thoughtco.com/exploring-the-value-of-whole-group-instruction-3194549 on February 7, 2024.

Memis, M. R. (2019). A research on reading comprehension and morphological awareness levels of middle school students and the relationship between these concepts. *Journal of Language and Linguistic Studies, 15*(2), 649–677. Accessed at www.jlls.org/index.php/jlls/article/view/1292 on February 7, 2024.

Meyer, N. K., & Bouck, E. C. (2014). The impact of text-to-speech on expository reading for adolescents with LD. *Journal of Special Education Technology*, *29*(1), 21–33.

Mid-Continent Research for Education and Learning (McREL). (2015). *Righting your RTI/MTSS triangle*. Accessed at https://www.mcrel.org/righting-your-rtimtss-triangle on April 23, 2024.

Mid-Continent Research for Education and Learning (McREL). (2016). *A step by-step guide to building your intervention system*. Accessed at www.mcrel.org /a-step-by-step-guide-to-building-your-intervention-system on February 7, 2024.

Miller, S. S. (2006). *How teachers spend instructional time in the primary grades and how this influences student achievement*. Salt Lake City: University of Utah. Accessed at http://proquest.umi.com.proxy.usd.edu /pqdweb?did=1251862061&Fmt=7&clientId=44616&RQT=309&V Name=PQD on February 7, 2024.

Moats, L. (2019). Phonics and spelling: Learning the structure of language at the word level. In D. A. Kilpatrick, R. Malatesha Joshi, & R. K. Wagner (Eds.), *Reading development and difficulties: Bridging the gap between research and practice* (pp. 39–62). New York: Springer.

Mometrix Academy. (2022). *Reading comprehension*. Accessed at www.mometrix .com/academy/reading-comprehension on February 7, 2024.

Morin, A. (n.d.). *What is co-teaching?* Accessed at www.understood .org/en/articles/ collaborative-team-teaching-what-you-need-to-know on April 23, 2024.

Musdizal, M. (2019). The influence of visualization strategy on reading comprehension ability. *Jurnal Dimensi,* (8). DOI: 10.33373/dms.v8i2.2162

Myers, T. (2015). The relationship between fluency and comprehension. Goucher College Graduate Works. Accessed at https://mdsoar.org /handle/11603/1691 on April 23, 2024.

Myers, T. (2015). *The relationship between fluency and comprehension*. Accessed at https://mdsoar.org/handle/11603/1691 on February 7, 2024.

Nagy, W. E., & Scott, J. A. (2000). Vocabulary processes. In M. L. Kamil, P. B. Mosenthal, P. D. Pearson, & R. Barr (Eds.), *Handbook of reading research* (p. 269–284). Mahwah, NJ: Lawrence Erlbaum Associates.

Narra, A. (2019). *The scavenger hunt*. Bengaluru, Karnataka, India: Pratham Books.

National Center for Education Statistics. (2018). *Program for international student assessment (PISA)*. Accessed at https://nces.ed.gov/surveys/pisa/PISA on February 7, 2024.

National Center for Education Statistics. (2019). *NAEP report card: 2019 NAEP reading assessment*. Accessed at www.nationsreportcard.gov/highlight s/reading/2019/ on February 26, 2024.

National Center for Improving Literacy (2023). *The educator's science of reading toolbox: Explicit vocabulary instruction to build equitable access for all learners.* Accessed at https://improvingliteracy.org/brief/educators-science-reading-toolbox-explicit-vocabulary-instruction-build-equitable-access-all on April 23, 2024.

National Commission on Excellence in Education. (1983). *A nation at risk: The imperative for education reform.* Washington, DC: U.S. Government Printing Office.

National Council of Teachers of English. (1987). NCTE to you. *Language Arts, 64*(4), 450–457.

National Governors Association Center for Best Practices & Council of Chief State School Officers. (2010, June). *Common Core State Standards for English language arts and literacy in history/social studies, science, and technical subjects.* Accessed at https://learning.ccsso.org/wp-content/uploads/2022/11/ADA-Compliant-ELA-Standards.pdf on January 26, 2024.

National Reading Panel. (2000). *Report of the National Reading Panel: Teaching children to read.* Bethesda, MD: National Institute of Child Health and Development.

Neri, P., & Linde, S. (2022). *Independent reading: Strategies and value.* Accessed at https://study.com/learn/lesson/independent-reading-classroom-strategies-importance.html on February 7, 2024.

Ness, M. (2011). Explicit reading comprehension instruction in elementary classrooms: Teacher use of reading comprehension strategies. *Journal of Research in Childhood Education, 25*(1), 98–117. Accessed at www.tandfonline.com/doi/abs/10.1080/02568543.2010.531076 on February 7, 2024.

Ness, M., Couperus, J., & Willey, M. (2013). A comparison study of the effectiveness of the Lexia reading program. *Kairaranga, 14*(1), 16–24.

Northwest Evaluation Association. (2019). *Measurements of academic progress.* Portland, OR: Author.

Norton, S. W. (2018). *Impact of research-based literacy programs, used for response to intervention (RTI), in Tennessee fourth-grade English/Language Arts (ELA) students.* [Dissertation].

Novridewi, N., Wachyunni, S., & Sulistiyo, U. (2023). Reciprocal teaching as a strategy to improve students' understanding of reading content. *Jurnal Ilmiah Universitas Batanghari Jambi, 23*(1), 761–766. Accessed at www.academia.edu/110851109/Reciprocal_Teaching_as_a_Strategy_to_Improve_Students_Understanding_of_Reading_Content_Reading_Skill_ on February 27, 2024.

Oczkus, L. D. (2018). *Reciprocal teaching at work: Powerful strategies and lessons for improving reading comprehension* (3rd ed.). Arlington, VA: ASCD.

Ohio Literacy Advisory Council, (2021). *Explicit intervention in fluency.* Accessed at https://allohioliteracy.org/learning-modules/decision-rules-flowchart -interventions/explicit-intervention-in-fluency on April 23, 2024.

Olson, M. (2021). The importance of vocabulary instruction [Blog post]. *Kids Discover.* Accessed at https://kidsdiscover.com/teacherresources/the -importance-of-vocabulary-instruction/ on February 7, 2024.

Olsson, E. (2021). A comparative study of CLIL implementation in upper secondary school in Sweden and students' development of L2 English academic vocabulary. *Language Teaching Research.* Accessed at https://journals .sagepub.com/doi/10.1177/13621688211045000 on February 7, 2024.

Osborn, J., Lehr, F., & Hiebert, E. (2004). *A focus on fluency: Research-based practices in early learning series.* Honolulu, HI: Regional Educational Laboratory at Pacific Resources for Education and Learning (PREL).

Pak, S. S., & Weseley, A. J. (2012). The effect of mandatory reading logs on children's motivation to read. *Journal of Research in Education, 22*(1), 251–265.

Parrish, N. (2020). *5 ways to support students who struggle with reading comprehension.* Accessed at www.edutopia.org/article/5-ways-support-students -who-struggle-reading-comprehension on February 7, 2024.

Pearson Education. (2018). *The Iowa statewide assessment of student progress(ISASP).* Accessed at https://iowa.pearsonaccess.com on February 7, 2024.

Pendergast, M., Bingham, G., & Patton-Terry, N. (2015). Examining the relationship between emergent literacy skills and invented spelling in prekindergarten Spanish-speaking dual language learners. *Early Education and Development, 26*(2), 264–285. Accessed at www.tandfonline.com/doi/abs/10.1 080/10409289.2015.991083 on February 7, 2024.

Pinnell, G. S. (2000). *Teacher decision making in literacy education: Learning to teach.* Posted by Dorothy Brandon Home and Family. Alabama A&M and Auburn Universities.

Pourhosein-Gilakjani, A., & Sabouri, N. B. (2016). How can students improve their reading comprehension skills? *Journal of Studies in Education, 6*(2), 229.

Presto, E. (n.d.). *Visual Literacies and Young Children's writing: creating spaces for young children's voices and engaging in authentic writing experiences.* [Dissertation]. Accessed at https://digitalcommons.odu.edu/teachinglearning _etds/85 on April 23, 2024.

Pufpaff, L. A. (2009). A developmental continuum of phonological sensitivity skills. *Psychology in the Schools, 46*(7), 679–691. Accessed at https:// onlinelibrary.wiley.com/doi/10.1002/pits.20407 on February 7, 2024.

Read Naturally, Inc. (1999). *Read naturally.* St. Paul, MN. Publisher. Accessed at https://www.tandfonline.com/doi/abs/10.1080/19388079909558310 on March 11, 2024.

Reading Done Right. (n.d.). *Sounds first phonemic awareness program.* Accessed at www.readingdoneright.org/programs-by-grade#:~:text=The%20Best%20 for%20All% 20Sounds,students%20who%20might%20need%20 reinforcement on February 7, 2024.

Reed, D. K., & Hinzman, M. (2018). *Teaching sight words as a part of comprehensive reading instruction.* Accessed at https://irrc.education.uiowa.edu /blog/2018/06/teaching-sight-words-part-comprehensive-reading-instruction on January 26, 2024.

Regis College (2023). Child illiteracy in America: Statistics, facts, and resources. [Blog Post]. *Regis College.* Accessed at https://online.regiscollege.edu/ blog/child-illiteracy on April 23, 2024.

Renaissance Learning. (2016). *The magic of 15 minutes: Reading practice and reading growth.* Accessed at www-fca.stjohns.k12.fl.us/media/wp -content/uploads/sites/4/2021/06/The-magic-of-15-minutes_-Daily-reading -practice-and-reading-growth.pdf on February 7, 2024.

Renaissance Learning. (2019). *FastBridge CAT and CBM reading assessments.* Accessed at www.renaissance.com/products/fastbridge/fastbridge-reading on January 26, 2024.

Reutzel, D. R., Fawson, P. C., & Smith, J. A. (2008). Reconsidering silent sustained reading: An exploratory study of scaffolded silent reading. *The Journal of Educational Research, 102*(1), 37–50. Accessed at www.tandfonline .com/doi/abs/10.3200/JOER.102.1.37-50 on February 7, 2024.

Reutzel, R., & Cooter, R. (2018). A closer look at early reading. *International Review of Education, 45*(1). Accessed at www.nctq.org on February 7, 2024.

Rodriguez, K., & Novak, K. (n.d.). *Understanding the relationship between MTSS and special education.* Accessed at www.doe.mass.edu/sfss/mtss/mobilization /relationship-mtss-sped.docx on February 7, 2024.

Roe, B. D., Smith, S. H., & Burns, P. C. (2005). *Teaching reading in today's elementary schools* (9th ed.). Boston: Houghton Mifflin Company.

Rothman, R. (1987, December 2). *Critique terms basal readers outmoded, urges spread of "real book" alternatives.* Accessed at www.edweek .org/education/critique-terms-basal-readers-outmoded-urges-spread-of-real -book-alternatives/1987/12 on February 26, 2024.

Routman, R. (2017). *What matters most: Ensuring literacy engagement, achievement, and equity for all learners.* Accessed at www.wsra.org/assets/Convention /handouts2017/Regie%20Routmans%20Saturday%20Handout.pdf on February 7, 2024.

Samuels, S. J. (2002). Reading fluency: Its development and assessment. In A. E. Rarstrup & S. J. Samuels, *What research has to say about reading instruction* (3rd ed). Newark, DE: International Reading Association.

Sanden, S. (2014). Out of the shadow of SSR: Real teachers' classroom independent reading practices. *Language Arts*, *91*(3), 161–175.

Santoro, L. E., Chard, D. J., Howard, L., & Baker, S. K. (2008). Making the very most of classroom read-alouds to promote comprehension and vocabulary. *Reading Teacher*, *61*(5), 396–408.

Schechter, R., Macaruso, P., Kazakoff, E., & Brooke, E. (2015). Exploration of a blended learning approach to reading instruction on low SES students in early elementary grades. *Computers in the Schools*, *32*(3–4), 183–200. Accessed at www.tandfonline.com/doi/full/10.1080/07380569.2015.1100652 on February 7, 2024.

Schmidt, C. (2020). *Leveled texts are "Exhibit A" for the soft bigotry of low expectations*. Accessed at www.edpost.com/stories/leveled-texts-are-exhibit-a -for-the-soft-bigotry-of-low-expectations on February 7, 2024.

Schmoker, M. J. (2011). *Focus: Elevating the essentials to radically improve student learning*. Arlington, VA: ASCD.

Schmoker, M. J. (2019). *How to make reading instruction much, much more efficient.* Accessed at www.edweek.org/teaching-learning/opinion-how-to-make -reading-instruction-much-much-more-efficient/2019/11 on February 7, 2024.

Schoolyard, S. (2017, July 10). Why is English language arts so important? [Blog post]. *School Specialty*. Accessed at https://blog.schoolspecialty.com/english -language-arts-important on April 23, 2024.

Schroeder-Van Cleve, J. (2007). The advantages and challenges of fluency instruction. *Graduate Research Papers*, 1485. Accessed at https://scholarworks .uni.edu/grp/1485 on February 7, 2024.

Schuele, M., & Murphy, N. (2014). *The intensive phonological awareness program*. Baltimore, MD: Brookes Publishing.

Sela, H., Davis, N., & Hulse, J. (2019). Making math social with dialogue protocols. *Mathematics Teaching in the Middle School*, *24*(4), 226–232. Accessed at www.jstor.org/stable/10.5951/mathteacmiddscho.24.4.0226 on February 7, 2024.

Serafini, F. (2011). Expanding perspectives for comprehending visual images in multimodal texts. *Journal of Adolescent and Adult Literacy*, *54*(5), 342–350. Accessed at https://ila.onlinelibrary.wiley.com/doi/10.1598/JAAL.54.5.4 on February 7, 2024.

Shaman, S. (2014). *Using the picture word inductive model (PWIM) to teach English vocabulary*. Accessed at https://ortesol.wildapricot.org/resources/ Documents/Publications/Journals/2014/Using%20the%20Picture%20 Word%20Inductive%20Model%20(PWIM)%20to%20Teach%20 English%20Vocabulary%20(49).pdf on April 23, 2024.

Shanahan, T. (2015). To group or not to group, that is the question [Blog post]. *Shanahan on Literacy.* Accessed at www.readingrockets.org/blogs/shanahan-on-literacy/group-or-not-group-question on April 23, 2024.

Shanahan, T. (2016). Does independent reading time during the school day create lifelong readers? [Blog post]. *Shanahan on Literacy.* Accessed at www.readingrockets.org/blogs/shanahan-on-literacy/does-independent-reading-time-during-school-day-create-lifelong-readers on April 23, 2024.

Shanahan, T. (2017). The instructional level concept revisited: Teaching with complex text [Blog post]. *Shanahan on Literacy.* Accessed at www.shanahanonliteracy.com/blog/the-instructional-level-concept-revisited-teaching-with-complex-text on February 7, 2024.

Shanahan, T. (2018). Should reading be taught whole class or small group? [Blog post]. *Shanahan on Literacy.* Accessed at www.shanahanonliteracy.com/blog/should-reading-be-taught-whole-class-or-small-group on February 7, 2024.

Shanahan, T. (2019a). Isn't independent reading a research-based practice? [Blog post]. *Shanahan on Literacy.* Accessed at https://shanahanonliteracy.com/blog/isnt-independent-reading-a-research-based-practice on February 7, 2024.

Shanahan, T. (2019b). Why not teach reading comprehension for a change? [Blog post]. *Shanahan on Literacy.* Accessed at https://shanahanonliteracy.com/blog/why-not-teach-reading-comprehension-for-a-change on February 7, 2024.

Shanahan, T. (2020a). Planning lessons with complex text [Blog post]. *Shanahan on Literacy.* Accessed at www.shanahanonliteracy.com/blog/planning-lessons-with-complex-text on February 7, 2024.

Shanahan, T. (2020b). Will challenging text put a crimp in students' motivation? [Blog post]. *Shanahan on Literacy.* Accessed at https://shanahanonliteracy.com/blog/will-challenging-text-put-a-crimp-in-students-motivation on February 7, 2024.

Shanahan, T. (2022). Should kids pick out their own reading texts? [Blog post]. *Shanahan on Literacy.* Accessed at www.shanahanonliteracy.com/blog/should-kids-pick-their-own-reading-texts on February 7, 2024.

Shapiro, E. S. (n.d.). *Tiered instruction and intervention in a response-to-intervention model.* Accessed at www.rtinetwork.org/essential/tieredinstruction/tiered-instruction-and-intervention-rti-model on February 7, 2024.

Slavin, R. E., Lake, C., Baye, A., Dachet, D., & Haslam, J. (2019). *A quantitative synthesis of research on writing approaches in grades 2 to 12.* Accessed at www.bestevidence.org/word/writing_grades2to12 on February 7, 2024.

Slavin, R. E., Lake, C., Davis, S., & Madden, N. A. (2011). Effective programs for struggling readers: A best-evidence synthesis. *Educational Research Review, 6*(1), 1–26. Accessed at www.sciencedirect.com/science/article/abs/pii/S1747938X10000400?via%3Dihub on February 7, 2024.

Slavin, R., & Cheung, A. (2016). *Effective reading programs for middle and high schools: A best evidence synthesis.* Accessed at www.adlit.org/article/28285 on February 7, 2024.

Smith, S. (2008). *McGuffey readers. Faculty Publications and Presentations.* Accessed at https://digitalcommons.liberty.edu/educ_fac_pubs/101/ on April 23, 2024.

Solity, J. E., & Vousden, J. (2009). Real books vs reading schemes: A new perspective from instructional psychology. *Educational Psychology, 29*(4), 469–511. Accessed at www.tandfonline.com/doi/full/10.1080/01443410903103657 on February 8, 2024.

Sood, I. (2019). *7 Characteristics of a good question.* Accessed at https://elearningindustry.com/characteristics-of-a-good-question-7 on April 23, 2024.

Sparks, S. (2022). *Classroom reading groups: 5 lessons from recent studies.* Accessed at www.edweek.org/teaching-learning/classroom-reading-groups-5-lessons-from-recent-studies/2022/03 on April 23, 2024.

Sparks, S. D. (2018). *Are classroom reading groups the best way to teach reading? Maybe not.* Accessed at www.edweek.org/teaching-learning/are-classroom-reading-groups-the-best-way-to-teach-reading-maybe-not/2018/08 on February 8, 2024.

Spear-Swerling, L. (August, 2006). *The importance of teaching handwriting.* Accessed at www.ldonline.org/spearswerling/The_Importance_of_Teaching_Handwriting on April 23, 2024.

Spear-Swerling, L., & Zibulsky, J. (2013). Making time for literacy: Teacher knowledge and time allocation in instructional planning. *Reading and Writing, 27*(8), 1353–1378. Accessed at https://link.springer.com/article/10.1007/s11145-013-9491-y on February 8, 2024.

Staake, J. (2022). *What is the science of reading?* Accessed at www.weareteachers.com/what-is-the-science-of-reading on February 8, 2024.

Stack, R. (2017). *Putting grade-level texts in the hands of all students.* Accessed at www.ascd.org/el/articles/putting-grade-level-texts-in-the-hands-of-all-students on February 8, 2024.

Stahl, S. A., & Fairbanks, M. M. (1986). The effects of vocabulary instruction: A model-based meta-analysis. *Review of Educational Research, 56*(1), 72–110. Accessed at https://journals.sagepub.com/doi/10.3102/00346543056001072 on February 8, 2024.

Stetter, M. E., & Hughes, M. T. (2010). Computer-assisted instruction to enhance the reading comprehension of struggling readers: A review of the literature. *Journal of Special Education Technology, 25*(4), 1–16. Accessed at https://journals.sagepub.com/doi/10.1177/016264341002500401 on February 8, 2024.

Strasser, K., & Rio, F. (2013). The role of comprehension monitoring, theory of mind, and vocabulary depth in predicting story comprehension and recall of kindergarten children. *Reading Research Quarterly*, *49*(2), 169–187. Accessed at https://ila.onlinelibrary.wiley.com/doi/10.1002/rrq.68 on February 8, 2024.

Study.com. (n.d.). *How does literacy rate affect economic development?* Accessed at https://homework.study.com/explanation/how-does-literacy-rate-affect-economic-development.html on January 26, 2024.

Suggate, S. P. (2016). A meta-analysis of the long-term effects of phonemic awareness, phonics, fluency, and reading comprehension interventions. *Journal of Learning Disabilities*, *49*(1), 77–96. Accessed at https://journals.sagepub.com/doi/10.1177/0022219414528540 on February 8, 2024.

Swanson, E., Denton, C. A., Wolters, C. A., York, M. J., Kulesz, P. A., & Francis, D. J. (2015). Adolescents' use of reading comprehension strategies: Differences related to reading proficiency, grade level, and gender. *Learning and Individual Differences*, *37*, 81–95.

Swartz, S. (2019). The most popular reading programs aren't backed by science. Accessed at www.edweek.org/teaching-learning/the-most-popular-reading-programs-arent-backed-by-science/2019/12 on April 23, 2024.

Tang, S., Asrifan, A., Chen, Y., Haedar, H., & Agussalim, M. (2019). The humor story in teaching reading comprehension. *Journal of Advanced English Studies*, *2*(2), 77–87. Accessed at https://jaes.journal.unifa.ac.id/index.php/jes/article/view/65 on February 8, 2024.

Taylor, B. M., Pearson, P. D., Clark, K., & Walpole, S. (2000). Effective schools and accomplished teachers: Lessons about primary-grade reading instruction in low-income schools. *Elementary School Journal*, *101*(2), 121–165. Accessed at www.journals.uchicago.edu/doi/10.1086/499662 on February 8, 2024.

Texas Center for Learning Disabilities (2023). *Five research-based ways to teach vocabulary.* Accessed at https://texasldcenter.org/teachers-corner/five-research-based-ways-to-teach-vocabulary/ on April 23, 2024.

Texas Education Agency (2002). *Comprehension instruction.* Accessed at https://tea.texas.gov/ academics/subject-areas/english-language-arts-and-reading/redbk2.pdf on April 23, 2024.

The WfP Center (2021). *What do world-class writing teachers do that makes the difference?* Accessed at https://writing4pleasure.com/2021/08/05/what-do-world-class -writing-teachers-do-that-makes-the-difference-seminar-presentation-ukla -national-conference-2021/ on April 23, 2024.

The Zoog Team. (2022, May 9). 10 ways to encourage grade-schoolers to read [Blog post]. *Zoog.* Accessed at www.getzoog.com/how-encourage-kids-read /#:~:text=Choose%20Age%%202DAppropriate%20%20Books,their%20 age%%2020and%20development%20level on January 26, 2024.

Therrien, W. J., Wickstrom, K., & Jones, K. (2006). Effect of a combined repeated reading and question generation intervention on reading achievement. *Learning Disabilities Research & Practice, 21*(2), 89–97. Accessed at https://journals.sagepub.com/doi/abs/10.1111/j.1540-5826.2006.00209.x on February 8, 2024.

Thierer, K. (2019). Protocols in the classroom—Creating a reflective learning community for students [Blog post]. *School Reform Initiative.* Accessed at www.schoolreforminitiative.org/blog/protocols-in-the-classroom-creating-a-reflective-learning-community-for-students on February 8, 2024.

TNTP, New Teachers Project. (2018). *The opportunity myth: What students can show us about how school is letting them down—and how to fix it.* Accessed at https://eric.ed.gov/?id=ED590204 on February 8, 2024.

Tomesen, M., & Aarnoutse, C. (1998). Effects of an instructional programme for deriving word meanings. *Educational Studies, 24*(1), 107–222.

Toonder, S. & Sawyer, L. (2021). The impact of adaptive computer assisted instruction on reading comprehension: Identifying the main idea. *Journal of Computer Assisted Learning, 37*(5), 1336–1347.

Topping, K. J., Samuels, J., & Paul, T. (2007). Does practice make perfect? Independent reading quantity, quality and student achievement. *Learning and Instruction, 17*(3), 253–264. Accessed at www.sciencedirect.com/science/article/abs/pii/S095947520700028X?via%3Dihub on February 8, 2024.

Torppa, M., Vasalampi, K., Eklund, K., Sulkunen, S., & Niemi, P. (2020). Reading comprehension difficulty is often distinct from difficulty in reading fluency and accompanied with problems in motivation and school well-being. *Educational Psychology, 40*(1), 62–81. Accessed at www.tandfonline.com/doi/full/10.1080/01443410.2019.1670334 on February 8, 2024.

U.S. Department of Education, Office of Elementary and Secondary Education. (2002). *No child left behind: A desktop reference.* Washington, DC: Educational Publications.

U.S. Department of Education. (1965). *Elementary and Secondary Education Act of 1965 H.R. 89th Congress, Public Law 89-10.* Washington, DC: U.S. Government Printing Office.

U.S. Department of Education. (2015). *Every student succeeds act (ESSA).* Accessed at www.ed.gov/ESSA on February 8, 2024.

U.S. Department of Education. (2019). *National Assessment of Educational Progress (NAEP).* Institute of Educational Sciences, National Center for Education Statistics. Accessed at https://nces.ed.gov/nationsreportcard/subject/participating/2019/public/2019_facts_for_teachers.pdf on April 23, 2024.

U.S. Department of Education. (2022). Institute of Education Sciences, National Center for Education Statistics, National Assessment of Educational Progress (NAEP), 2022 Reading Assessment. Accessed at www.nationsreport card.gov/highlights/reading/2022/ on April 23, 2024.

Ulerick, S. L. (2018). *Using textbooks for meaningful learning in science.* Accessed at https://narst.org/research-matters/using-textbooks-for-meaningful-learning on February 8, 2024.

University of Oregon, Center on Teaching and Learning. (2018). *Understanding the research behind DIBELS® 8th Edition (Technical Report 1801).* Accessed at https://dibels.uoregon.edu/sites/default/files/DIBELS8thEdition_Tech Rpt1801_ResearchBrief.pdf on February 8, 2024.

U.S. Department of Education. (n.d.). *No child left behind: Elementary and secondary education act (ESEA).* Accessed at www2.ed.gov/nclb /landing.jhtml on February 27, 2024.

University of Oregon. (n.d.). *Group students with similar needs for small group instruction.* Accessed at http://oregonliteracypd.uoregon.edu/topic/group -students-similar-needs-small-group-instruction on February 8, 2024.

Valencia, S. W., Wixson, K. K., & Pearson, P. D. (2014). Putting text complexity in context: Refocusing on comprehension of complex text. *The Elementary School Journal, 115*(2), 270–289. Accessed at www.journals.uchicago.edu /doi/10.1086/678296 on February 8, 2024.

Van Zant, S., & Volpe, N. (2018). *Small group instruction: How to make it effective.* Accessed at www.corelearn.com/small-group-instruction-blog on February 8, 2024.

Victoria Department of Education. (2018). *Independent reading and writing (emergent literacy).* Accessed at www.vic.gov.au/literacy-teaching-toolkit-early -childhood/teaching-practices-emergent-literacy/independent-reading on February 8, 2024.

Walczyk, J. J., & Griffith-Ross, D. A. (2007). How important is reading skill fluency for comprehension? *The Reading Teacher, 60*(6), 560–569. Accessed at https://ila.onlinelibrary.wiley.com/doi/10.1598/RT.60.6.6 on February 24, 2024.

Walsh, J., & Sattes, B. (2016). *Quality questioning: Research-based practice to engage every learner.* Thousand Oaks, CA: Corwin.

Wang, C., Algozzine, B., Ma, W., & Porfeli, E. (2011). Oral reading rates of second-grade students. *Journal of Educational Psychology, 103*(2), 442–454. Accessed at https://ila.onlinelibrary.wiley.com/doi/10.1598/RT.60.6.6 on February 8, 2024.

Washburn, E. K, Joshi, R. M., & Cantrell, E. B. (2011a). Are preservice teachers prepared to teach struggling readers? *Annals of Dyslexia, 61*(1), 21–43.

Washburn, E. K, Joshi, R. M., & Cantrell, E. B. (2011b). Teacher knowledge of basic language concepts and dyslexia. *Dyslexia, 17*(2), 165–183.

Webb, S., & Nation, P. (2017). *How vocabulary is learned*. Oxford: Oxford University Press.

White, E. B. (1952). *Charlotte's web* (1st ed.). New York: Harper & Brothers.

Whyte, R. (2016). *Teach essential writing skills*. Accessed at www.eslwriting.org/wp-content/uploads/tews-sample0115.pdf on February 8, 2024.

Wilson, P. (2019, September 6). *Why low expectations are dangerous in education*. [Post]. LinkedIn. Accessed at www.linkedin.com/pulse/why-low-expectations-dangerous-education-paul-v-wilson-jr-/ on April 23, 2024.

Wilson, T., Nabors, D., Berg, H., Simpson, C., & Timme, K. (2012). Small-group reading instruction: Lessons from the field. *Dimensions of Early Childhood, 40*(3). Accessed at www.rcboe.org/cms/lib/GA01903614/Centricity/Domain/15506/Dimensions_Vol40_3_Wilson.pdf on February 8, 2024.

Wood, S. G., Moxley, J. H., Tighe, E. L., & Wagner, R. K. (2017). *Does use of text-to-speech and related read-aloud tools improve reading comprehension for students with reading disabilities? A meta-analysis*. Accessed at https://journals.sagepub.com/doi/10.1177/0022219416688170 on February 8, 2024.

Yu, F.-Y. (2009). Scaffolding student-generated questions: Design and development of a customizable online learning system. *Computers in Human Behavior, 25*(5), 1129–1138. Accessed at www.sciencedirect.com/science/article/abs/pii/S0747563209000703?via%3Dihubon February 8, 2024.

Zimmermann, L., & Reed, D. K. (2017). *Attributes of effective explicit vocabulary instruction*. Accessed at https://irrc.education.uiowa.edu/blog/2017/10/attributes-effective-explicit-vocabulary-instruction on February 8, 2024.

Index

The Power of Effective Reading Instruction
Karen Gazith

Through research-supported tools and strategies, this book explores how children learn to read and how neuroscience should inform reading practices in schools. K–12 educators will find resources and reproducible tools to effectively implement reading instruction and interventions, no matter the subject taught.

BKG104

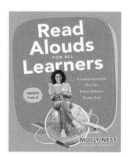

Read Alouds for All Learners
Molly Ness

In *Read Alouds for All Learners: A Comprehensive Plan for Every Subject, Every Day, Grades PreK–8,* Molly Ness provides a compelling case for the integration, or reintegration, of the read aloud in schools and a step-by-step resource for preK–8 educators in classrooms.

BKG116

The Literacy Triangle
LeAnn Nickelsen and Melissa Dickson

Accelerate learning with high-impact strategies. Beginning and veteran teachers alike will find insights and practices they can use immediately. No matter what content area you teach, this book will help you develop the strategic reader in every student.

BKF983

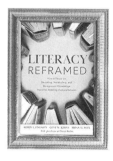

Literacy Reframed
Robin J. Fogarty, Gene M. Kerns, and Brian M. Pete

Discover a game-changing new way to think about—and teach—literacy at all levels. *With Literacy Reframed*, you will discover a dynamic path forward for creating classrooms that fully support students on their literacy journeys and prepare them to become lifelong lovers of reading.

BKF959

Solution Tree | Press

a division of

Solution Tree

Visit solution-tree.com or call 800.733.6786 to order.